CIRCLES OF HOPE

A Historical Novel

JAMES C. THOMAS

CIRCLES OF HOPE

A Historical Novel

This novel is an interpretation of actual facts and events.

Published by

S. Ross Publishing, Inc.
1621 S. Harvard Ave • Tulsa • Oklahoma • 74112

Library of Congress Cataloging-in-Publication Data
on file with the Library of Congress

ISBN   978-0-9888872-0-6
Copyright © 2013 by James C. Thomas
All Rights Reserved

Printed In The United States Of America

October 2013
First Edition, First Printing

CHAPTER ONE

$\mathcal{H}$e had made this walk numerous times on instructions from his mom. "Michael, run down to the mail box to see if the postman left us something." She didn't care what they might get, it was just the thing to do. The mail box was about a quarter of a mile down the dirt road from the farm house located on top of one of the highest hills in the area, a spot just east of Billings and about ten miles west of Blackwell in north central Oklahoma. Michael, the oldest and only boy of the four children of Tyler and Bessie Grimes, could, from the time he turned thirteen years of age, run down that dirt road from the house to the county road, get the mail, and run back in three minutes flat. That is, if he wanted to impress his mom with his speed. "Nobody is as fast as me," he would proudly boast to his mom.

Many times though, maybe most, Michael would take his own sweet-time, sometimes extending the short quarter mile distance to the mail box many times over, as he often times veered off the road and disappeared in the wheat fields surrounding the house. In whatever direction you looked from the Grimes' hilltop, wheat fields reached out as far as the eyes could see. This sea of wheat was broken only by hedgerows that followed the underground water flow and the dirt roads, cutting across the land to provide access to other homes in the area. Ever since he was old enough to claim the freedom to wander, Michael used the wheat fields as part of his private world. Whether he veered into his private world of wheat depended on the moment and his mood, or on the added instructions his mom sometimes gave him. "Get back as quickly as you can, Michael!"

The Grimes' house was built on a hilltop, the highest point on their 640 acres, giving Michael and his grandpa Mose Grimes, a great vantage point, to see for miles in all directions. Often times, the two would sit on top of that hilltop and just stare into the vast space around them. They would do this for long periods; it was their periods of tranquility. On occasion, Tyler would join his father and son in the early evening and the three of them would sit in their self-assigned green wooden lawn chairs anchored into the hillside by the passage of time, facing westward, always facing westward. Grandpa loved the sunsets. They are a gift from God he would say. And he wanted to share this gift with his son Tyler and then Michael.

Grandpa believed and kept telling Michael that one who can accept the beauty of nature that sketches her wonders across the western sky in the evening as God's portrait of colors and shapes, will find peace. The Grimes-men, Grandpa, Tyler and Michael, had all captured that special gift. The three of them could sit in those three green chairs for long periods sometimes saying nothing, taking in the sounds of silence, broken only by the punctuations of nature – the wind, the birds, the buzz of the insects, the crickets and the call and smell from the house that told them when dinner was ready. Most times, it was only Michael and his grandpa sitting in the chairs. Tyler was too busy running the wheat farm to sit for long spells, but he had been there when he was younger and held fond memories of those times spent with his dad. He enjoyed the moments sitting there, listening to all the wild, wonderful and beautiful stories his father had told him in the past and was now telling Michael.

On occasion, the whole family would come out to the three green chairs, though always remembering that the chairs were reserved for Mose, Tyler and Michael. The chairs always faced westward so they could see the evening sky, and no one ever dared move them. With the passage of time, the chairs had seemingly anchored themselves into the ground, and over that time, the spot had in a secular sense become a sacred area. It became a spot for self reflection and grandpa's stories, stories he was now passing on to his oldest grandchild.

The family cemetery, located about 100 yards south of the green chairs, was the spot recognized by all as the real consecrated place on the farm. There, the grave stones told the stories of the true pioneers and the many personal struggles that went into the building of what now was paradise. In the center of the family plot were the grave stones of Walter Grimes and his wife Sarah East Grimes. They were the true family pioneers who had taken part in the 1893 Land Run with great success. Ten grave stones were in the family plot in 1967, including three children who in life

never reached the age of seven. Walter had staked his claim to
the land and then he and Sarah defended their claim and held
the raw land and brought it to life. Their headstones in the
family cemetery preserved the story of their personal
struggles.

Walter and Sarah had come to the Cherokee Strip from
Alabama after learning that public land was about to be
opened to settlers by order from President Benjamin Harrison
in the year of 1893. They had six children and Mose was the
second oldest. But, three of their young children who had
come to the land with them had not been strong enough to
survive the great ordeal of homesteading, and now, each rested
in the family cemetery. Their grave stones added one more
enduring part to the expanding history of the courageous
pioneering families who took part in the settlement of
America's west and in what would become the State of
Oklahoma. On this hill in Noble County, Oklahoma, resting at
a spot overlooking a productive, living valley, Walter and
Sarah and their three young children who did not survive the
harshness of life on the prairie and who had to let go, now
rested in peace in the family cemetery. Yet, even in death,
they still cast their presence on all who lived. This is how it
was on the Grimes' wheat farm.

The Grimes family was close-knit, with each member
sharing in the duties of a farm-family. But, it was not all
work, and they all shared in the pleasures of life. During the
summer months on the farm, the family frequently gathered
around the three green lawn chairs to make and eat homemade
ice cream, with the flavors changing quiet often – strawberry,

lemon, peach or peppermint. No one in the county could make better ice cream than Michael's mom, Bessie Grimes. For her prized ice cream, she refused to use anything except the richest cream of the cow's milk and the freshest of berries off the vines. No shortcuts were ever taken. On occasions, with the number of times increasing as the girls in the family grew older, the Grimes-farm became the centerpiece and meeting place for teenagers.

Sarah Jean, approaching her fifteenth birthday, was the most active of the three girls. She was a tall girl, strikingly beautiful for a 14 year old, but a tomboy who loved going out on the wheat combines with her father. And, like her brother Michael, she too was athletic at school, playing basketball and volleyball. Quite frequently, Sarah Jean invited all her teammates and friends to come over for a cookout, and sometimes her dad or brother took them on a hay ride. On these occasions, she and her friends always preferred her brother Michael to hitch the team and drive the hay wagon. Michael and his girlfriend Suszette actually enjoyed this role. On occasion, Sarah Jean would invite her younger sisters, Cindy Kay, age 12, and Kathy Ann, age 9, to come along. Other times, Cindy and Kathy would simply climb on the wagon uninvited and go on the hay rides. During the hay rides with the younger kids, Suszette would lead them into songs, with the sound carrying for miles. They were that loud. When the singing was over, Michael turned the eyes of the kids skyward for watching and competing over the identification of groups of stars that form shapes in the nighttime sky.

Michael had become an expert in identifying a number of the constellations from his sky watching with his grandpa. One of the favorite things Michael and his grandpa liked most to do while sitting in their green chairs, just as early evening began to set in, was to watch the big Oklahoma sky – always looking westward.   Often times they sat in stone silence, watching the brilliant sunsets, made more brilliant by the rich red dirt found in the area that often blew toward the horizon by the steady Oklahoma winds that also powered the water-pump windmills.   They always liked to see how the sunset in the western sky at times cast its glow over the wheat fields and brought a tinge of gold down to earth. Their favorite time was in May when the wheat turned golden as it began to ripen, evidenced by the gentle waves created by the evening breeze. As the wheat reached the level of ripeness needed for harvest, the breeze moving through the drying stems of wheat gave off the light rustling or whispering sounds that the crop was ready for harvest.

Michael and his grandpa also loved watching the storms as they moved in from the south and west. At times, they loved the storms as much if not more so than the sunsets. Storm watching generated a different, higher energy-level feeling than watching the more peaceful sunsets.   They would watch the violent storms that moved in across the prairie bringing to earth the extraordinary power of lighting that in their minds removed all doubts about the existence of a God.   An Oklahoma lighting storm occurring sometimes without rain and with some frequency presented a pageantry of light far more grand than the most technologically advanced fireworks display. Accompanying these visual patterns of erupting flashes of light were the intermitting drum-roles from the claps of thunder, creating at times the likeness of a war zone battlefield.

On occasion, the whole family would come out to join Michael and his grandpa to watch the dramatic display of Oklahoma weather, except when the storm turned to rain, then they hurried to the house for shelter. A tornado or twister was scary enough to send everyone, including daring Michael and his grandpa, into their protective tornado shelter – an underground thick concrete bunker that had no comforts of home. But tornados quickly pass over without lingering too long, allowing the family to resurface to assess the damage if any. Earlier experiences had taught the family to recognize when it was time to head to the safety of the bunker. They had experienced the destructive force of an Oklahoma tornado that could lift a grain combine in the air or turn a barn or a house into small kindling scattering it over many acres. This was the Oklahoma, Michael would long remember and love.

But none of this, neither the storms he loved nor the beauty of the land was on Michael's mind as his eighteenth birthday started drawing closer, bringing with it an increased level of anxiety that the next thing he picked up at the mail box, a quarter mile down the hill from his house, might be his draft notice. All of his buddies graduating from Billings High School in 1967, faced the same hurdle and choices in their young lives: get accepted in a college with a draft deferment or simply take a chance that your number would not be pulled. None of the boys really wanted to go to Vietnam, but they were not opposed to the war as so many people were, including Suszette Andrew, Michael's steady girlfriend since the sixth grade.

The two of them had been inseparable, and both had worked the wheat harvests on the Grimes's wheat farm from the time they became teenagers. But as Michael reached the age of possible military service and Vietnam, a conflict erupted between Michael and Suszette.   It was inevitable. Suszette's parents had taught her to hate the Vietnam war, if for no other reason than out of a sense of justice and humanity. She saw no sense to the war that was killing American combat soldiers as well as the Vietnamese people. Michael, on the other hand, saw Vietnam as a sacred battle against the evils of Communism. He had been told so many times that if he lived in Russian or China his family's wheat farm would be taken by the State. Living on a wheat farm in Oklahoma, he thought, put him in a very special, historic Americana role. But this thought of patriotism that ran through Michael's head was not deep enough to lead him into volunteering. He would continue to wait for the official notice instructing him to report to the draft board in Oklahoma City. This war was causing for the first time a separation of Michael and Suszette. As it had divided the nation, the Vietnam war now was dividing these two teenage sweethearts.

People who have lived long on the land in north-central Oklahoma wheat country do indeed hold an historic Americana role, reaching back to the presidency of Abraham Lincoln. Serving as President from March 4, 1861 to the dark day of April 14, 1865, that fateful day he was shot, with death coming early the next day, the 16th President of the United States was more than the wartime Commander in Chief, trying to keep the country united. For sure the Civil War became the most visible stain on his administration. But Lincoln was also a man of peacetime vision – a pioneer, a farmer and an industrial adventurer. During his second year in office, the year of 1862, President Lincoln signed three important Congressional enactments into law. These laws would help lead to the settlement of America's vast continent westward, and on a smaller scale, the creation of the Grimes' wheat farm in Noble County, Oklahoma.

On May 15, Lincoln signed the bill that created the United States Department of Agriculture, an agency that helped turn America into the bread-basket of the world. Kansas and Oklahoma became the leaders in the production of wheat. Lincoln signed the Pacific Railroad Act, a move by Congress intended to expand rail transportation through heretofore uncharted territory heading westward and continuing until they reached the Pacific ocean. Most importantly, at least to Michael Grimes, President Lincoln signed the Homestead Act of 1862. Free land would be offered to all those fast enough to stake-out their prime quarter-section of land, and strong enough to defend and develop that land for five years. Those who succeeded in this great American experience, needed heart, stamina, staying power, a willingness, and the capability of spending five harsh years, turning raw solid ground into productive farms on which to raise and educate children. And out of the struggles, civilization was brought to the raw prairie land.

From the stories grandpa told, Michael could trace his family history and the story of their wheat farm all the way back to the great *Cherokee Strip* Land Run of 1893. Michael knew all the stories, at least as they were told to him by his grandpa during the many hours they sat in their green chairs, looking out over the wheat fields towards the sunsets or into the approaching storms. Subject of the stories grandpa told changed, depending on whether they were watching a storm come in or were marveling at the tints of color that appeared and moved with the setting sun. Grandpa never hesitated about embellishing the stories, stored up in his personal memory of the history of the great Land Run.

Walter Grimes had been able to beat thousands of other land-hungry settlers to claim as his own, 160 acres of free land. From the moment he drove his claiming stake into the ground, Walter Grimes sensed it was a perfect piece of land. And it was. The land had fertile soil and a good water supply from a spring-feed stream that ran through the property. The land was claimed at first by driving a wooden claim-stake in the ground. But, then, when need arose, these settlers had to defend their claim with a rifle. Now, the land only needed the work Walter Grimes and his wife Sarah had been willing to supply. Listening to all the stories about his pioneering family, Michael did not care how much grandpa embellished and dramatized the events. He could never get enough of the pioneering tales that had shaped his own young life.

It had been grandpa's parents, Walter and Sarah Grimes, who came to the Oklahoma Territory as hardy pioneers, who survived the great Land Run of 1893, and staked out their claim for a new life on the prairie. Walter had traveled from Alabama to join the thousands of other hungry land seekers who dreamed of the promise of free land under President Lincoln's Homestead Act. His wife Sarah and their children stayed back in Alabama on their small farm outside of Clanton, while Walter took his place among the throng of people gathering in what would become the State of Oklahoma. This great congregation of people were all there for the same reason. Walter was a big man, six feet, five inches tall, capable of handling himself against the best of them, and sometimes, he was put to the test.

For the great Land Run, Walter had the added advantage of owning one of the swiftest horses, that would take him to his promised land. He had come to the Oklahoma Territory and Indian country with a deep determination to make the historic dash for what he hoped would be the most productive piece of land he could reach before some other settler claimed the spot. How this Alabama farmer was able to reach his "Promised Land" was one more story Michael had heard from his grandpa. And, just as Walter had dreamed many years before, the land blossomed into a flower that, in time, yielded a bounty in hard red winter wheat that brought prosperity to the farm during the years when the wheat market was healthy. But now, other things were beginning to occupy the mind of Michael Grimes as he approached his eighteenth birthday.

During his senior year of high school in Billings, Michael, standing over six feet, four inches tall and weighing

230 pounds, had been the star high school quarterback. He was being highly recruited by several leading universities, including the University of Oklahoma, Texas, and Oklahoma State University, the State's agricultural college, located in Stillwater, not too far from the wheat farm. Suszette Andrew, Michael's high school sweetheart, tried to talk him into accepting the OSU football scholarship that had been offered him. She wanted him to enroll at OSU, where she had already been accepted. "If you don't," Suszette pleaded, "you are going to get drafted and sent to Vietnam." But Michael had already decided to take the chance that he would not be drafted. He didn't want to be drafted. What he wanted was to delay college a few years despite the risk of the draft. He wanted to become more involved in the operation of the wheat farm with his dad, knowing that one day he would be the one in charge of running the operation, just as his dad, his grandpa and his great grandpa before him. Michael's decision put a heavy strain on his long-time relationship with Suszette.

Suszette had been listening to her parents wail against the Vietnam war since before 1967. She had even attended a few highly active and charged antiwar rallies with them." And, she has joined in the chants, "Hey, hey, LBJ, how many kids did you kill today! Hey, hey, LBJ, how many kids did you kill today! Hey, hey, LBJ, how many kids did you kill today!" This chant began ringing out in Suszette's head, and would in time spread across the country. At all the antiwar demonstrations, attended by ten people or ten thousands or more, the chant could be heard on college campuses, on city streets and in the nation's capitol. "Hey, hey, LBJ, how many kids did you kill today!"

Michael refused to attend any of the antiwar demonstrations with Suszette and the two had argued over the meaning of them. He wasn't afraid of going to Vietnam and thought the people in the demonstrations were being disloyal to America. He did not want to get drafted, he wanted to stay on the farm to help raise wheat. But, he wasn't afraid of the draft. He faced the reality that chances were good that once he turned eighteen, he would be drafted and probably sent to Vietnam. In some ways, Michael thought, it was his duty to go if called, and he refused even to think about running from a fight against the Communists.

"If we don't stop them there," Michael once told Suszette, "we will be fighting them on the shores of the United States and then maybe even on our wheat farm." He had heard these domino-theory thoughts expressed during grange hall meetings he attended with his grandpa and dad. It didn't matter if there was truth or no truth in the thought. It was simply the thought that made him pause about trying to get out of serving his country, even in Vietnam if he got the call. Vietnam was, Michael thought, a war against Communism. This is what President Lyndon Johnson was telling the nation, and the Grimes family had listened and believed. If the call came, he would go. Until then, he wanted to stand with his father and be a wheat farmer, preparing for the 1967 harvest, which they expected to be a good crop, maybe even the best per acre yield for their 450 planted acres.

Harvest time was the busiest time on the farm, leaving little or no time for star gazing. Once the harvest began, completing the operation as quickly as possible before an Oklahoma storm suddenly appeared and devastated the crop, became top priority. During harvest time, everybody worked, and they worked long hours.   During his young life, Michael had already gone through several wheat harvests. As a small kid, he frequently rode on the big grain combines driven by his grandpa or dad as they harvested the wheat crop with the broad sweeps of the blades. From the safety of the cab, Michael would watch the big machines cut through the stems of wheat, and separate the chaff from the grain, with the wheat kernels pouring into the grain hopper of the combine. When the grain hopper became full, it is transferred from the combine to the trucks, and transported to the farm's storage elevators if there was space or to the local coop elevator.

The operation looked magical to the kids. By the time he was fourteen, Michael could handle one of the combines almost as skillfully as the men and could drive the grain trucks even better.   Without a doubt, this Billings High School football star was cut-out to be a wheat farmer and that is exactly what he wanted to do in life. He even liked going to the grange hall meetings where the farmers shared information about their wheat crop, the weather and what the grain market looked like. For this, they all relied on market information published by the United States Department of Agriculture, and mailed to the farmers.   Each time Michael saw the USDA's *Wheat Situation* arrive in the mail, he knew he was about to go to another grange hall meeting with his dad and grandpa.

The *Wheat Situation* was the official USDA quarterly publication distributed to the farmers during the months of

February, May, August and November. Congress had directed the USDA to collect current market data needed by the farmers to make informed decisions and to intelligently adjust their operations and practices to meet domestic and world market conditions. That Department was also required to conduct investigations abroad regarding factors affecting and influencing the export of wheat from the United States, and then to honestly report back to the farmers. The USDA's *Wheat Situation* contained vital information on wheat production levels, inventories, loan activity, domestic and export market prospects, and price projections. During the grange hall meetings, each farmer always held in hand his personal copy of the most recent *Wheat Situation* report as they discussed and made collective decisions, based on their reports. This was the way it was in wheat country; the farmers made collective decisions and took care of each other. Attending the grange meetings from the time he became a teenager, Michael took in every word, and after each meeting, he bombarded his dad or his grandpa with questions. Most of Michael's questions were directed to his grandpa because he seemed to have more patience.

As his eighteenth birthday approached, Michael began to experience a deep feeling that 1967 might be his last wheat harvest for awhile. It was a hot, muggy Monday, the first part of July, when he received the word. As he had most days, Michael walked or ran the quarter mile down the dirt road to the mail box, and on this day, there it was, just as he had suspected. The letter was addressed to him, and it was from the draft board. He was ordered to report to the draft board offices in Oklahoma City on July 12, 1967, for his physical examination. That evening, with letter in hand, Michael, his dad and his grandpa headed for their green chairs and there they sat for the longest time in complete silence. Not saying a word, they kept looking out over the fields and into the cloudless sky as the evening turned into a moonless night that allowed them to escape into the star-filled wonder and for a time travel down the milky-way path of stars, with no worry about the draft or Vietnam. Finally, the silence was broken by Michael's words.

"I don't want you all to worry," he said. "I know I will pass the physical, and if I have to go, I will go." Then he added in a boastful voice, "If I get sent to Vietnam, woe to those Communist bastards." Michael didn't really believe any of these words, the same words he had told his mom. But he thought they might help to keep his grandpa from worrying. The words though didn't help very much at all, with his dad or his grandpa. They would worry. They had both silently hoped Michael would have listened to Suszette and had enrolled at OSU where he would have received a good education and a draft deferment. Yet, that wasn't Michael's decision, and his dad and grandpa respected the decision he had made. So the three wheat farmers sitting in the green chairs returned to their silence and continued gazing into the star-filled sky.

CHAPTER TWO

$\mathcal{N}$ot surprising to anyone in the Grimes family or to Suszette, Michael passed his physical examination and soon thereafter received his induction notice three days before Thanksgiving.   Michael was ordered to report for military duty, and with that the reality of war became very real for the Grimes family.   Whatever feeling of pride there may have been, it did little to dull their sense of fear.   As Michael and the other inductees began boarding the bus that would transport them to their basic training camp, all the young men right out of high school could see the crowd of antiwar demonstrators gathering. They were assembling and lining the road leading out of the induction center.   This was the first time Michael had witnessed a live demonstration against the war in Vietnam and against the draft, and now it was against him, he thought. He had seen it on television. But now, it was first hand, in sight and sound."Hey, Hey, LBJ, How many kids did you kill today?" came the growing and repeated chant from the crowd. "Hey, Hey, LBJ, How many kids did you kill

today?   Hey, Hey, LBJ, How many kids did you kill today?"
The sound kept ringing!

At the very front of the line of the demonstrators stood
Michael's girlfriend, Suszette Andrew, and her parents.   She
was leading the group in chants and slurs directed at the army
and the new inductees. Michael was so confused. How could
these people be standing against the soldiers who were risking
their lives in the fight against the evils of Communism, and in
defense of America's homeland?   My God, this is America!
he thought. A tear rolled down his cheek, as he felt so deeply
hurt, seeing Suszette standing with the demonstrators, yelling
slurs at him. My God! they had been sweethearts since
elementary school.   How could Suszette of all people be out
there standing as an antiwar demonstrator against him?
Michael could not understand. But soon, the sound stopped as
the bus speeded up and the crowd was left in the distance.

During basic training, a grinding period, spanning
some eight weeks, Michael learned through repetition the
skills of weaponry, marksmanship, explosives, killing and
map reading. The art of killing had become a taught skill to
the soldiers who would be going into battle of survival — kill
or be killed. You are America's soldiers, Michael and the
other draftees were repeatedly told.   Physical conditioning
was also a big part of basic training: daily workouts, two-mile
runs then three-miles then four.   For Michael, this basic
military training was a lot like his high school football
training, except that instead of the coaches yelling at the
players, it was now the sergeants And, just as the young
soldiers, with muscles aching, thought their day was coming to

an end, the sergeant called them out for a ten mile march with full gear. On top of all of this physical and war stuff, the soldiers attended mandatory propaganda classes on the evils of Communism and why America needed to send her young combat troops to Vietnam. "We are over there," the sergeant shouted out to the troops, "to kill Communists so that your families and all American people can feel safe." Then he added with increased emphasis, "if you don't kill them, they will kill you!"

During his basic training, Michael found moments of leisure when he allowed his mind to drift back to the wheat farm in Oklahoma and to the pioneering stories he had heard more than once from grandpa Mose. When his army buddies opened the door by asking Michael about Oklahoma, the cowboys and Indians or the Dust Bowl days of the '30s, Michael willingly obliged. When that door was opened, he would tell some of the stories he had heard from his grandpa, adding of course, as his grandpa had done, his own embellishment. Telling the stories helped him get through the stressful life of a soldier, who just wanted to go home when it was all over.

"Back before the greatest of the five Land Runs that opened Oklahoma to settlers," Michael began one of his stories, "the Cherokee Indian Tribe was, as were the other tribes in Oklahoma, assigned by treaty to vast areas of land." The land assigned the Cherokees in the Oklahoma Territory had been intended to replace the farm lands stolen from them in Georgia. Driven off their lands in Georgia, the tribe was forcefully relocated to what would become Oklahoma

Territory. "In addition to this assigned land," Michael
continued, "the Cherokee Tribe was also granted rights or
easements over a strip of land along the Kansas border that
was about 58 miles wide and 226 miles long, providing the
Indians access to their hunting grounds." Michael paused,
then added, "This 226 mile strip of land became known as the
'Cherokee Outlet.'"

Before Michael could complete the story, the sergeant
ordered the soldiers back into formation for a run to the rifle
range for mandatory qualifying. Later that evening back at the
barracks when things quieted down, Michael was urged to
complete the story about the Cherokees. He did not hesitate,
for it took him back home to the wheat harvests and to his
green chair and the evening sessions with his grandpa.
Michael began, "The Cherokees had been given the right to
use the Outlet for accessing their hunting areas." But, then,
sounding a level of personal disappointment, he added, "this
land was also taken away from the Cherokees after the Civil
War, as a form of retribution for their siding with and aiding
the Confederacy. After Congress created the Oklahoma
Territory by the Organic Act of 1890, the Cherokee Strip was
then opened to the settlers." Michael stopped here, telling his
army buddies that the Land Run was a different story, and he
needed to stop because he wanted to get his weekly letters off
to his mom and dad and grandpa before going to sleep. He
wanted to tell his family that it was looking like he would
soon be shipping out for Vietnam, and for them not to worry.
Two weeks later, he was on his way.

By the time Michael reached Vietnam, he had been

trained to be suspicious of everybody in that country, including the women and children. He had been trained and trained to kill all the Communists he could find. But, he never learned how to tell for sure which Vietnamese was Communist. Just kill them! The means mattered not – bombings, field artillery, helicopter gun-ships, napalm or hand-to-hand combat. Kill! Kill! Kill! Michael was one of the ground troops and frequently reminded about why they were there in the jungle. "This is a war against Communism, and forgetting it might cost you your life." Michael knew why he was there, and he did not need such constant reminder of what was before them. Basic training had made him ready, but it would still be November, nearing Thanksgiving, before his unit faced actual combat.

The first field operation for Michael and his fellow combat troops was an assignment to capture a hill that had a number instead of a name. It was a hill on which North Vietnamese troops were firmly entrenched. Capturing this nameless hill would not be easy, nothing was in Vietnam. But after intense bombing with napalm that filled the air with the smell of burning flesh, followed by many ground attempts, resulting in hundreds of casualties on both sides, the American troops finally captured the unnamed lonely hill. There they waited, for what, the troops could never understand. Waiting and waiting brought loneliness and boredom, one of the biggest problems facing the soldiers in Vietnam. Few of the combat troops including Michael could understand the military strategy for all this waiting. For the soldiers, it simply made no sense. But, their's was not to think. They were soldiers! They were not supposed to think!

Not long after going out on their first field operation, Michael and the other troops learned that the Communists had launched a major coordinated offensive that had reached all the way into Saigon, the American embassy, and other urban areas previously believed impenetrable. They called it the Tet offensive. Five American soldiers died during the Communists' attack on and capture of the Embassy. It mattered little that American troops quickly regained control of the Embassy. The lasting images of the raids, played and replayed on American television screens, belied the empty optimism the American military leaders had been feeding the American public. "Hey, hey LBJ, how many kids did you kill today?" The chant could be heard in all regions of America, and in Vietnam, among many of the troops, who still stood day-to-day and faced the threat of death.

Back in Oklahoma, Michael's mom and dad heard the news of the Communists' surprise Tet offensive that began on January 1, 1968, and with that dismal news, they began questioning the sense of the war. Their growing doubts were reinforced one evening, as they were listening to the CBS News, a daily event on the farm, and heard the words of Walter Cronkite, "What the hell is going on? I thought we were winning the war!" Michael and his fellow soldiers heard these same reports and they too began wondering what the hell they were doing over there. News can travel fast on the battlefield. The soldiers quickly learned that the Communists had embarrassed the U.S. military, shattering America's myth of invincibility. The Communist Tet offensive effectively destroyed the public's confidence in the Johnson Administration. Still Michael was a soldier, willing to follow orders and do his duty, even if the orders made no sense to him. The system controlled the thinking of Michael and the other soldiers.

But out in the fields of battle, Michael had one advantage over many of the other troops who suffered from loneliness and boredom. He could always lift his head and gaze up and into the sky and the clouds if there were any, with their many formations. This is what his grandpa had taught him. This is what his grandpa was probably doing right then, back in Oklahoma. That was their private linkage. His loneliness could be broken by the memories of home, his visions of the Oklahoma wheat fields, his own green chair and his long evening sessions listening to his grandpa's stories. In time, however, after witnessing the evidence of war and death on a daily basis, these once cherished memories began to fade as Michael, so typical with the soldiers in Vietnam, began withdrawing, no longer caring or finding pleasure in telling his stories to his fellow soldiers.

Though Michael began mentally withdrawing from the outside world as the death of war pushed out the beauty and peacefulness of the Oklahoma wheat fields he once remembered, he could still find some solace as brief as they might be in letting his mind drift back to the stories his grandpa told as the two of them sat alone in their green chairs. But he no longer wanted to share the stories. He just kept to himself. Mentally isolated on a lonely hill or in the jungle infected with danger, one of his favorite thoughts that brought him some relief from his combat loncliness was the one about his great grandpa's race for the free land.   At nighttime, he could lie back on the ground and look up at the stars and allow his mind to move into a different time zone, all the way back to the year 1893.

Thousands of hopeful settlers on horseback, wagon and on foot lined up and waited for the signal on this beautiful cloudless day.   All the land-hungry settlers anxiously waited for the signal that would set them free to reach out and grab their future, if they could.   When the signal finally sounded, the race was on, and, at that very moment, the air was filled with the sounds of racing horses, wagon wheels and vocal screams of excitement and anger from the men racing toward the horizon, leaving behind only a cloud of dust that quickly blotted-out their visual images to those remaining back at the starting line.   They were all reaching out, hoping to find an open spot to drive their claiming-stake on their prized 160 acres.

As Michael allowed his mind to drift back to the spot where his grandpa was probably still visiting each day, the spot of the three green chairs, he could look up to the nighttime sky in Vietnam and see the same milky-way that he and his grandpa had watched together back on the wheat farm. The path of the milky-way brought him home just for a moment. For that moment at night, the soldiers waited on top of that unnamed hill, just waiting for orders to move off the hill. In all this, Michael could still look up at the milky-way and sense the presence of his own private linkage back to his home in Oklahoma. He was always certain his grandpa was linked to the other end of the same milky-way, giving him a sense that they were still connected.

After several days of holding the unnamed hill, the troops were suddenly ordered to move off the hill they had captured and move out on a search and destroy mission. As ordered, the unit moved through the jungle in search of the enemy and when found, to kill them – "search and destroy." Unfortunately, some units, carrying out ordered search and destroy missions, went far beyond acceptable behavior. One such event took place in the early morning of March 16, 1968, in the hamlet of My Lai, located in the jungle about one hundred miles northeast of Saigon. On that morning, a platoon of American combat troops moved into the village on a search and destroy mission and opened fire on old men, women and children running from their dwellings. Those in the village not killed on the initial entry were gathered up and led to a large ditch where they were systematically shot. Some girls as young as five and six were first raped and then shot. When the slaughter was over, 200 to 500 men, women and children had been ravished and killed. Facing such atrocities in a war that was beginning to make less and less sense, many American soldiers fighting in Vietnam, began turning against the war. Questions too were being raised in the mind of Michael Grimes as he began to go deeper and deeper into withdrawal.

Back in America, the media's increased coverage of the atrocities in Vietnam, without offsetting news of advancements toward victory or settlement, began creating a progressively deepening disenchantment among the people.

In 1968, a year of recurring calamities, the Vietnam war became one of the dominating issues in presidential politics. President Johnson, hit with one calamity after another, the assassination of Martin Luther King, Jr., the riots that followed in many major American cities, and the assassination of Robert Kennedy, decided to called it quits. LBJ decided to forego his bid for a second full term as President as he withdrew from politics and headed back to his ranch in Texas. On March 31, 1968, speaking to a nationwide television audience, he made his surprise announcement: "I shall not seek, and I will not accept, the nomination of my party for another term as your President."

Suszette Andrew, Michael's former girl friend, along with other anti-war activists, were thrilled, and took some credit for President Johnson's decision not to run for reelection. She had remained enrolled at Oklahoma State University to complete her spring '68 semester. But that summer, Suszette decided to go with her parents to Chicago during the Democratic Convention, where Vice President Hubert Humphrey was vying for the nomination to be the Democratic candidate for President. That week in Chicago convinced Suszette not to return to OSU for her fall semester. She had decided to devote her full-time efforts to the antiwar movement. Her strong opposition to the Vietnam war that led to her estrangement from Michael grew stronger as she came to believe that the war had already caused too much suffering, and too many losses of lives. Suszette helped organize marches in Washington against the war. During her efforts, she was arrested numerous times and beaten by the police more than once. All this seemed to add more fuel to her burning energies. She hated the war and the soldiers fighting in the war and was beginning to hate the country that was allowing young men to be drafted and killed for no damn reason.

Her thoughts about the soldiers fighting in Vietnam were always tempered by her realization that most of them had been drafted and were not there by choice. This was a politician's war! The politicians in Washington financed the war to let it happen, but none of them was facing the dangers of that war that could bring instant death or some maiming injury that might cause one to wish for death. As Suszette fought the battles of the streets, she at times momentarily reflected back to her days in Oklahoma. She could never bring herself to hate Michael Grimes, even though she was angry that he had not sought to avoid the draft by enrolling at OSU. Had he just done that, Suszette thought to herself, she too might have stayed in school.

• • • •

During his 1968 presidential campaign, Richard Nixon promised to end the Vietnam war if he were elected President. He kept repeating that promise, and based on that promise, Nixon was elected President in a campaign against Democratic candidate Hubert Humphrey, albeit by a razor-thin nationwide margin of only 510,000 votes. With that victory, Vietnam suddenly became Nixon's war, and from the first day he took office, the antiwar activity on college campuses and in

the cities across the nation intensified and kept getting hotter
and more violent day-by-day.

From the moment he took office, President Nixon
seriously sought a quick solution. He wanted to proclaim
peace with honor, during his first year in office. In his
inaugural address, the new President and man of peace made
clear that his first priority as President was to find an answer
to Vietnam. "Let us take this as our goal," Nixon told the
nation, "where peace is unknown, make it welcome; where
peace is fragile, make it strong; where peace is temporary,
make it permanent." He saw no limits to how far he was
willing to go to deliver on his campaign promises of peace.
"We are caught in war, wanting peace. We're torn by division,
wanting unity. We see around us empty lives, wanting
fulfillment. We see tasks that need doing, waiting for hands to
do them." Nixon truly and boldly believed he would become
known as the man of peace, and that he could reach a peace
agreement within his first year in office.

As he strolled down the beach soon after the election,
still basking in his narrow victory, Nixon told H.R. Haldeman,
"I'm the one man in this country who can end the Vietnam
war." With this high level of confidence, Nixon, as President-
elect, set out toward achieving his goal of peace, bringing into
his administration Henry Kissinger, a tenured Harvard
professor, who possessed the expertise Nixon thought might
be helpful. But then he took office. And, nothing seemed to
work. During Nixon's first two years in office the war
continued. Combat troops kept dying and soldiers were being
sent home maimed. Michael Grimes was still in Vietnam,

risking his life, going out regularly with his unit on search and destroy missions.

But finally, in March, 1970, Michael Grimes received the good news that all soldiers relished with deep anticipation. He was going home – target date, April 15. Could it be true? He had been there for so long, maybe even overlooked by the brass. Now, if all goes well, he might even get back to Oklahoma, in time for the 1970 wheat harvest. At that moment though, the wheat harvest no longer excited him. The war had taken its toll, and it would get worse. A few days before he was scheduled to ship out, Michael was sent out on one more search and destroy mission. There had been so many. This time his unit became involved in a heavy firefight with the Vietcong, and Michael was seriously wounded. Shrapnel tore through his body as he went face down in a muddy rice field. On that day, the field turned red with his blood and the blood of his comrades.

When Michael went down and was facing death, a quick call went out for a helicopter to lift him out to safety and transfer him to a field hospital. A young pilot, who had been on a bombing raid was heading back to the base when he heard the call. Without hesitation, he responded in the face of great danger. His Cobra helicopter dropped down out of the sky and somehow Michael's damaged body was loaded on the Cobra, and he was taken out of harms reach to a highly advanced field hospital. There he remained until the doctors got him stabilized, and then Michael was flown home to the army hospital in Texas, where he would remain for an indefinite period.

In a strange twist of things going bad, Michael's grandpa had died of a sudden heart attack two days after Michael was wounded. He was eighty-seven years of age. Sadly, Michael would not be home for his grandpa's funeral. He was not even told about his grandpa's death until after the doctor's were sure the news would not cause a setback in his recovery. In time, Michael fully recovered physically from his wounds, after the doctors had so skillfully removed all the shrapnel. Mentally, his prognosis remained uncertain. The war had scattered Michael's dreams. No longer was there the pioneering spirit that had been instilled in him by his grandpa. Whether he would ever regain the depth of those dreams, only time could tell. With his grandpa's comforting words now gone, the uncertainties became more uncertain.

As soon as Michael arrived at the army hospital in Texas on April 21, 1970, his mom and dad were there. His mom stayed by his side until the physical danger had past. But with the 1970 wheat harvest approaching, his dad had to get back to the farm. Still he called every day to check on his son, hoping he would soon be home. Michael remained in the army hospital for three more months for physical treatment and mental counseling. He was finally cleared on August 10, 1970, to go home, and immediately, plans began for a big celebration on the Grimes wheat farm. Sarah Jean, now 17 years of age, took the lead, and together with her sisters, they decorated the house and the yard in great anticipation of their brother's return.

When the day arrived, Tyler drove to Texas to pick up Michael at the hospital. But, Tyler's trip to pick up his son turned out to be a demoralizing experience. During the drive back home, Tyler for the first time realized the changes his son was exhibiting. No longer was he the vibrant, spirited boy who loved going out on wheat harvests. Now Michael was a withdrawn, dispirited man who didn't give a damn about anything, and who could at any given moment, display fits of violence, as if he were still back in Vietnam, fighting some invisible enemy.

Before he was drafted and sent to the army, Michael was happy, confident, excited about life and his future. He was always talkative and inquisitive. He had a work ethic few men could match. Now, the person heading back to the Grimes farm was someone Tyler did not know and did not like. Michael was totally withdrawn from the present and refused to be drawn into conversation. He did not even ask about grandpa Mose, who would no longer be waiting at the farm for his arrival. He did not ask about his sisters. He didn't even ask about his mom. Nothing seemed to matter to him!

Mile after mile, Tyler drove the highway toward the farm, constantly trying to get his son to talk. Nothing came out, that is until he started screaming at his dad. Then he would apologize. It was an agonizing experience. In time, silence replaced the screaming — Michael, out of need for an isolated world; and Tyler, out of deep frustration. They said nothing to each other, nothing at all. Back at the farm, Michael's sisters were excited, happily waiting to launch their big celebration, the moment their brother arrived. They had worked so hard planning for his return.

As they got closer to home, Tyler thought things might get better. They didn't. Michael was back home, but yet he was not. Tyler began to think that maybe Michael's own soul had been lost to Vietnam. As they drove toward the house, Tyler stopped and paused at the mail box that Michael had checked so often. Anything to spark a memory. Then he drove slowly up the dirt road toward the house, hoping Michael would see something that might break him out of his silence. Tyler wanted to hear Michael scream-out, "Yes, I am back home." But nothing! Only more silence! The silence seemed so loud to Tyler.

Before going into the house where the girls were waiting with their home coming celebration, Tyler tried to get Michael to walk over to the family cemetery plot, to spend a moment with his grandpa, but he wasn't ready. Then, Tyler tried to get him to go over to the three green chairs, to sit with him for awhile as he had done so often with his grandpa. But, Michael seemed to have forgotten all about the three green chairs and their liberating force. So had Tyler. Michael wasn't ready; he wasn't ready for anything.

After reaching the house, Michael was blind to all the decorations his sisters had put up in celebration of his homecoming. They simply did not register. He just wanted to go in the house and escape to his room. When they entered the house, Michael was met by three screaming girls, "Welcome home Michael! We love you.!" The room was full of balloons with a big "WELCOME HOME- MICHAEL" sign. And his mom was standing in the middle of the room with tears streaming down her face, her arms outstretched ready to embrace her son. Michael stood in silence for a long period, just gazing at the balloons and his sisters, showing no emotion, no expression, not saying a thing, not even a thank you. When Michael's mom and sisters tried to embrace him, he defensively drew back, not wanting to be touched. Finally, he went to his room, slammed the door, and went to bed at four o'clock in the afternoon.

Michael's mom and dad decided to just leave him alone and hope that in time his mind too would finally come home to join his body. Sarah Jean, and her younger sisters, Cindy Kay and Kathy Ann, could not understand the coldness in their brother. Kathy, now 12 years of age, began crying and the two older girls tried to comfort her, but they couldn't understand either. "Doesn't Michael love us anymore?" Kathy ask her mom. Her mom did not answer.

Michael was scheduled to go to the VA hospital in Oklahoma City on a weekly basis, for treatment of his physical and mental war wounds. He had been diagnosed with post-traumatic stress disorder. PTSD was a common occurrence for Vietnam veterans who had personally witnessed and felt the atrocities of war, a war that began to make no sense to them. His mom took him to his weekly visits to the VA hospital and clinic. There, the doctors expressed the view to her that Michael's PTSD may have been further aggravated by the death of his grandpa that he had learned about while in the hospital. He had not been able to go through his needed period of mourning.

Michael so loved his grandpa and the peaceful times the two of them were together, sitting in their green lawn chairs, watching the heaven's masterpieces being painted across the evening sky. The choreographed lightning displays and the star-studded skies at night gave them a feeling of worth. At times, the two of them would sit in their green chairs for long periods without saying a word. But now, with grandpa gone, none of this seemed important to Michael. He no longer saw the beauty in the sky. He remained withdrawn, sheltered in the privacy and protection of his own room. Michael's room became his shelter. No one was allowed to enter, except for Sarah Jean who refused to accept any boundaries and would just barge in at any time, and get away with it.

Sitting in the silence of his room, Michael's emotions kept building with no release until, at unexpected moments, he felt his head and body about to explode. When this happened, he raced out of the house and started running. He just kept on running for miles, until physical exhaustion took over his body and mind. Right at that point, he just stopped. On the positive side, the running helped keep Michael physically fit, and temporarily it released his pent-up emotions and anger. For these few moments, he found peace, but still no interaction with people. When he got back home, he always headed back to the solitude of his room, as if those surrounding walls gave him protection from harm.

As time passed, Tyler began losing patience with Michael. Yet, out of his love for his son, knowing what he must have gone through, Tyler did his best to remain calm. It was a struggle, and the struggle was getting harder. His one real escape was work. He had a farm to run and that was a big job. The Grimes farm was 640 acres, with 450 of those acres cultivated in wheat.   After the Land Run in 1893, homesteading settlers received 160 acres, but after the Dust Bowl days when farming became harder, hopeless for some, many farmers just gave up and left the land. Grandpa Mose, after taking over operations of the farm from his pa, stepped in and purchased his neighbors' farms, more to help them out than simply to increase his acreage.   Many of the farmers escaping the residual effects of the dust storms simply abandoned their land or lost it in subsequent tax sales.

Grandpa Mose paid the neighboring farmers who wanted out, a fair price for their land.   The dust storms had been centered farther west, out in the Oklahoma Panhandle, but the drought left residual effects on the farmers in Noble County. When Tyler took over the farm, he was content with keeping it at the 640 acres his dad had put together. But he added a lot of improvements, including two large grain storage terminals.   He also kept his mom's vegetable garden that during the season provided fresh vegetables to the family, and he added more fruit trees. Tyler also expanded the herd of cattle, running some 100 head at the time Michael got home from Vietnam.

A year after Michael got home from Vietnam, with all the medical care he received at the army hospital, Michael seemed no better. He remained deeply withdrawn, closing his eyes to the beauty of the Oklahoma skies, and showing no interest in helping on the farm, even as the 1971 wheat harvest was approaching. For Tyler, he found relief that the harvest was about to start; it would serve as his personal distraction and escape from Michael. Once the harvest started, he didn't have to think about his son – he simply didn't have the time or energy. He let his wife do the worrying. But, she too was growing weary. The wheat harvest demanded so much time, but Tyler was now more than ever using the harvest as an excuse for staying away from the house and his son. It was obvious to all who knew him, including his wife and daughters, that Tyler was having a hard time coping. He began staying away from the house and letting his wife, who had greater patience and love for their son, take on all responsibilities. This was his way of surviving. If Tyler could just stay busy, he would not have to feel guilty. So, he buried himself with work around the farm and with his grange duties.

● ● ● ●

Arrival in the mail of the May 1971 issue of the *Wheat Situation* from the Department of Agriculture was once an occurrence that excited Michael. Now it only gave Tyler another excuse to stay away from the house. Tyler knew that once that publication arrived, the farmers would be heading to the grange hall to discuss the market prospects for their 1971 wheat harvest. Such discussions that could extend for days and on through harvest time offered one more escape for Tyler. But this time was time worth spending. The discussion was important to all the wheat farmers, who placed great reliance on the accuracy of the USDA *Wheat Situation*. This official publication was made more useful by the farmers' careful analysis of the information. The May 1971 issue of the *Wheat Situation* was the most important of the four annual issues because it arrived just before harvest time. It was the issue that contained the most critical market information, including the amount of wheat held in storage nationally, the expected production level of wheat, a forecast of the demand for wheat within the domestic and export markets, as well as projected prices the farmers could reasonably expect during the spring and summer of 1971.

This May issue of the *Wheat Situation* reminded the farmers they had the option of either selling their 1971 wheat harvest outright on the grain market at the current market price (about $1.32 per bushel), or they could take out a government non-recourse crop loan of about $1.25 per bushel, and take a chance without risks that market prices would experience a big jump. Farmers electing to take the loan had to pledge their wheat crop as security with the USDA's Commodity Credit Corporation (CCC). That agency took physical possession of the grain and stored it under USDA contracts with many private grain elevators scattered around the countryside. Later, if market prices increased high enough beyond the market price of $1.32 per bushel, farmers could redeem their wheat from the CCC by repaying the crop loan plus accrued interest and storage charges. They would then be free to sell their wheat on the open market at the higher price. This critical decision turned on the accuracy of the information the farmers received from the USDA.

For the farmer to win on the loan option, market prices for wheat would need to increase high enough for the farmer to repay the crop loan, plus the loan interest, storage charges, and an increase in market prices that would leave them a profit margin. Absent that, the farmers could simply let the CCC take clear title of the wheat, without further obligation on them. They were relieved of all obligations under the loan, including accumulated interest and storage charges. This important option is what the farmers needed to discuss among themselves at their grange hall meeting. As the years passed, the USDA's Commodity Credit Corporation, had become the owner of mammoth quantities of wheat that would be added to the growing vast wheat surpluses. These huge, ever growing, wheat surpluses created economic and costly problems for both the CCC and the farmers.

America's mountainous wheat surplus had resulted from bountiful harvests, slow markets, and the nature of the system itself. And as long as the surpluses existed, farm wheat prices would remain depressed. This was something the farmers discussed at their grange hall meetings, but it was not something they could change. After the farmers reviewed all the data in the USDA *Wheat Situation* and after listening to all the discussion, Tyler announced that he had decided to sell his 1971 wheat crop to either the Farmers' Coop or to one of the big independent grain companies – Continental Grain, Cargill Incorporated or the Bunge Corporation, that bought grain in Oklahoma. He decided against taking a crop loan because the May issue of the USDA *Wheat Situation* offered no positive indicators that the market would be getting any better. Taking the $1.32 market price now seemed better than taking the $1.25 crop loan, with the expectation that things would get better. They weren't, not according to their government. The USDA made everything about the market look so negative and bleak. The May 1971 issue of the *Wheat Situation* gave the farmers a gloomy forecast that left them with little hope for improvement. Most, if not all, the farmers attending the grange meeting made the same decision as Tyler — to sell their 1971 wheat crop on the open market.

Oklahoma wheat was ready for harvest by the end of May and into early June, and this year's wheat crop was looking good. It was an annual event when the big combines, on signal, started their motors and began cutting through the Oklahoma grain fields. With the big combines, the farmers begin the process, collecting the precious kernels of wheat that go into making rolls and bread. When the time arrived, Tyler once again tried to convince Michael to come to the fields and ride with him in the combine as he had done so frequently as a kid. But, he wasn't ready! That's what Michael's mom kept telling Tyler. "Give him more time." But Tyler thought he had given Michael enough time.

"Come on Michael," his dad spoke, almost in a pleading voice.

"I don't feel like it," Michael told his dad.

Tyler kept pressing the issue as he began showing his loss of patience, "Get off your lazy ass and come on!" Tyler barked, this time more as a command than a request, just as if he were in the army.

"Get off my fucking back," Michael blurted out in an angry voice as he started screaming at his dad. And without waiting for his stunned father to say anything, Michael raced back to the house to the protected safety of his room.

Tyler did not go after him. As his own anger built, all Tyler could think of was to tell Michael "to hell with you." As his escape, Tyler headed back into the wheat fields and climbed back into his combine, trying to get the harvest completed before the weather changed. He tried not to think about what he had just experienced. But more and more and more, he was losing patience with Michael, and was close to telling him to get the hell out of his house and not return until he was ready to do his share of the work. He didn't know what else to do. But Michael's mom always intervened and shielded her son and Tyler was always glad she did. She held on to her faith and hope, knowing in her mind that Michael would soon find his way back home.

While Michael Grimes was still in Vietnam, his father and his grandpa, until his death on April 14, 1970, had looked after the operation of their wheat farm. Some evenings the two of them would go out and sit in their green chairs, think about Michael, and watch the waves of wheat roll with the rhythm of the light Oklahoma breezes. They always recalled how much Michael had loved the land and the wheat harvests, the high point in the year for all the wheat farmers. With grandpa gone and Michael still trying to find his way back home, Tyler alone carried the burdens of the farming operation. Except that Sarah Jean was beginning to show more interest in the wheat harvest and riding the combine with her dad, and driving one of the grain trucks.

Hope within the Grimes family was raised by an announcement of a new treatment for PTSD that included intense group sessions and an experimental drug developed by the VA. On recommendations from his doctor, Michael was checked into the mental wing of the VA hospital in Oklahoma City, on September 6, 1971. This new experimental plan was a thirty day inpatient treatment plan during which time no visitation by parents or anyone else would be allowed. Michael's doctor believed the treatment plan had promise. Tyler was happy for his son, but he saw something else about the thirty days. During the time Michael remained in the hospital with no visitation allowed, Tyler saw this as a time of peace on the farm, when he could enjoy his wife and three daughters. And for this, Tyler expressed no guilt feelings at all.

But when the thirty days came to an end, and Michael returned home, it was back to the same. Bessie could see nothing the new treatment had done for her son. Everything reverted back the way it was. When he arrived back home from the VA hospital, he seemed as deeply withdrawn if not more so than when he was checked in. Nothing seemed to be working. And now, Bessie too began experiencing growing despair, thinking that it might not ever get any better. It's that god-damn Vietnam war! she kept thinking.

CHAPTER THREE

$\mathcal{A}$s the antiwar scene became more intense, violent and expensive, Suszette Andrew became more deeply involved, and lost all contact with her childhood sweetheart. She did not know Michael Grimes had returned home from Vietnam, a shell of a man, living at home on the wheat farm. She did not know he had been seriously wounded and was still suffering from his battlefield scars. In her mind, she saw Michael as one of the many casualties of that damn war, but so was she. While Michael stood and fought as a soldier against the Communists in Vietnam, Suszette stood as a soldier of peace, fighting President Nixon who was escalating the war instead of bringing it to an end, as he had promised the voters. Suszette stood firmly committed to a cause for peace without war. Her activism against the war led her into joining up with antiwar groups that had become progressively more militant and committed to an unending increase in a pressure-building campaign against President Nixon. Their campaign would continue until Nixon or his successor in office finally announced an end to the war.

The longer the war continued, the more violent the antiwar activists became. The violence increased in direct proportion to the level of desperation. News reports chronicled the tactics used by antiwar groups: increased violence on college campuses, detonation of explosive devices in the nation's Capitol Building and other public places, burning draft board offices and draft cards. Then there was this more daring dramatic tactic that never got beyond the planning stages. The plan of one antiwar group called for Henry Kissinger to be kidnapped and tried for war crimes. But the plot was discovered by the FBI before it even materialized. When the threat was uncovered, the FBI notified the White House. And, in his act of drama, Kissinger wrote a personal letter to the President, urging him "to meet no demands of the kidnappers, however trivial." The letter continued, "If you should receive any communication from me to the contrary, you should assume that it was made under duress."

Facing growing pressure from antiwar groups, White House security was tightened, with the FBI handling the major part of the increased security needs. President Nixon's concern about information leaks led him to adopt the strict security practices used by his predecessors. He signed off on a plan to continue an active program of wiretapping certain White House staffers, suspected of leaking information to the press, just as his predecessor had done. As Nixon placed his focus on finding a way out of Vietnam, White House officials grew increasingly concerned over leaks of classified information, particularly information relating to his highly secret policies relating to Vietnam, China, and the Soviet Union.

Responding to the seriousness of these information leaks, Nixon, met with his top advisers soon after being sworn into office. He met with Attorney General John Mitchell, Henry Kissinger, and J. Edgar Hoover in late April 1969, to discuss the serious problems arising out of information leaks. Based on these early discussions, President Nixon approved a White House security plan to be run exclusively by the FBI. Under the approved plan, either the President or Kissinger could unilaterally without court supervision authorize the FBI to wiretap individuals suspected of leaking information. It was all part of the FBI's program of electronic surveillance. Seventeen wiretaps were placed on thirteen government officials and four newsmen, all of whom had been suspected of leaking or receiving classified documents.

In May 1969, FBI Director Hoover informed Kissinger that one of his National Security Council members, Morton Halperin, was suspected of leaking information about the President's decision to expand the war by carrying out bombing raids in Cambodia. Hearing this, Kissinger instructed Hoover to install wiretaps on Halperin's and three other individuals' telephones. Once the wiretaps were in place, FBI agents closely monitored the intercepted telephone communications and prepared logs of the conversations. From the daily monitoring logs, FBI agents summarized the discussions and forwarded them to FBI Director Hoover for transmittal to the President and Dr. Kissinger. Quite clearly, under Nixon's wiretap program, the FBI held an important and critical place at the very center of White House security, with open access to the most sensitive of information.

The watchful eyes of the FBI insured the White House of security. It was a security system, probably the most efficient in the world. Director J. Edgar Hoover had served eight Presidents and eighteen attorneys general. During his forty-eight years in office, he had developed a highly disciplined and efficient law enforcement agency within the Department of Justice. Whatever it took, he was willing to do. Under Hoover's leadership, the FBI evolved into a highly sophisticated law enforcement operation with an elaborate surveillance system, operated by highly disciplined undercover agents and paid informers.

Security needs of the White House sometimes led to deeper problems and embarrassment. On May 4, 1970, for example, a platoon of National Guardsmen armed with loaded M-1 rifles opened fire on a group of student demonstrators. Four students were killed and eight wounded. These students and bystanders became additional casualties of the Vietnam war. Out of that tragic incident flowed such a negative backlash, it sent shockwaves through the peaceful suburban middle-class, already beginning to have second thoughts about the war. And that backlash was quickly felt by Nixon and the Republican Party, as measured by their 1970 midterm-election losses.

Kent State had become a wake-up call to thousands of middle-class parents who had been sitting on the fence, torn between loyalty to "the nation" and love for their children. Back in Billings, Bessie and Tyler Grimes had followed the news of the Kent State tragedy, and more and more they were beginning to regret their son's decision to take a chance with the draft. Nixon, too, saw Kent State as one of the darkest moments of his presidency. And the darkness of that moment was made even darker by the committed antiwar leaders, who used Kent State as an inspirational call for increased waves of anti-war protests.

In efforts to quell the rising tide of violence, National Guard troops were called out in sixteen states. Still the antiwar revolutionaries continued down their road, pressing for peace without regard to cost. Suszette Andrew experienced one of the most dramatic moments in the antiwar movement during the 1971 Washington Mayday demonstrations, when the protestors' mission was to literally shut down the federal government, if only for a day. Previous to this stand, Suszette had already been jailed five or six times. She had been beaten by the police, spit on by passing citizens, and cursed as a traitor to America. For a while, all the arrests and beatings had only added fuel to her burning energies. But now she was beginning to feel tired and lonely. She needed home, but she had lost her way.

During the 1971 Mayday demonstrations, Suszette was working sixteen hour days, days that included drinking and partying with the demonstrators to help keep them charged up. Their master plan was to lead the demonstrators into sensitive street positions with the goal of paralyzing the federal government. This radical plan was their way of adding a final touch to their month-long series of anti-war demonstrations in Washington during the month of April, that culminated in a mass rally on May 1, attended by over 200,000 people. Following that mass rally, Suszette and other protest leaders encouraged the thousands of demonstrators to remain in Washington to help carry out the ambitious plan of blockading the streets leading into the center of government. Their goal was to shut down government on the target dates set for Monday and Tuesday, May 3 and 4.

While waiting for the target dates, the core group of demonstrators electing to remain in Washington for the big day, camped out in West Potomac Park near the Lincoln Memorial. There they were entertained by music, food and love. Suszette and the other organizers stayed busy keeping the protestors churned for action. The number of protesters assembling in West Potomac Park kept rising, considerably beyond everyone's original estimate. Everything was looking good as the protest leaders, seeing success at hand, began celebrating. But this same vision of success did not go unnoticed by the White House, and, in fact, raised serious concern, reaching a level of alarm. The White House suddenly faced the reality that with the number of anti-war protestors assembling in West Potomac Park, the group just might succeed in their plans, something President Nixon could not allow to happen.

Such success by a bunch of antiwar activists would give off a signal that the President of the United States had lost all control, and that would surely invite more trouble. Nixon made it clear, he would not tolerate any chance of success by the demonstrators. As leader of the Nation, President Nixon made it clear, the demonstrators would be stopped, regardless of the cost, and even if he had to brush aside the Constitution. Maintaining stability and the integrity of government was more important to Nixon than the demonstrators' constitutional rights. So out of a real fear of the protestors' success, the White House initiated plans to guarantee failure of the planned protest. For Nixon, and Attorney General Mitchell, the end justified the means.

The White House's plan was to launch a quick preemptive strike against the growing antiwar group. Under Nixon's plan, the administration would summarily revoked the protesters' permit to camp in West Potomac Park, basing the preemptive action on trumped up drug charges. The idea was to cut off the entertainment venue in the park with the hope and expectation that the young, less radical demonstrators, would go home. If that worked, it would reduce the number of protestors available to block the streets. So, at the moment set, the preemptive plan was placed into action. The metropolitan police, on signal, moved in at dawn on Sunday, May 2, and ordered all demonstrators out of the park. And, just as Nixon had anticipated, nearly three-fourths of the crowd of 45,000 people headed home to diverse points around the country, as soon as the music stopped.

The 10,000 protestors remaining in Washington were the most militant of the crowd, with the leaders capable of adapting to the circumstances and willing to engage in violence. Pushed out of the park, the remaining militant demonstrators began engaging in guerilla-like hit and run tactics, emerging for an instant, then disappearing again. Suszette led the charges at her designated intersections. Her protestor-group blocked traffic with trash fires and abandoned automobiles, dispersing as quickly as they appeared when the police arrived.

But in the end, President Nixon won the battle as he knew he had to, and the government remained open. It was surely a battle where the end justified the means, and the means were harsh, as the protestors' objective of halting government operations was crushed. On directions from Attorney General John Mitchell, the protestors and anyone standing near them were arrested in mass, without regard for anyone's Constitutional rights. The police were instructed to make no distinction between the innocent and the lawbreakers. And with this official command from the White House, the police herded the people arrested into makeshift detention centers. Suszette Andrew was one of the protestors caught up in one wave of the mass arrests. When she was identified as one of the protest organizers, she was repeatedly clubbed by the police and thrown in the detention center that had no shelter, no sanitary facilities, no food, and no water. The administration had quickly converted an outdoors football practice field into a concentration camp. Suszette, seriously hurt from the police clubbing, was bleeding from a head wound and left with no medical care. That was the price she willingly paid for her stand against the Vietnam war.

Lying on the ground with a broken body, suffering inordinate pain from her head wounds, Suszette also received the residual effects of tear gas grenades lobbed into the midst of the crowd pressing against the fence of the makeshift prison. But as she laid there in pain with a weakened voice,

Suszette still joined in the antiwar chants ringing throughout
the football field detention center. "We shall overcome, We
shall overcome . . . ." The words kept ringing out, and it
didn't really matter whether anyone listened to the words of
the chants and songs. It was enough that the protestors found
inner strength in the songs. As she laid on the ground of the
makeshift detention center without water or food, Suszette
kept her eyes focused on the clouds in the sky to help her find
even the slightest moment of serenity. She remembered the
lessons of Michael's grandpa told during her more peaceful
days when she visited Michael on the Grimes wheat farm back
in Oklahoma. Grandpa always told them to keep their eyes
turned to the sky, particularly during moments of despair.
This is where you will find peace, he told them. There had
been other moments, but right then, Suszette needed a feeling
of peace more than ever. She needed to take a break from the
violence and the emotional state of constant fighting a
government that kept justifying the Vietnam war, a war that
was killing so many human beings — Americans and
Vietnamese.

      During her moments of pain, Suszette began reflecting
back to her days in Oklahoma where her surroundings had
always been so peaceful. She remembered Michael telling her
that if the Communists weren't stopped in Vietnam, we would
all be fighting them on the shores of the United States. In her
mind, Suszette now knew this was Michael's way of justifying
his going to war. That was his war and maybe he was still
over there or maybe he had been killed. She had not kept up
with him or his family. She had not even been back home to

Billings. She had become a casualty of Vietnam. Suszette and the other antiwar activists may not have faced the same level of battlefield violence the combat soldiers faced, but, the antiwar activists faced a level of violence from the government of the United States, that created a lasting level of psychological trauma and shock.

After being released from the misery of the football field detention, Suszette and the other antiwar activists finally accepted the reality that they had failed in their campaign to shut down the government. Their struggle had been met by the more powerful arm of government and Attorney General Mitchell's police force. But the American people had watched it all unfold on national television, and they grew more weary of the war. Public pressure began building for the President to end the Vietnam war, and Suszette and the other protestors remained committed toward the fight to end the Vietnam war. But their energy level had been drained.

• • • •

As 1971 moved toward its close, the strategy of the protestors began shifting from violent confrontation to political activism. Their stored up energy would now be directed toward electing an antiwar candidate for president who would end the war. Suszette joined the antiwar group that began applying their collective energies toward getting George McGovern, the most outspoken antiwar presidential candidate, nominated as the Democratic candidate for president. They began working in the McGovern campaign that kept expanding with antiwar activists around the country.

George McGovern was the Democratic candidate running for president who stood for stopping the Vietnam War if he were elected. That was enough for Suszette and the thousands of other activists and members of antiwar groups who no longer cared what the cost might be or the means needed to achieve their goal. Now working within the political system, the end still justified the means. They were willing even to clean up their act, at least up to a point. Interestingly and unknowingly to Suszette and her activist friends, Richard Nixon, as President, had reached that same level of desperation. Just as they, Nixon had reached the point of accepting as a reality that the end justifies the means. He too wanted and needed to find a way to end the war before he had to again face the voters. He knew that failure to achieve this goal before the elections, would mean his defeat for a second term as President.

• • • •

Back in Oklahoma, work on the wheat farms continued without regard to the antiwar activity around the country. On Thursday, Tyler Grimes received his copy of the February 1972 issue of the USDA *Wheat Situation*. For him, this meant the farmers would soon be coming together at the Grange Hall for another state-of-the-crop report. On the day of the meeting, before the serious business began, the farmers had coffee or a cold drink and milled around talking about all subjects, the weather, family matters, the war, politics, and whatever. All the farmers who came to the meeting wanted to know how Michael was doing. They all remembered when he use to come to the meetings with his dad and grandpa and how inquisitive he was after the meetings. But Michael wasn't there that night. He hadn't been since getting back home from Vietnam. And Tyler didn't want to talk about it. He heard enough about Michael at home, and now at the grange meeting, this was one of his escapes. He didn't want to tell the other farmers that Michael was just as withdrawn as he was when he first got back home. When asked directly about his son, Tyler always said the same thing, "He's coming along!"

Tyler was happy when the questions stopped and the meeting began.

CHAPTER FOUR

*T*he February meeting at the grange hall finally started at 7:30 p.m., when the chairman called the group to order and announced that they were here today to discuss the February issue of the *Wheat Situation*. Reviewing that official government publication page-by-page, the wheat farmers found no encouraging words on any improved prospects for their 1972 wheat crop. The February issue of the *Wheat Situation* offered a gloomy USDA forecast, leading the farmers into believing that for another year, they had little choice but to sell their harvested wheat on the open market before prices dropped any farther. From the February edition of the *Wheat Situation*, the farmers were told that the larger world wheat crop meant lower expectations for any increase in wheat exports, and higher surpluses should be expected by them. What does this mean, the farmers wondered out loud. Tyler Grimes had carefully studied the February *Wheat*

Situation, and took the floor at the grange meeting to help give meaning to the words. He explained that according to the USDA report, world wheat producing countries were having record production of wheat due to favorable weather and increased acreage planted. Tyler then added that this increase in world production would reduce import demands for those countries and thereby result in lower prices for the farmers.

The grange meeting ended at about 9:30 p.m., with many of the farmers coming up to Tyler to wish Michael a speedy recovery. He thanked them but didn't want to talk about his son. Heading home, Tyler decided to stop at the bar in Blackwell for a couple of beers to help him unwind, as if he had to justify the stop. Tyler didn't drink much, but on occasion he would stop at Jake's Place, located on the outskirts of Blackwell, to relax before heading back home. The occasions of his visits to Jake's place began to increase in frequency as Michael retreated farther into his own world with no visible signs of improvement.

Tyler had long reached the point of hating the Vietnam war, the war that had destroyed his son. He stayed mad enough to have joined the antiwar demonstrators, except he had a farm to run. As he sipped on his first beer, Tyler, mentally went over the wheat report he and the farmers had just finished discussing. He ran the figures through his mind and knew that 1972 was looking no better than 1971. But he kept thinking because, when he stopped, it would be time to head home and listen to more sad stories about Michael. Finally, finishing his third beer, he left the bar and headed home, hoping everyone in the family would be sleeping. Tomorrow, he thought, would be another day, maybe it would be better.

The May issue of the *Wheat Situation* confirmed his own negative forecast, projected from the February issue. Wheat farmers in Noble County received their copy of the May 1972 issue of the *Wheat Situation*, just about the time their harvest was approaching. When Tyler Grimes received his copy, he studied the report more closely because it was the last report before the wheat harvest. Whatever the USDA included in that issue would determine the success or failure of the wheat farmers' year. That's how much reliance the farmers placed on the government's market publication.   As he had in the past, at least for the last several years, Tyler spent time prior to the meeting, preparing to make his report to the farmers attending this important grange hall meeting.

Before heading off to this meeting, the last before the harvest, Tyler again tried to get Michael to go with him, but without success. With all the passage of time since he got home from Vietnam, it was still as if Michael remained in the jungles of Vietnam looking for a way out. He seemed to move as if he suspected the enemy to open fire. He was suspicious of everyone, including his dad and his sisters, and less so, his mom.   Battlefield stress is a serious mental condition that many veterans experience, some coming out of it quicker than others. The doctors had told Tyler not to expect a miracle, and that Michael's post traumatic stress disorder could be permanent, last for years, or suddenly end. The doctors told Tyler and Bessie, the end could come suddenly and without notice. We just don't know, the doctors kept telling them. That was one reason Tyler kept urging Michael to come to the grange hall meetings with him and listen to the discussion of the *Wheat Situation* and the market prospects for their 1972 wheat crop. But Michael continued to say "NO!" in a way that Tyler knew he should no longer press the issue. "Let him find his way back home without pressuring him," the doctor had advised. But this advice was getting harder to follow for Tyler who at times wanted to scream out at his son.

So, as he had since grandpa died, Tyler went by himself to the meeting, leaving Michael at home in the sanctuary of his room. Remembering that for this May meeting, the grange always staged a big barbecue to celebrate a successful wheat harvest for all, Tyler left early for the meeting. The 1972 wheat crop did look like the farmers would have a good year in yield per acre, that is if they could bring the crop in before one of Oklahoma's unexpected destructive storms hit. Getting the wheat from the fields to the elevators would be something to celebrate. Tyler was harvesting 450 acres of wheat so he was optimistic that as for as his production level, the year 1972 looked good. How good, of course, depended on the market and the demand for wheat. That is what made this meeting at the grange hall so important to the farmers.

After everybody had had their fill of barbecue and after a pause to regain focus, the meeting was called to order. The chair then called on Tyler Grimes to make his preliminary analysis of the USDA crop report. He had done this a number of times before. Tyler opened the May issue of the *Wheat*

Situation and began reading. "Exports are running sharply lower and total wheat disappearance is expected to fall about 5% from last season's" – not good news for the farmers. He then noted that the disappearance of wheat held in storage was expected to fall, meaning that the nation's wheat surplus was increasing. And this translated into lower prices. None of these revelations from the USDA bode well for the farmers. Faced with the USDA's pessimistic report of an ever expanding surplus, the highest level since 1963, the farmers were left with little visible choice. Sell your 1972 harvest with no delay, at the depressed market prices, and wish for a better year in 1973.

Tyler next read from the report, "Farm prices for the season will average moderately above the loan rate and close to the $1.33 per bushel of last season." He then added from the USDA report, "World wheat prices have dropped 10 to 20 cents a bushel as a result of larger supplies, lower import demand, and lower feed grain prices." After Tyler had presented his review of the official government information supplied to the farmers, the chair opened the meeting to discussion. At first, there was long silence leading the farmers into accepting their fate as part of being a farmer. These farmers trusted their government. They had supported the candidacy of President Nixon and knew in their hearts that he would never betray them. If the May issue of the 1972 USDA *Wheat Situation* stated that prices would remain low, they accepted that as a reality. In their minds, the government doesn't lie!

None of the farmers held any positive view of the

economic situation and most had already settled on the idea that if they could get $1.33 a bushel on the market, they would be better off selling their '72 crop without exercising an option they had of taking a crop loan of about $1.25. That is what the farmers, including Tyler Grimes, did. They sold their 1972 wheat crop on the open market at the depressed market price of about $1.33 a bushel. This was their most logical decision, based on the information the USDA provided. But, as always, came the optimistic tone of farmers, "Maybe next year will be better." This was the collective thought of the farmers of Noble County, meeting that night at the Grange hall. Farmers never give up hope. For if they did, it would be all over. In their positive tone, passed on through the years from one generation to the next, farmers have experienced different levels of tragedy: drought, Dust Bowl, tornadoes and insect invasion with their enduring belief. Next year will be better! For them, it will always be better, the next year.

Relying on the USDA's negative forecast, most farmers sold their 1972 wheat harvest for an average price of about $1.33 a bushel. Having made this irretrievable decision, Tyler and the other farmers were stunned when they later heard Walter Cronkite read his CBS evening news report for September 27, 1972. They all watched and listened in disbelief in the disparity of that news report and the May issue of the USDA *Wheat Situation*. Cronkite began his three-part expose on some kind of wheat deal that had been made with the Soviets. Reporting this huge increase in wheat demand, Cronkite reported that the wheat farmers in Texas, Oklahoma and Kansas had been cheated by the government. Of all things, Walter Cronkite explained, the farmers were cheated by the Department of Agriculture and the big grain exporters. They were cheated when the USDA falsified information published in the May issue of the *Wheat Situation*. Richard Nixon, the President who had been supported by the farmers, had betrayed them when his USDA withheld valuable information about the magnitude of the Soviets' need for wheat.

Deprived of this essential market information, the wheat farmers prematurely sold their wheat harvest at depressed prices. It was only after they heard the Cronkite report that they began to suspect that maybe they had sold their wheat too quickly. Selling when they did, they lost the market advantage of knowing the true magnitude of the Soviet wheat deal. It became crystal clear when the Soviet wheat deal finally became known to the public and after the information reached the market mechanism. At that moment, the market price for wheat skyrocketed. But by then, the farmers had already sold their wheat. Truly, they had been sacrificed by the Nixon administration. What the hell is going on, the farmers wanted to know.

During September and October of 1972, there began what appeared to be an intense inquiry by Congress and the news media into the Soviet wheat deal. They were trying to find answers to the farmers questions. More than anything, however, the Soviet wheat deal had gained national prominence by Walter Cronkite's CBS news coverage. His three-part special report began on September 27, 1972, when he explained that the "giant wheat sale to Russia, first regarded as part of President Nixon's triumphal summit meeting, is now the subject of no less than five separate governmental investigations." Charges under investigation, he reported, included "conflict of interest, windfall profits for six large grain exporters, and suppression of information." The immediate economic impact of the higher wheat prices, Cronkite reported, translated "into higher flour prices" and thereby higher prices for bread and other baked goods for American consumers. As a result of the Soviet wheat deal, American bakeries ironically faced the need to pay substantially more for wheat grown in this country than what the Soviets were paying.

One day before Cronkite closed his reporting on the Soviet wheat deal, President Nixon called for the FBI to investigate the wheat deal in his effort to silence all critics. During a news conference on October 5, 1972, Nixon explained that "if there was any impropriety, if there was any illegality, we want to know it. The way to find out is to put the best investigative agency in the world to work at finding out." But one was left to wonder whether Nixon ever intended for the FBI to make an independent and complete investigation into all the surroundings of the Soviet wheat deal.

The farmers of Noble County were astounded by the inflaming news reports about the 1972 Soviet wheat deal. Soon after they heard Walter Cronkite's report on the wheat deal, they quickly called a special meeting at the grange hall to discuss the subject. They wanted to know why the Nixon administration had not included information about the Soviet wheat deal in the May issue of the *Wheat Situation*. Tyler had already begun collecting news stories published in the *New York Times*, *Washington Post*, and other papers. Based on these news accounts, the wheat farmers more firmly believed they had been cheated by President Nixon, and now they wanted to know the truth.

One reporter who had already turned her serious attention to the Soviet wheat deal was Amber Nicole Highlander. This freelance journalist out of Washington, D. C. always insisted on using her full name. After hearing the Cronkite Report, Highlander turned her attention to the wheat deal with a determination to find out what it was all about. The story fascinated her and she sensed there was a bigger story in the deal. As a freelance reporter she had the independence to take chances, if only she had the financial backing. Several of her articles on the wheat deal had already been published in several newspapers, and these papers were showing a continuing interest in the subject.

Amber was a tall, stately, beautiful women with blue eyes and blonde hair that gleamed like gold in the sunlight. Her natural beauty was further complimented by the fact that she was intelligent, well read, shrewd, calculating and a daring investigative freelance reporter. One additional advantage she held over other reporters was that she had a close friend working at the White House. He was one of H. R. Haldeman's assistants.

Through her research, Amber learned that wheat farmers had long placed almost complete reliance on the

USDA publication, *Wheat Situation*. So she visited the USDA and picked up a copy of the February and May, 1972, issues. Carefully studying these public documents, she began to wonder why the publications had made no mention of the Soviet wheat deal. It made no sense to her in terms of her understanding of economics. She decided to search for answers, exploring this question independently, using different sources available to her. For a head-start she asked her friend at the White House, Joshua Walker, why the information about the wheat deal had not been furnished to farmers. She could tell the question itself had hit a sensitive nerve the moment she made the inquiry. She could tell by looking into the eyes of her friend. Amber had known Josh too long not to be able to measure his pulse by looking into his eyes.

Josh and Amber were never romantically involved. Her heart had long been given to Robert Jefferies or RJ as he was called. Josh and RJ, who was raised in Atlanta, had been roommates at the University of Alabama. Josh and Amber though were life-long friends, both raised in Clanton, Alabama, a small town between Birmingham and Montgomery, the state capitol. They attended the same high school and started and graduated together from the University of Alabama. All during college, it was Josh, RJ and Amber, the inseparable threesome. RJ was the brain, Josh the athlete and music man, and Amber, the news hound.

While at the University of Alabama, RJ, majoring in aeronautical engineering, made straight "A"s, with dreams of a career in aviation, designing aircraft. Josh ran on the Crimson Tide track team, played in the "million dollar band,"

and was active in student government. His major was political science. His dream for after graduation was to head to Washington, the seat of government, and get a job at the White House. Amber majored in journalism and was a staff member of the student newspaper. She and RJ became a couple during their senior year, and began talking of marriage. But, they decided to wait until each had first had an opportunity to work in their chosen careers.

After the threesome graduated, RJ with honors, each went in separate directions to explore the world before settling down. Josh went to Washington. Amber went home to Clanton and, after a few years working as a reporter for a small town newspaper, she too came to Washington. RJ ended up in the Air Force where he became a "Cobra" attack helicopter pilot and was later sent to Vietnam. The "Cobra," also called the "Snake," was a highly armed attack ship, with side-pod gun turrets, rockets and Gatling guns. It was a mainstay in Vietnam, used for air assaults, armed patrol and escort, reconnaissance and medical evacuation. Back in Washington, Josh and Amber frequently got together, and reminisced about the good old days at the U of A.

Just as he had dreamed, Josh had worked his way into a job at the Nixon White House, with the political help of one of Alabama's U. S. Senators. He became one of the assistants to H. R. Haldeman. As the junior assistant to Haldeman, Josh had been given the assignment of collecting and summarizing all the newspaper articles on the wheat deal. His job also was to file all the memos coming through Haldeman's office. Being a curious person, Josh read a lot of the memos. So he probably knew more than he needed to know about the wheat deal, though he did not feel comfortable talking about it. When he was permitted to invite a guest to a White House function, he would invite Amber, and sometimes he gave her background help on stories she was writing. But when Amber asked him about the Soviet wheat deal and keeping information away from the farmers, he froze for a moment and was reluctant to talk to her about the deal. It was obvious to Amber that Josh got nervous when the subject was raised. But, he did tell her that the White House was for some reason very sensitive about all the publicity surrounding the international wheat transaction that had stirred so much controversy.

Amber never pressured her friend to supply her information if he were reluctant. She would just find another source, even going to the top of the USDA, in her search for answers. She had met Secretary of Agriculture Earl Butz at a White House function, and had been invited to his office for an interview. Her interview with Butz lasted an hour and a half. As soon as it started, even before Amber's first question, Secretary Butz began vigorously defending the Soviet wheat deal as something good for the farmers and good for America. He let it be known that he could not understand all the controversy, and he directed his strongest of negative comments toward the coverage by the press. Amber understood that the Secretary was trying to soften her before she could ask her first question. Then after his momentary bash of the press, Secretary Butz returned to his defense. "The sale of grain to Russia was good for America," Butz told

Highlander. "The sale provided the farmers stronger markets, higher prices and more freedom to plant."

"If it was so good for the farmers," Amber asked, "why wasn't the information about the sale included in the May issue of the USDA's *Wheat Situation?*"

This question caught the Secretary by surprise. There was a long pause. Finally, the silence was broken when he spoke. "At the time the information for that publication was being collected, we simply did not know what the Russians intended," Butz then added, "I emphasize that nobody knew then – neither the Department of Agriculture nor the trade – just how much the Russians would buy. The export traders were not telling each other how much the Soviets were booking with them. The exporters did not tell the Department of Agriculture. Nor were the Russians talking."

"Mr. Secretary," Highlander inquired, "how do you explain the fact that the May issue of the *Wheat Situation* was advising the wheat farmers that they could anticipate a wheat price no higher than $1.33 for their crop during the coming year?"

"Again, Ms Highlander, as I have already said, nobody anticipated the magnitude of how much wheat the Soviets would buy from the private exporters. But let me assure you," Secretary Butz emphasized, "if we had known the intent of the Soviets in time, we would have truthfully conveyed that information to the farmers. In any case, the transaction was a good deal for the farmers because it eliminated the wheat surplus," Butz repeated. He then kept repeating that phrase, "It eliminated the wheat surplus; It eliminated the wheat surplus; It eliminated the wheat surplus."

Amber remembered Earl Butz had been a close adherent to the farm economic model Ezra Taft Benson had advocated when he was Secretary of Agriculture during the Dwight Eisenhower presidency. Benson was the most vocal opponent of mammoth grain surpluses owned and supported by the government. He served eight years in the Eisenhower Administration, during which time he freely expressed the view that government had no rightful place in the business of farming. In his book, *Freedom To Farm*, Benson wrote: "It will cost taxpayers over a billion and a quarter dollars for transportation, handling, storage and interest just to hold the surpluses."

In a philosophical sense, Benson needed to get rid of the surpluses not only because of their extraordinary cost to the government, but also because they took away from the farmers, their God given independence. Eisenhower's idealistic and optimistic Secretary of Agriculture believed farmers were competent to run their own affairs. He believed strongly in the individual capacity of American farmers to make independent business decisions without the government dictating to them on what to plant, how much to plant, or when to plant. He preached to all who would listen that price support payments had to be eliminated so farmers would be liberated and "free to farm." Despite Secretary Benson's philosophical belief, the farm bloc's political forces thought otherwise, and they held the power to prevent Republican Ezra Taft Benson from dismantling the New Deal farm programs. With one out of every five Americans still living on a farm in

1950, farmers did not care whether the government's extensive involvement was desirable in philosophical or economic terms. To them, it was a matter of economic survival. Government subsidies and price support programs gave them the level of stability not otherwise available in the free and open market.

Still Benson's eight years in the Agriculture Department left behind a lasting imprint, now carried on by his economic disciple Earl Butz. Benson's economic views, at least among the grassroots farmers, were mostly unpopular. Preach as he might, Benson could not bend elected officials to his ideals. Any politician, attempting to eliminate the government largesse, would be considered an enemy to the farmers, and would not long remain in office. These possible political consequences made change come slowly, if at all. As a result, the government stood firmly locked into a system of support that led farmers into consistently producing too much grain, and from there, an unmanageable and costly surplus. Benson's Assistant Secretary of Agriculture, Earl Butz, became Nixon's Secretary during the second half of his first term as President.

Amber Nicole Highlander did not think Secretary Butz gave her anything she had not already gleaned from the Congressional Committee's wheat deal hearing transcript of testimony. So she kept investigating and, just by chance, was able to interview Henry Kissinger, a rare moment indeed for her. She had been invited by Joshua to attend a White House function which Kissinger attended. When Kissinger noticed her entrance into the room, he was immediately struck by her beauty, and quickly moved in to engage her in conversation, not knowing who she was. It was commonly known within White House circles that Kissinger was attracted to beautiful women, and before he was married, he had a reputation as a socializing bachelor. Nixon had, Amber discovered, admonished Kissinger on his need "to be more discreet with women when in public, especially in Washington," suggesting that it might be "OK" what Kissinger did in New York, Florida and California. But not so in Washington or at White House functions. As a precaution, Haldeman had been instructed not to "put Kissinger by glamorous women at White House dinners, give him the intelligent women instead."

Amber Highlander was both glamorous and intelligent and she wanted to talk with Kissinger about the Soviet wheat deal. When the right moment opened, she asked him whether the big sale of wheat to the Soviet Union was a White House operation.

"No!", Kissinger retorted without hesitation. But the question made Kissinger nervous and Amber's beauty no longer matter. Suddenly, she began to look like a ghoul, trying to reach into his body and take out his soul. But he didn't want to be impolite, so he did not shut her off, though he might have words for Joshua Walker later, for even inviting her.

"As National Security Adviser to the President," Highlander said, "you must have had prior knowledge of what the Soviets were planning and their intent on buying huge quantities of wheat from either the CCC or the private exporters."

"No!" came Kissinger's single word response. But this time, Kissinger, beginning to show a loss of patience with Amber, attempted to distance himself from the controversial wheat deal by claiming his personal lack of knowledge. "The Soviets simply outwitted the United States, and got away with it because no senior official -- except possibly Butz – understood what they were doing."

"So, are you saying that the wheat deal was solely a private transaction between the Soviets and the private exporters?", Amber asked.

"That's the way it was," Kissinger added. "The Soviets were quick to take advantage of the competitiveness of our grain companies. They gave us a lesson in the handicaps a market economy has in negotiating with a state trading enterprise. Each of our grain companies, trying to steal a march on its competitors, sold the largest amount possible and kept its sale utterly secret, even from the US government." Then he added, "Without knowledge, we could not alert our own wheat farmers."

Before Amber could pose another question, Joshua came up and saved Kissinger who looked relieved. "Thank you, Mr. Kissinger," Amber said. "That was interesting," Amber commented to Joshua as he handed her a drink.

"What did you learn?"

"I guess I learned that no one in the administration is willing to admit to having any information about the Soviets' intention to buy large quantities of wheat in time to alert the farmers before they sold their 1972 wheat harvest. And, without that information, what happened to the farmers was unavoidable."

"Maybe they didn't know," Josh suggested.

"I don't believe it," Amber retorted in an emphatic tone of voice. "The answers given by Butz and Kissinger were almost identical, as if they had rehearsed their lines."

In a newspaper article she published, Amber summarized her conversations with Secretary of Agriculture Earl Butz and with Kissinger, but she explained that the explanations received were, in her opinion, hard to accept. Something was still missing she thought, and she ended her article with a question: "What is this all about?" Joshua told Amber that her last article had made Kissinger mad as hell. This only delighted Amber and made her even more committed to her search for answers.

She had studied the grain industry and learned that Canada was also a major wheat producing country, but with more government controls than the United States. So she made arrangements to travel there to talk with officials of the Canadian Wheat Board. When she arrived, she found the Canadians far more cooperative than Secretary Butz and Kissinger. She knew that since 1943, wheat farmers in Canada had been required by law to sell their wheat to the CWB. From her talks with CWB officials, Amber learned that during 1971 and 1972, the Soviets had sought to buy large quantities of Canadian wheat. The Soviet Union's wheat production had been greatly destroyed by harsh winter weather, when at the same time, the country's consumption needs had appreciably increased. These two factors of supply and demand had created a level of desperation on the part of the Soviets, to find a reliable, long-term source of wheat. Unfortunately for the Soviets, in 1971-72, the only reliable source of wheat was North America, the United States and Canada.

During her talks with the Canadians, Amber got caught up in the dynamics of the international wheat trade and its potential leveraging power.   She learned that the Soviets, in searching for much needed wheat to feed her people, realistically assumed that, in view of the Vietnam War, they could not rely on the United States as a dependable supplier, despite the well known fact that the U. S. had a huge surplus of wheat, the largest in the world. In times of history, as long as Nixon was President, the United States could not be expected to entertain any notion of supplying wheat to feed the Russian people, not as long as that Communist country stood as one of the major suppliers of military weapons to North Vietnam.

Facing this reality of international politics, the Soviets turned to Canada, wanting to purchase all the wheat they could get. But the Soviets were turned away by the CWB. Canada's wheat supply had already been over-committed.   The Canadians told Amber that the only available world wheat supply during 1971 and 1972 was the United States. She was astounded when she learned that the CWB had on February 28, 1972, notified USDA Secretary Earl Butz by letter that the Russians were in desperate need for wheat and that the CWB had been unable to fill their desperate needs. It was suggested to Secretary Butz that because the United States held a monopoly position in wheat, with no other major stocks available in the world, it had an excellent opportunity to take advantage of this monopoly position in the international marketplace by charging higher prices.

When Amber returned to Washington, she began recording all the information she had gained from the CWB officials. From this, she began to suspect that Secretary Butz and Kissinger had not told her the full truth about their lack of knowledge of the Soviets' high demand for wheat. They had withheld from her and from Congress the fact that the United States held a worldwide monopoly in the wheat market. Not sure of what was fueling the Nixon administration with regard to the Soviet wheat deal, but sensing a bigger story, Amber decided not to write any article disclosing her findings from her trip to Canada. She decided to dig deeper before disclosing the facts she had discovered. She had been left with more questions in her mind than answers. As with the life of a freelance journalist, she had exhausted most of her funds needed to pay for extended investigation. So, before advancing her wheat project, she needed to sell a couple of articles.

She was determined to find an answer to the question in her mind as to why the government in its May '72 issue of the *Wheat Situation* advised the wheat farmers that there was an anticipated increase in world supply of wheat. That representation was a lie, when in fact the USDA knew that the United States held a worldwide monopoly. She queried, what would be the motivation behind the USDA's deception of the wheat farmers? Amber knew that the USDA, as early as February of 1972 had knowledge of the United States' monopoly position in the worldwide wheat market. Amber began speculating that the wheat sale to the Soviets during the summer of '72 might in some way be connected to the White House's efforts to settle the Vietnam war.

She had no evidence of this, but the very thought of such a possibility made her tingle as a journalist. This very thought also made her angry and sad, for had Nixon ended that war before June 28, 1972, Amber would still have her fiancée, Robert Jefferies, instead of only his memory. This was Amber's belief and she could not be moved away from that belief. RJ had been killed on June 28, 1972, at 6:06 p.m., when his Cobra helicopter was shot down while he was on one of his many evacuation missions, removing a wounded soldier from the battlefield. Amber was determined personally and as a journalist to find the answers and didn't care what she had to do to get there. Truth would be hers! And then, it would be the world's!

CHAPTER FIVE

*T*yler Grimes closely followed the news coverage on the giant wheat sale to the Soviets, and had discovered material differences between the news reports and the information the government provided the farmers. He was particularly impressed with the articles by Amber Nicole Highlander. He liked the way she refused to fully accept the explanations offered by Kissinger and Butz, and her apparent willingness to challenge high government officials. Tyler began to think she might be the person who could best help the farmers find the truth. That is what the farmers needed and wanted: the truth!

Based on Tyler's recommendation, the grange members voted in favor of a resolution on trying to hire Amber Nicole Highlander to investigate the Soviet wheat deal and to report back to the grange. They thought that with her being a Washington insider engaged in political type

investigations, she might be the best person to look behind the
surface of the wheat deal and find the truth. Reading some of
her articles once again, the farmers were all impressed with
the details and thoroughness of her reporting.   So, having
agreed to try to engage her services, Tyler was given the
assignment of calling and inviting her down to Billings to
meet with the wheat farmers.

When she got the call from some Oklahoma wheat
farmer, Amber was surprised and at first skeptical.   But after
listening to Tyler's explanation, she became intrigued and
agreed to come to Billings, thinking that if nothing else, she
might get a good story out of it. Little could she have known
what might lie ahead for her.   Tyler picked her up at the
Oklahoma City airport on a Thursday, late on October 26 of
1972. It was a crisp, Fall day when Tyler brought her out to
the Grimes wheat farm, where she would stay as a guest
during her three day visit. As they drove toward Billings,
Tyler told Amber about Michael, not wanting her to be
shocked when they got to the house. He told Amber how
Michael had been sent to Vietnam after he had been drafted,
and after two years in combat, he had been seriously wounded.
And, after months in the hospital, he finally came home and
has ever since been totally withdrawn from everything and
everybody.   This brief story about Michael immediately
caught Amber's imagination. Her fiancée RJ had also gone to
Vietnam as a pilot, flying the Cobra assault helicopter. But he
was not coming home! He was killed when his helicopter was
shot down during one of his medical evacuation missions, but
Amber said nothing to Tyler about her fiancée being killed in

Vietnam. She had personally experienced Vietnam from going there on assignment and from writing several news stories about that war. She had come to Billings to talk and learn about wheat farming, and she needed to keep her mind focused on that single subject.

She didn't really need to say anything after leaving the airport. Tyler talked the entire way and had not even finished the story when they began the drive up the dirt road to the house. Amber would stay with the Grimes family in their guest room that seemed perfect for a writer. The room had two big windows looking out over the green fields of the new wheat crop, with a good-size worktable and an Underwood typewriter. When she got out of the truck, she looked around and could immediately sense the peacefulness of this wheat farm in Noble County. They entered the house through the back door into the kitchen where she met Bessie and the girls. Amber was also introduced to Michael who was sitting at the kitchen table, but he never got out of his chair or even looked at her. He just stared at the ceiling while she kept talking about her own trip to Vietnam. After introductions, with the awkwardness of meeting Michael, Amber was shown the guest room and given time to rest and freshen up. As she sat by the window looking out over the vastness of the young wheat crop, she used the time alone to think and work a little on her planned presentation to the wheat farmers, scheduled for that same evening. She was too excited to take a nap.

Bessie served an early dinner, about 5:00 o'clock., to give Tyler and Amber time to get to the grange hall for the meeting scheduled to begin at 7:00. When they arrived at the hall, Amber was at ease, and comfortably moved around and talked with individual farmers. She was not expected to make any lengthy presentation at this initial meeting. The farmers just wanted to get acquainted with her before deciding on whether to retain her to investigate the wheat story, beyond Walter Cronkite's report.   After Tyler introduced Amber Nicole Highlander, she confidently took the floor, immediately commanding the attention of the farmers by her beauty, self-confidence and intelligence.

"I was born and raised in a little town in Alabama," Amber began, "where the farmers raised peaches instead of wheat. I left Clanton for the first time when I enrolled at the University of Alabama, where I majored in journalism. When I graduated, I returned to my hometown, the town we all claim to be the peach capitol of the country. I was hired by the Clanton Courier, the town's daily newspaper. I worked there reporting news for about five years, and left only when I was invited to join the staff of Alabama's newly elected U.S. Senator, Craig Williamson. I was hired to be his press secretary in Washington." Amber paused here for a moment, as if to place emphasis on her next remark. "I quickly accepted that position," she continued, "and moved from the little town of Clanton to the big city of Washington, the center of the universe, I thought at the time."

Amber wanted the farmers to know everything about her, because she had already decided she wanted this assignment. She needed the money! She had been working on the wheat deal ever since listening to the same Cronkite report that had stirred these farmers, and, with that work, she had exhausted her funds. Now, if retained by the farmers, she would have the money needed to continue her project. So she wanted to convince the farmers she was capable of handling the assignment. "As press secretary for Senator Williamson," Amber explained, "I gained invaluable exposure to the workings of Washington; met a lot of people who became and still remain good contacts; and most importantly, I was introduced to investigative reporting." When she mentioned "investigative reporting," Tyler and the other farmers could see her face light-up in a heightened level of excitement. "Once I became exposed to investigative reporting," Amber told the farmers, " it changed my life. And, when my urge to engage in investigative reporting made it difficult to continue working as the press secretary, I resigned and went out on my own as a full-time freelance reporter."

A voice in the back of the hall interrupted Amber with a question, "Have you ever regretted that decision to go out on your own?"

"No!" came Amber's emphatic reply. "I have never looked back with any regrets." Then she explained, "As a freelance journalist, I have the same independence and freedom that you wheat farmers have, but with the advantage of not having to face the added risk of the weather." Then, she stopped for a moment to let the farmers reflect on what she just said. "Since making the decision to go independent," Amber explained, "I have led a busy and interesting life and traveled to many countries including Vietnam, China and the Soviet Union. I was selected as one of the reporters who accompanied President Nixon on his historic trip to China in

February of 1972." After another short pause, Amber
continued, "And, out of all my assignments, the wheat deal,
that brought me here to Billings, is the one story that straight
away caught my attention as being one of the most interesting
and puzzling."

Here she paused once again as she looked around the
grange hall, her eyes directly meeting the eyes of each farmer,
as if she were measuring and evaluating the farmers' thoughts
and reactions to her. Then she asked, "Are there questions?"

"Ms Highlander," one of the farmers inquired, "when
did you get interested in the big wheat sale made to the
Russians?"

"Well, I wasn't," Amber admitted, "until I heard the
story coverage by Walter Cronkite. It was after listening to
that story that bells started to ring in my head as a journalist. I
began to sense a deeper story." Then, she told the farmers, "I
tried to get more information from the White House about the
wheat deal, but what I got was a claim that the Nixon
administration had nothing to do with the sale. I interviewed
Secretary of Agriculture Earl Butz and Henry Kissinger and
they both supported Nixon's denial of having any prior
knowledge about the wheat transaction." Another pause, and
then Amber commented, "If the President and Henry
Kissinger did in fact not know anything about the wheat deal,
then I am wrong in my personal assessment. But if I am right,
which I believe I am, then the whole Soviet wheat deal had to
have been part of a bigger plan, with the White House sitting
at the very center. They claim in the White House that it had
all been a big surprise to them. They claimed the wheat sale

was solely a commercial transaction between the private exporters and the Soviets." Then after one of her longest pauses, Amber added, "I don't believe they are telling the truth." This comment led to a loud applause from the farmers, with echoes running through the group, "Yeah, yeah, yeah!"

Amber told the farmers that from the moment the White House denied involvement in the Soviet wheat deal, she had strong inner doubts. "Even before I received your invitation to come to Billings," Amber said, "I had conducted my preliminary investigation into the wheat deal, and from what I have learned, I do not believe we are hearing the truth out of the Nixon White House." Amber paused once again, then added, "If I can work with you, I believe the truth will surface. I already suspect that the Soviet wheat deal was part of some kind of highly secret White House operation and that the private exporters were being used as surrogates to conceal the details of the sales."

As a freelance journalist, Amber was casting a lot of doubt on what the farmers had been told in the February and May issues of the USDA's *Wheat Situation* publications. "What its all about," Amber admitted to the farmers, " I don't know yet. It's all supposition for now based, of course, on my early investigation." Here she stopped as if waiting for a question or just a moment of self reflection, then added, "I believe the White House's planning for the Soviet wheat deal had its beginning in early 1971, and was firmly in place by late 1971."

"Excuse me," came a voice from the back of the hall, "if the wheat deal was firmly in place by late 1971, why was it not mentioned in the USDA's February and May issues of the *Wheat Situation?*"

"Quite frankly," Amber spoke in a firm, resounding voice, "President Nixon needed the farmers out of the equation."

"Why!" the farmers screamed out. "We have all been supporters of Richard Nixon. Don't we deserve better?"

"There lies the mystery," Amber replied. "I have carefully studied the February and the May issues of the *Wheat Situation,* and I have strong suspicion, though without conclusive evidence at this time, that the White House was, from the beginning, putting together some secret financial deal with the Soviets." She did not mention to the farmers that she had already gotten a lot of secret White House information from her reliable confidential source who had only put her in the right direction to discover the truth. That's all Amber needed, for she was a hell of an investigator. As she was bringing her remarks to a close, she added in a more softened voice, " I believe the White House has been using the wheat farmers for some reason by engaging in activity designed to keep wheat market prices as low as possible. The prices were kept low by falsification, distortion and suppression of market information, as published in the *Wheat Situation.*" Amber was now making some strong accusations without a lot of evidence, but she cautioned, "I do believe that President Nixon was at all times, acting in good faith. If the White House was doing what I suspect, President Nixon had a reason. Perhaps," she paused, "it was his way out of Vietnam."

At the end of the meeting and her full and honest

responses to all the questions raised by the farmers, Amber received a standing ovation. She had truly impressed even the most hardened wheat farmers. With all the individual farmers wanting to personally thank her, Amber did not get away from the hall until after 10:30 p.m., when Tyler finally pulled her away. Heading back to the Grimes' farm, Tyler told Amber that she was truly impressive and had made a strong impression on the farmers. On the way home, Tyler decided to stop at Jake's Place for a beer with the acquiescence from Amber. She could use a beer after her presentation. When they entered Jake's, they saw a number of the farmers who had already arrived and joined them for a few beers and conversation. They finally got home at about midnight, and Amber went to her room to summarize her mental notes.

The next day, she got up early and took a stroll around the farm. When she came to the family cemetery, she stopped to read each grave stone, realizing she was in the presence of early Oklahoma history. This made her want more than ever to talk with Michael about his experiences in Vietnam, and she hoped to get the chance at the breakfast table. After reading all the headstones, she left the cemetery and caught a glimpse of the three green wooden lawn chairs seemingly growing out of the hillside. The chairs were Kelly green and were sunk into the ground just enough to make them appear as if they were growing out of the ground. Later that morning, Tyler took her around the farm and explained to her the operation of wheat farming.

After lunch, Amber helped Bessie clear the table and hoped to get her talking about the job of being the wife of a wheat farmer. But, what Amber really wanted Bessie to talk about was Michael. "That is a subject harder to talk about," Bessie told Amber. "Since he got home from Vietnam back in 1970," Bessie quietly said, as a tear slowly rolled down her cheek, "he has remained withdrawn, always looking so sad, bewildered and lost." More tears flowed.

"How was he before he went to Vietnam?" Amber asked.

"Let me show you his high school senior picture," Bessie answered, as she hurried to get the picture to show Amber, before Tyler came in to take her to next planned stop. She was scheduled that afternoon to go visit a couple of other wheat farms. So while she had someone who wanted to listen, Bessie wanted to talk about Michael. "When Michael was in high school," Bessie began, "he was the star quarterback on the football team and had scholarship offers from Oklahoma State University and other big schools, including the University of Alabama."

"That's my old school," Amber said proudly.

"I know," Bessie said.

"What happened? Why did he not take one of the scholarships?" Amber asked. "Did he get drafted?"

"Michael wanted to work with his dad and grandpa as a wheat farmer before going off to college, just as his dad had done." In his day, Tyler had delayed college for two years to work on the wheat farm with his dad, Mose Grimes. Then he went to OSU on a baseball scholarship where he played second base. He graduated with a degree in Agricultural Science and Management. He was a good student and an excellent baseball player. After graduation, he had an offer to join the pros, but he chose to come home and work with his dad on the wheat farm."

"Did you meet Tyler at OSU?" Amber asked.

"Yea," she said shyly. "He was a Senior and I was a sophomore from Enid, Oklahoma, the wheat terminal center of the region. My father was a doctor and wanted me to go into medicine. But I was smitten with Tyler Grimes and we were married after he graduated."

"Did you go back and finish at OSU?"

"No," Bessie said in a soft voice that revealed a tinge of sadness. "I don't really regret dropping out of OSU after two years. I got pregnant with Michael and decided I would come to the Grimes farm and work and raise children." Then Bessie added, "It's been a good life!"

"So, when Michael graduated from high school, he too wanted to follow in the footsteps of his father?" Amber asked.

"Yes." Bessie said. "But he did not seek any deferment from the draft, thinking he had a duty to go fight the Communists if he got the call. And he did get called by his draft board. So, he went, and here we are."

Just then, Tyler came in to see if Amber was ready to head off to the next wheat farm. Soon, the two of them were gone, heading over to the Weaver wheat farm, their first stop. As he drove the dirt roads that connected all the farms, they talked about wheat farming operations – the planting, the field work required and then the harvest. It's a task full of risks. Driving down the dirt road, the trail of dust blotted out where they had been. And Tyler kept talking and inviting Amber back for the 1973 wheat harvest. He told her that if she came back down, he would teach her how to drive one of the big combines. When they got to Scott Weaver's farm, Amber was given a quick tour, including a climb on a combine, with a short lesson on how it worked. Then they were off to the next farm. As they were driving down the dirt road approaching Billings, Amber told Tyler that she would like to stop by Henry Bellmon's farm and visit with him, if he were home. She had met the Senator in Washington, and thought he was nice and very accessible to reporters, particularly reporters not associated with the *New York Times* or the *Washington Post*. They weren't far from the Bellmon farm, which Tyler had visited a number of times, but when they got there, the Senator was not home; he was still in Washington.

So Tyler brought Amber back to the farm. It had been a long day for her and she was ready to rest a little and record her notes while her thoughts were still fresh. She was thankful she had the Underwood typewriter so handy. After dinner, Amber again helped Bessie in the kitchen and the two picked up on the conversation they had started earlier in the day. Bessie fixed them a drink, hers gin and tonic and Amber's scotch and water, and they sat at the kitchen table and talked. After about thirty minutes, Michael walked in to get a drink of water, and his mom tried to get him to sit down and talk with them. He did sit for awhile but said nothing while Amber kept talking to him about other Vietnam veterans she had met. Then, without warning or apology, Michael got up from the kitchen table, not saying a word, and went back to the safety of his room.

On the last day of her visit, Amber had breakfast with Bessie as they kept talking about the problems facing wheat farmers. Then they got back on the subject of Michael. Amber had become convinced she needed to write a story about PTSD and how Vietnam had altered the lives of so many young American combat soldiers like Michael, but also the families of the soldiers, who also suffered. When talking on this subject, Amber's thoughts always went back to her fiancée who had given his life in Vietnam. She saw this as her personal story and a story of human tragedy of destroying the dreams of many young soldiers and their families. She also thought the story as it applied to Michael was not too far off from her more current story about wheat and the deal she suspected Nixon had made with the Soviets.

Sitting at the kitchen table drinking coffee, Amber asked Bessie about those three green chairs. "Is there some significance to those three green chairs that seem to be growing out of the ground?"

"I guess they have by now become part of the heritage of this farm," Bessie explained. "It was started by Michael's grandpa who died at about the same time Michael was wounded in Vietnam. The story I heard from Tyler was that his pa had built those chairs himself to match chairs he saw in an old Sears catalog. He painted them Kelly green only because he already had that paint in the barn. After painting them, grandpa placed them exactly where you see them; they have never been moved." Bessie then added, "Grandpa and his son Tyler started sitting out there for long periods just talking, and when anyone else showed up while they were talking, grandpa would just shush them away." And then she repeated once again, "the chairs have not been moved from the spot grandpa placed them. And they probably never will be."

"But, why three chairs?" Amber inquired.

"Grandpa wanted a grandson! After Michael was born," Bessie explained, "his grandpa began taking him out to the green chairs, and there they would talk or not talk. Grandpa wanted Michael to love Oklahoma's land and the sky and to understand and appreciate the power and beauty of the weather. He wanted him to love the feeling of peace he could experience from just looking into the skies, the sunsets in the evening, the stars at night and the mighty storms that sweep across the Oklahoma prairie."

"What a heritage to give to a boy and what a story," Amber said exhibiting a level of excitement in her voice.

"Well, that's the three green chairs," Bessie said. "The custom on this farm has been that no one sits in those chairs unless Grandpa says it's OK, and now he's dead. Today, with Grandpa gone, the chairs are for Tyler and Michael, but neither of them have been spending any time in the chairs. They just sit there, but no one else uses them. Michael has been too withdrawn and Tyler too angry to spend time in the chairs that had in the past brought so much peace to them. So the chairs sit unused at their fixed spot, as if they too were waiting for Michael to finally come home from the war."

Just then, Tyler entered the room and interrupted the kitchen conversation, telling Amber it was about time to head to the airport. While Bessie and Amber were engaged in their kitchen talk, Tyler had been conferring with the other farmers

who had met at the grange hall. Without a single negative
vote, they agreed to retain Amber Highlander to investigate
the controversial Soviet wheat deal. The farmers had been so
impressed with her investigative skills, they wanted to see if
she could determine if there was anything they could or should
do. They drafted an agreement for her to sign if she accepted
the terms of the proposal, along with the retainer advance.
Tyler was to present the proposal and retainer to Amber on
their way to the airport.

During her short visit, Amber felt she had personally
fit into the lifestyle of the wheat farmers and enjoyed every
moment; her three day visit had gone by so fast. But now, as
they headed to the airport, she was ready to get back home to
Washington. She wanted to visit Senator Bellmon's office
and tell him she went to visit him on his farm in Billings. She
wanted to tell him the story of the concern of the wheat
farmers, hoping to get his comments and information he might
have about the Soviet wheat deal.   As they drove down
Interstate 35,Tyler handed Amber the retainer agreement he
and the other farmers had drafted with their check for one-half
of the proposed retainer fee. The other half would be paid
after she submitted her final report to the farmers. She read
the agreement, had no changes and told Tyler she accepted the
terms. She then signed the agreement with this closing
comment, "Thank you for being so very generous. I am
looking forward to getting the project started."

As they approached the airport in Oklahoma City,
Amber thanked Tyler for his family's gracious hospitality,
then added, "I hope you will invite me again to stay with your

family."

"Your welcome at any time," Tyler said.   And, he added, " Bessie told me to extend a double invitation to you from her. She enjoyed her conversations with you."

"I'll keep you and the other farmers informed on my progress, and will try to have a preliminary report in your hands by the end of March of '73," Amber told Tyler. At the airport, Amber got out of the car and headed toward the terminal door as she heard Tyler's parting words.

"Don't forget your invitation to come down for the wheat harvest," Tyler yelled out the window.

Amber turned, smiled at Tyler and waved, and then disappeared into the terminal, ready to get back to Washington. Tyler headed back home to Billings.

CHAPTER SIX

$\mathscr{A}$mber got back to Washington after her walk through the fields of new wheat, where she experienced the sounds of the wind and the sounds of silence, and she heard the sounds of anger from the wheat farmers who knew they had been cheated by the Nixon Administration. Now back home, she was wired with the excitement of a journalist, and immediately began her search for more answers toward the real truth. Already she had interviewed Secretary Butz and Henry Kissinger without much success, getting only denials of personal knowledge. She had already gone to Canada where she did get a lot of useful information from the Canadian Wheat Board. This CWB information confirmed what she suspected, that Secretary Butz's denial of having knowledge of the wheat deal was untrue. She began to suspect that the Nixon administration was holding something back from her, something big. But, now with the information gained from the CWB, she might be able to leverage that to gain the full truth.

Setting out in her new direction, Amber first turned to the staff members of the House of Representatives' Committee On Agriculture that had held hearings on the Sale of Wheat to Russia. That hearing, extending over a period of three days in September of 1972, offered her little help. The Committee staff members she talked with only confirmed and reinforced the denials made by Secretary Butz that the USDA had no advance knowledge that the Soviets were planning to buy large quantities of wheat from the private grain exporters. Amber believed that the House Committee had simply accepted as a fact that the wheat deal was just a private transaction. What's with this wall of silence? Amber thought.

She realized that if Earl Butz had admitted personal knowledge of the wheat deal, he then would need to explain why his Department of Agriculture lied to the wheat farmers in the February and May issues of the *Wheat Situation*. Such a visible conflict caused Amber to suspect that Secretary Butz was holding something back even from Congress. She also suspected that the Soviet wheat deal was probably at the very center of some big White House secret international deal with the Soviets.. The mystery kept getting deeper and this only excited Amber even more, knowing now that with the Oklahoma wheat farmers' generous advance, she could financially afford to follow up on the leads she was gaining.

With the Nixon administration offering her so little credible information, Amber decided to go for broke and go talk directly with officials of the private grain exporters. So, she traveled to New York, hoping to get company officials at

Continental Grain and the Bunge Corporation to talk with her. What she discovered was that these private grain companies were as closed-mouth as the Nixon administration. The company officials were courteous to her when she arrived at their headquarters. They too had been following Amber Highlander's news articles published in several major newspapers. But still, they displayed no willingness to give her any information about their wheat sales to the Soviets. At Continental Grain, she was introduced to Clarence Palmby, but she did not get a chance to talk to him alone. Palmby, she remembered, had been Nixon's Assistant Secretary of Agriculture before going to work for Continental Grain. He came under the employ of this large grain exporter at about the same time that company made its huge sale of wheat to the Russians on July 5, 1972. But Amber was not allowed to interview Palmby while she was at Continental's home offices. She was told, he had to leave on assignment. She returned to Washington empty handed.

Arriving back home, Amber experienced a little frustration over all the closed communications about one of the largest international grain sales that had ever occurred, and this one to the Soviet Union, a major ally to North Vietnam. Thinking longer about the embedded silence with which she had been confronted, she began to see the Administration's silence as part of the story. She realized that what she now needed was someone with whom she could talk who might help make sense out of this pervasive pattern of silence. She also needed a drink. So she called her close friend Joshua Walker and met him for drinks at their popular Washington

hangout. They had talked before about her interest in the
wheat deal but they had not talked much since she returned
from Oklahoma.

As they sipped on drinks, Joshua asked how her
Oklahoma trip went and what Oklahoma wheat country was
like. She quickly summarized the story and then started
telling him about Michael's dreams of becoming a wheat
farmer, and how those dreams had been dashed by the injuries
he experienced in Vietnam. She told Josh she wanted to write
a story about the "Michaels" who returned home from
Vietnam, suffering from the destructive post traumatic stress
disorder to show how that disorder affects the lives of not only
the veterans but their families as well. But for now, she told
him, her focus had to stay on the wheat deal and its effect on
the wheat farmers.

Joshua was impressed with Amber's story about the
wheat farmers and Michael's Vietnam tour and his injuries.
"More and more," Josh told Amber after his second drink,
"the people in growing numbers are opposing the Vietnam
war. In fact, he added with emphasis, "I believe that unless
the President brings that war to an end, he will not be
reelected. He might not even be re-nominated."

"I hear the same thing everywhere I go," Amber added.
"Even the Oklahoma wheat farmers who almost always voted
Republican were criticizing the war. With Michael's serious
medical condition, they suddenly began seeing the tragic side
of that war, first hand."

"I know," Josh said. "Let's have one more drink
before heading home."

"OK," Amber agreed. But now she wanted to get to her problem of trying to find some start toward gaining information about what the wheat deal was all about. "Josh, you know I have been working on the wheat deal since I first heard Cronkite's report. But I am having a hell of a time getting information. Everybody in the administration and the companies is stonewalling as if they are hiding something."

There was a long pause before Joshua volunteered, "They are! But, if you want answers, you need to go back to early 1971, to understand the need for all the silence."

Just then, their last drinks arrived and Amber picked up the check, hoping that Josh would continue talking. They took a moment to enjoy their drinks, and then Amber asked: "Josh, tell me, what the hell was going on with the wheat deal in 1971? Why all the silence?"

Another long moment of silence, finally broken by Josh, "What the hell, I'll tell you what I know, but you can't report what I will tell you without firm confirmation."

"I agree," Amber said.

"Recognize this," Josh began, "my personal knowledge is limited, but it might help you gather additional information through other sources. I told you that the wheat deal began in 1971, just how early I don't know, maybe as early as February. It seemed to have begun with all the agonizing talk at the White House over the Republican Party's dismal showing in the midterm elections, a disaster, I heard it called. Facing that national political defeat, it seemed that everybody in the White House began searching for some bold new direction. There was even discussion in the White House about Nixon's possible failure to even get re-nominated by his own Party." Josh stopped here to take another drink and to think, then added, "With elections coming up so quickly, Nixon's failure to bring Vietnam to a close began appearing as his biggest stumbling block that could threaten his bid for a second term. I heard Nixon tell Haldeman that with his inability to end Vietnam, the first months of 1971 were the lowest point of his first term as President."

"If he were stressed out that much, Nixon might be more willing to take on greater risk through more drastic action," Amber summed up.

"That's right!"

"This distress could have even generated the idea of making a deal with the Soviets — a secret deal of exchanging American grown wheat for some kind of settlement in Vietnam." Amber was reaching out here, drawing from the information she had obtained earlier from the Canadian Wheat Board and then adding her own inferences.

This comment from Amber brought a moment of silence from Joshua. It seemed like a long moment. Then he spoke, "Where in the world did you come up with that idea?" Josh asked, not really expecting Amber to answer that question. He knew she had developed a lot of sources for information and probably knew more than him. "Amber, you need to further explore that drastic idea."

"Lets get one more drink," Amber suggested. "I don't live far from here, so we won't need to drive." She did not want Josh to stop talking, and she had a tape recorder going to preserve what he was saying.

"OK," Josh agreed, as he was now ready to keep talking. "One day, during June of '71, I heard Kissinger railing against some maritime union official who had refused to talk to him about loading grain on Soviet ships." Josh then told Amber the story that he had later put together. "It's a story that will make you laugh," Josh added, as he began to chuckle to himself.

"It might be the drinks," Amber suggested.

As he was beginning the story about the White House's efforts to get the maritime unions to load grain on Soviet ships, Josh told Amber that he only had surface information that he had overheard at the White House. He suggested that she go to the union halls and talk with the union leaders and try getting the details needed from them. "One of the funny things I heard was how Kissinger thought his personal power of persuasion would be enough to convince the union leaders to allow their members to load the grain on Soviet ships. Kissinger had so much faith in his accomplished and highly touted skills in diplomacy." Suddenly, Joshua began to laugh almost out loud, suggesting to Amber that they had had enough.

"Let's head home Josh." Amber suggested after paying the tab. They began walking toward her apartment, with Josh still laughing.

Josh could not stop laughing, as if he needed to complete his story about Kissinger's attempt to use his diplomatic skills to convince a bunch of labor union leaders to do something in the name of peace. Josh thought the image was so comical. "I believe it was in June of 1971," Josh began, "when Kissinger invited two union officials to meet with him at the White House to talk about the planned Soviet wheat deal. I can't remember their names except for one, I believe his last name was Gleason. Kissinger and the President knew that no wheat deal could be made with the Soviets if the maritime unions opposed the deal. The ships would simply not be loaded without union support. But, Kissinger never got a chance to open his mouth to use his diplomatic skills." Josh continued his story, as he again began laughing.

"I can't wait to hear how this story is going to end," Amber interjected. "It sounds so funny, as I view the image of Henry Kissinger."

"It's funny to me," Josh added as he continued laughing. "These hardened anti-Communist union leaders slammed the door shut on Kissinger, not even giving this highly touted international diplomat a considerate reception." Joshua started laughing again at the image he was creating, an image he thought was so hilarious.

At just the right time, they reached Amber's apartment and as soon as they were in, Josh went to bed and fell asleep. Amber had held back on her drinks, and wanted to make some quick notes while she had her attention focused on the image that had become so hilarious to Josh when he was telling the story about Kissinger and the union leaders. Then she got ready for bed and went to sleep. After Joshua and Amber awakened the next morning, thankful it was a Saturday after a little too much to drink the night before, Amber fixed breakfast with no words spoken. After breakfast, she served coffee and then they talked about the wonderful years they had spent at the University of Alabama with RJ. When Robert Jefferies' name came up, Amber began to cry. This was her personal loss from that goddamn Vietnam war.

"That was such a loss!" Amber sobbed.

"I agree," Josh added with sadness in his voice. "RJ was my closest friend. He was smart and had so much to offer to the world. I will never forget the moment you called to tell me he had been killed. If the war could just have been ended sooner," Josh said, as a tear rolled down his cheek.

The two close friends who had briefly shared life with RJ embraced, until Amber said, "I'm OK Josh." Then after one more cup of coffee, Josh headed home, and Amber welcomed the solitude. After Josh left, she took a long walk, reflecting back on the happy days, she had had with Robert Jefferies. While on her walk, she remembered leaving her car at the pub the night before, and walked over to pick it up and drive home. Now, with a clearer mind, she would get back on her project. For this, Amber was thankful she had recorded Josh's remarks the evening before as they were having drinks, for she would never be able to remember everything said. She sat at her kitchen table, drinking coffee and listening to the tape, then listening again to Josh's story about the maritime unions. One thing that struck her as she listened was his repeated caution that she needed to go directly to the union hall to get more details. As she kept listening to the tape, making notes of what she considered the most important, Amber thought it interesting when one union leader told Kissinger harshly, "We won't let you sell the American people down the Volga or down the Yangtze."

So many questions without answers were coming to Amber's mind. Why would Kissinger be trying to convince the unions to load grain on the Soviet ships? He had told her he knew nothing about the Soviets' interest in buying wheat. In her mind, things were not stacking up in any orderly fashion. She knew she needed to talk with the union leaders, and she was confident enough to have no hesitation to contact them. These union leaders it seemed had stood at the very center of the whole plan as indispensable active participants. The White House's ability to effectuate the plan to sell wheat to the Soviets could work only with the full help of the unions. Amber theorized that these guys would have, as a condition for their help, probably insisted on being told what the plan was all about. If, Amber reasoned, the unions' ultra American patriotism and their contemptuous disdain toward the Communists was the thing blocking their willingness to allow their members to load the grain on Soviet ships, the White House knew it faced a serious obstacle. The plan could not advance unless and until the unions agreed to cooperate. So, Amber decided to go talk with the union leaders face to face and hope they too were not closed-mouth.

Before attempting to make contact with the maritime union, Amber conducted research and identified the two union leaders: Jay Lovestone, international affairs director for the AFL-CIO; and Thomas W. "Teddy" Gleason, President of the International Longshoreman's Association. After her preliminary investigation, Amber headed to the union hall unannounced, just taking a chance that someone at the hall would talk with her. It was a cold December 14, 1972, with snow covering the ground, when Amber arrived at the union hall. She was led to a conference room and offered a cup of coffee. Someone will be in shortly, the receptionist told her. Amber had been in a number of union halls and felt completely comfortable with the guys who represented working people. Hopefully they will not hold back information in any sense of loyalty to Richard Nixon and the White House. Soon one of the union officials entered the room and greeted Amber who was known to them from her news articles. From those articles, the union leaders knew that Highlander was a friend of the working people. When the union official introduced himself to Amber, he said, "You can't use my name or identify the source of anything you hear in this room. Do you agree with these terms?"

"Yes, that's agreeable with me. I truly appreciate your meeting with me." Amber then told the union official about the wheat farmers and about Michael and her reasons for exploring this story.

"OK, what do you want to talk about?" the union official bluntly asked.

Amber had to pause because she had not expected such openness, but then she said, "I want to know about your talks with Henry Kissinger and his efforts to convince you to let your members load wheat and other grains on Soviet ships and your initial refusal to go along with the plan. With your refusal to load the Soviet ships, weren't you depriving your union members needed work?"

"Ms Highlander, let me . . . ."

"Call me Amber!"

"Amber, let me remind you that we are at war with the Soviet Union.   Maybe not directly, but that Communist superpower along with China is supplying North Vietnam with military supplies and weapons being used to kill our soldiers in Vietnam."   The Union official paused for a moment, but did not want to stop explaining the story to this young freelance news reporter. "I have supported President Nixon's efforts to win the war against the Communists in Vietnam, and could not at first understand why the President was suddenly willing to extend his hand of assistance to feed them.   I   remember," he   kept   talking,   "during   the administration of our friend John Kennedy, when Richard Nixon criticized the same kind of wheat sale to the Soviets."

"Was President Kennedy proposing a wheat sale to the Soviets?" Amber inquired.

"He was, and we went along with the plan, and agreed to load the grain on Soviet ships."   The Union official then explained, "When the wheat sale to the Soviets was first advanced by President Kennedy back in 1963, Nixon and Barry Goldwater accused Kennedy of betraying the United States to Communism.   Nixon called the decision the worst foreign policy mistake of the Administration."   After a short pause to think, the union official continued. "I remember the substance of what Nixon told members of the press. He told them that Kennedy was subsidizing Khrushchev, allowing him to divert the Russian economy into space and into military activities that he otherwise would have to keep in agriculture."
The union guy, who did not want his name used, paused again

and then added. "Nixon kept criticizing Kennedy's wheat sale to the Soviets, claiming that the United States was entering the most dangerous period of the cold war since it began." Another pause in the union official's explanation and a short break. "You want another cup of coffee Amber"

"No thank you," Amber responded. "But you could direct me to the rest room."

"Go out this door, take a right and it's the first door on your right."

"Thank you," Amber said. When she returned to the conference room she discovered two additional union officials in the room.

"Amber, I have asked these two gentlemen to join us just in case I miss something, but none of us want our names used. So I am not going to introduce them by name, simply because we don't want you to slip up and drop one of our names in an article you might write. It's not that we don't trust you; it's just a precaution. Is that OK with you?"

"Absolutely!" Amber assured them. "And, I am not offended by your anonymity. Again, I appreciate your willingness to give me the information which I will confirm with an independent source before I publish anything. That will protect you."

"That's good," the official responded. "Getting back to my story about Nixon's objection to President Kennedy's wheat sale to the Soviets, I remember so clearly the statement he made about the bear being most dangerous when it has its arms stretched out in a gesture of friendship. Then, when

Kissinger approached us about an even bigger sale of wheat to the Soviets, I thought about Nixon's statement he had made against President Kennedy's sale to the Soviets."

"What was the difference between then and now?" Amber asked. "You agreed to load the Soviet ships for President Kennedy and you refuse when Nixon is offering to sell wheat to the Soviets. I don't understand."

"There were differences in the two international trade deals, but the biggest difference was the war, and the thousands of American soldiers who are losing their lives or come home crippled as a result of the Soviets' providing military supplies and hardware to North Vietnam. We took a hard line with Kissinger, because of our contempt for the Communists, and to make evident our contempt, we conveyed the message that our union members would only load the grain on the Russian ships, in exchange for American prisoners of war. Ms Highlander, I mean Amber, you have to understand just how staunchly patriotic our unions are. We would just as soon see the war continue until all the Communists on the battlefields of Vietnam were defeated or killed. We wanted an outright victory to prevent international threats of Communism from reaching the shores of the United States. And as long as the Soviet Union continued to enable the North Vietnam Communists to keep killing American soldiers, we would not load one grain of wheat on any ship heading to Russia."

"So, was there a time you changed your mind about loading wheat onboard Soviet ships?" Amber asked.

"Yes!"

"Well, that confirms my thought," Amber began, "that you did finally agree to allow your union members to load the wheat on Soviet vessels."

"Well, that's right, but how did you learn that?" the official ask.

"I can't disclose my sources!" Amber sounded with emphasis. "And, in the future, you can be completely confident, that you as a source will never be revealed."

"We believe you, and that is why we are willing to talk to you."   The three union officials then put their heads together to confer for a moment, and then the spokesman commented, "Excuse our interruption. After conferring with each other, let me tell you that a deal with the White House was worked out and we did agree to allow our members to load the wheat on the Soviet ships. But, we did not make our agreement with Henry Kissinger. One of the things that led to this agreement was Nixon's pragmatism in bringing in his trusted and more politically savvy assistant, Charles Colson, to talk with us. Colson has been one of our friends ever since Nixon was elected President, and he spoke our language."

"What did Colson add for you to cooperate with him?" Amber asked.

"Well, first, he respects the maritime unions' philosophical opposition to Communism and their reluctance to allow our members to load the Soviet grain ships. He treated us as equals. And, he didn't talk down to us. Charles Colson was able to sway us by carefully explaining and convincing us that the wheat deal was Nixon's way of fighting Communism and defeating North Vietnam by convincing the Soviet Union to pressure them into agreeing to a settlement that would end the war."

"So, the wheat deal became the quid pro quo for peace in Vietnam?" Amber sought reassurance.

"That's right!" the union official emphasized, "pure and simple. That is how Colson explained it to us. But to make it work, Colson stressed, the need for absolute secrecy as an imperative to Nixon's getting all the troops and POWs back home. That's one of the reasons we have kept our silence."

Amber interrupted to ask, "As a result of these negotiations between Colson and the union, when did things start coming together?"

"Well, in substance, we were all confident that an agreement was within reach by mid-July of 1971, with the final agreement not finalized until November. That was when our members actually began loading grain on Soviet ships."

"What I can't understand," Amber explained to the union officials, "is why President Nixon did not announce a Vietnam settlement agreement in 1971. If the grain deal with the Soviets was the quid pro quo for a peace agreement, why did Nixon start escalating the war by all his increased bombing raids? I don't understand," Amber remarked.

"We don't understand that either! But we can say that the November loading of grain was small in comparison to what occurred during the summer of 1972. We had been alerted by the White House that the Soviets were expected to be buying enormous quantities of wheat and other grains during the summer of '72. We later learned that the Soviets in fact purchased some 400 million bushels of wheat during that summer. And yet, the Vietnam war continued. The points were not connecting," the union official noted with a sound of puzzlement.

Amber had stayed with the union officials a good part of the day when one them suggested that they send out for sandwiches and a couple six packs of beer, even though it was cold outside. She liked the idea, thinking of just how productive her day had already been, even if nothing else occurred. When the sandwiches arrived, they sat around the table, slowly eating and drinking beer, as the conversation shifted over to several different subjects. As the Noble county wheat farmers had been so impressed with Amber, so were the three union officials. They supplied Amber a lot of useful information but those union officials were also enjoying themselves just being around their new acquaintance. They had made a new friend. After a couple of beers with her new friends, Amber thanked them and headed back home to begin digesting all she had learned. As she began driving, she kept repeating to herself that Nixon's secret wheat deal with the Soviets, exchanging wheat for peace, probably placed him in a position to end the war as early as July of 1971, and no later than November of '71. When she got home, Amber relaxed with a glass of wine and her favorite music, as she thought of the brilliance of Nixon in using wheat to end the war. Then she once again listened to the tape of Joshua's comments that were now making more sense.

She sat in front of her fireplace, just thinking about the idea of trading wheat to the Communists to gain their help in pressuring North Vietnam into a settlement. And, she thought it could have been done as early as July of 1971. Tears started rolling down her cheeks, as she suddenly realized that, that was almost a year before RJ's death in Vietnam. "Why didn't that son-of-a-bitch Nixon not end the Vietnam war?" Amber screamed out, though there was no one there to listen. After crying for a long period, Amber's sadness turned into anger. She became more determined to discover the full truth about the trade of wheat for some sort of settlement in Vietnam. She did not care what it took; she committed herself to discovering the truth.

She remembered when North Vietnamese Premier Pham Van Dong had made the announcement himself that he and Kissinger had reached a settlement agreement. There it was. Not in July of 1971, but right before the elections, Peace in Vietnam! "Can it really be?" the Washington *Post* editorialized on October 21, 1972, writing in positive tones, "[I]s it possible that the killing and wasting is finally going to come to an end?" And with that announcement, George McGovern's campaign for President collapsed, and Nixon went on to win a second term in a landslide vote. Nixon became the man of peace.

After it was publicly announced in October 1972, that America's involvement in Vietnam had finally come to an end, there was celebration in the streets throughout the land; through the ranks of the combat soldiers who would now be coming home; and among the cheering throngs of the antiwar activists. It was a personal victory for the antiwar activists, a vindication of their sacrifice and suffering. For them, it didn't matter that with the announcement of peace, President Nixon was swept back in for a second term as President. At that moment, even to them, he was the man of peace. Now, instead of violently clashing with the police, the antiwar activists were dancing in the streets and celebrating with their musical festivals, and with cheap wine and marijuana. But when that celebration was over, life as staunch antiwar activists ended. Now what?

The unswerving antiwar activists, including Suszette Andrew, began wandering off in different directions, many not knowing where they were going or what they were going to do in the future. Fighting the Vietnam war had become their life, and now that the war was over, their life as antiwar activists was over. "What are we going to do now?" one activist asked Suszette.

"I don't know!"

"Are you going back to Oklahoma?"

"No, not now. What about you?"

"I don't know either, but right now, I think I am going

home to Pennsylvania and spend some time with my parents. I haven't seen them for over two years."

"Good luck," Suszette said, as they headed off in different directions.

Suszette had not seen her parents for over two years either, but she could not go home. Not now. Without the war to fight, she no longer had direction, she did not know where to turn, except she was not ready to go back to Billings, Oklahoma. She crowded into an old VW bus of many colors, that some called the rolling graffiti, and hit the highway going West, heading for the "Farm," an agricultural commune in New Mexico. With the war over, many of the antiwar activists turned from the violence and street confrontations to a new state of pacifism and non-violent farm life. Suszette joined her comrades and worked hard in the fields, growing vegetables and tending the dairy cows and sheep. On the farm, they could cut out the world and search for their identity, or not.

In the evenings, Suszette once again turned to the night sky that allowed her mind to wonder along the path of the milky way to rest in peace among the stars that seemed to coexist so peacefully night after night. After about eight months on the farm as early fall of '73 was arriving, Suszette was back on the road, still searching for direction and meaning of life. In a way, her full meaningful life as an antiwar activist had pushed out everything else, but now, she felt empty. Without knowing it, Suszette was searching for the road back home, wherever that might be.

Scraping together enough funds, she decided to fly to Europe and move through the countries, visiting towns along the way and learning from the people, willing to take her into their homes, feed her for a few days and give her comfort. She never stayed more than three days with any one family or town. She just kept moving. When she came to the end of Europe, she moved on to Africa, and worked as a volunteer in a small hospital. In the evenings, Suszette spent time outdoors looking up into the sky at the brilliance of the stars. This was the one thing that kept her linked to her past. She had wandered the globe trying to find her way back home. And now, while still in Africa, Suszette, for the first time, began to feel homesick for Billings. She had long been silently heading home, not knowing what to expect, and in some ways not caring. She just wanted to go home. The road had been long to the place from which she had first begun her trip, and she still had a long way to go.

CHAPTER SEVEN

*I*n early March of 1973, Amber had prepared a preliminary report on the wheat deal and sent it to the wheat farmers in Billings. Her report, mailed to Scott Weaver, President of the Grange, included everything she had been able to discover up to that time. It was not complete, but it did confirm that the Nixon administration had indeed sacrificed the farmers, albeit in the name of peace. She promised to have her final report by harvest time in 1974. She needed that year to complete her investigation.

Amber's long meeting with the union leaders had helped put everything in clearer perspective, linking the Soviet wheat deal to the announced settlement in Vietnam. Now, she needed to establish confirmation of what she had been told. Toward gaining this confirmation, Amber decided to go to the public restaurant in the Department of Agriculture building, hoping to meet some insiders who may have worked on the wheat deal. By chance or fate, Amber was having lunch when she overheard two men at the next table complaining about the favoritism being extended to the private grain exporters that had sold wheat to the Soviets. After awhile, she walked over to their table and introduced herself. Amber never hesitated using her beauty and charm as an end to get people talking. She had reached the point when the end justified the means.

As soon as Amber introduced herself as a journalist, one of the men got extremely nervous and excused himself from the table. The other man remained and expressed a willingness to talk with her, but not in this public place, particularly the place where he was employed. As they were finishing lunch, he told Amber that he had been actively involved in the wheat deal since early in 1971, before and after Kissinger called for the Department to come up with a negotiating scenario in preparation of the big grain trade with the Soviets. Looking into Amber's deep blue eyes, the man introduced himself as Ken Downing, and suggested they meet after work at the C & O Bar & Grill in Georgetown.

"How about 6:00 p.m.," Amber suggested.

"That's fine," Ken said in a tone of excitement, as if he had made some big personal conquest.

Amber lived in Georgetown and knew the place, but she had never been there. She knew or thought she knew where this might be heading. In her mind, she figured the guy will be expecting her to go to bed with him. Her first thought was that going to bed with this guy to get information might be seen as an act degrading to all women. In some minds, it made her a prostitute. But did it? Amber had written news stories of female spies who had used sex to gain information. And these women did not view themselves as whores. She too was on a mission. After long thought, Amber reasoned, if that is what it takes to gain access to this important insider information, so be it.

She was willing to just let the guy fuck her, if that is what it took. In her mind, Amber thought that such a personal sacrifice was justified in view of this potential information-gold- mine. She was committed to mining every bit of information she could get, even if it required surrendering her body. It was early April, 1973, when Amber arrived at the C & O Bar & Grill. She was a little early and took a table located in a corner, away from the main path of customers. She ordered a drink, scotch and water, and waited for Ken. In picking this table, she wanted Ken to feel comfortable to talk with her. When he walked in, Amber stood and motioned him over.

"Hey Ken, what do you want to drink?"

"Hey Amber! I'll have a scotch and water."

"That's what I'm drinking."

At first, the two of them sat at the corner table, sipping their scotch and water, just chit chatting, with Amber taking care not to give him any personal information. She did not want to get stuck with the guy. After a couple of drinks, Ken began talking about why they were there. "Amber, I am glad you are writing articles about the Soviet wheat deal. I have read every one of your articles on the subject, and thought several times about trying to contact you to funnel information to you. It was just by chance that you came to the Department's cafeteria."

"What made you want to do that?" Amber asked.

"Well, it was partly out of anger at how they treated my long time friend, Will Griffin."

That was a name Amber had not heard before. "What happened to Will Griffin?"

"I have known Will for a long time, and remember how disappointed he was when he was told to back off his investigation of one of the private grain exporters. Later, that same private exporter became involved in the Soviet wheat deal. That was back in early 1971. Will had discovered evidence of some fraudulent grain practices occurring at Cook Industries' export grain terminal." Without telling Ken, Amber was recording their conversation. She wanted and needed to be able to document every word and every name she heard, like Will Griffin. After ordering another drink, they continued talking, and Amber learned that this guy really did know a lot about the Soviet wheat deal. He held a high level position within the USDA, and had played a significant part in putting together the Soviet wheat deal that summer of '72.

Ken had actually worked directly with Clarence Palmby on what he called "Kissinger's Soviet wheat deal," and he had traveled with Assistant Secretary Palmby to Moscow for the final negotiations with the Soviets that finalized the deal.   More excitingly, he told Amber that he had personally collected copies of all the documents relating to the Soviet wheat deal because he saw the documents as potentially having historic value.   After a few drinks and two hours of talking, they ordered dinner and another drink, and there was more talk.   Everything was going good with Amber recording it all.

After dinner, Ken invited Amber to go to his apartment a couple of blocks away to see the documents he had collected.   She agreed, knowing where this was likely to lead. She had not had sex with anybody since RJ left for Vietnam, and now he was dead because of Nixon's refusal to end the war.   So, now, she thought, sex at this moment was only a means to an end.   When they got to Ken's luxury apartment, he fixed her another drink and showed her a thick stack of documents on the Soviet wheat deal.   But, he held them back from Amber as they finished their drink.   "Amber," Ken said in a soft voice, "I don't feel much like going through all these documents tonight.   We have both had a lot to drink.   Why don't we go to bed, and look at them tomorrow?"

"OK," Amber said, almost as a reaction, as she thought, I'll let him fuck me, and that will be over with.   She kept justifying this use of her body by reminding herself that this was only a means to an end.   But as a side thought, she remembered it had been a long time since she had sex with anybody and now her fiancée was gone.   Amber and Ken then went to bed, and Ken was not so drunk to marvel over Amber's gorgeous body. Without too much foreplay, Ken took Amber and it was quickly over. The two went to sleep and remained asleep until 8:30 a.m., awaking thankful it was a Saturday. So now sober, Ken began to caress Amber's body and she let him. After about thirty minutes, their bodies were again interlocked, and this time, Amber felt some pleasure. It had been a long time.

After satisfying himself, Ken got out of bed and showered, and then while Amber was showering, he made coffee and fixed a fantastic breakfast. After breakfast, Amber told Ken that she was anxious to see the documents. The two then went to the den where Ken had started a fire, and Amber was handed a stack of documents. She found that the documents had been carefully organized by Ken, with his typed notes, added as explanations. This indeed was a gold mine of information. She wanted to take them home and to make copies, but for now, she wanted to go through the stack of documents with Ken's explanation.

Ken told Amber about efforts made by Will Griffin, a long time USDA employee who had, during the early 1971, tried to buck the system by initiating an expanded investigation into suspected fraudulent practices of the private grain exporters. According to the story, USDA Special Agent Willard W. Griffin was investigating one of the private grain exporters in late 1970 and early 1971 when he discovered evidence of the presence of the fraudulent grain practices, known as "short-weighing" and "misgrading" of PL 480 grain.

Ken explained that PL 480 grain was the grain from the government owned stores that Congress had made available to be sent to famine stricken countries under America's "food for peace" program, a program hailed by many as one of the greatest humanitarian ventures ever conceived.

As Griffin's investigation advanced, he had become more convinced that the short-weighing and misgrading of PL 480 grain was industry wide. Based on that belief, Ken explained, he recommended to our superiors at USDA to expand the investigation, with consideration of even filing criminal and civil charges against the offending private grain exporters. Ken turned to a specific document he held, and after studying it, he continued his explanation. Special Agent Griffin faced strong internal resistance and all his efforts to expand the inquiry into the suspected corruption were blocked by officials of the Department of Agriculture. Ken told Amber that he had talked with Griffin one evening over drinks and he was mad as hell after being ordered to halt his investigation into the private grain exporters and to turn his attention to other matters. Because he was so certain the exporters were stealing grain from poor countries, he refused to be silenced.

But when he persisted in his demands for an investigation, even attempting to take his finding to the United States Attorney, he was rebuffed as a "scandal monger." He was told to stop rocking the boat, and to back off from his probe. Ken told Amber that he knew no USDA career employee more committed than Will Griffin, and it really hurt him when he was ordered to back off the investigation of the private grain exporters. But, out of this frustration, Griffin did stop "rocking the boat." He finally took early retirement in June of 1972. After that, all grain fraud investigations were blocked, and the private grain exporters were given a green light to continue their stealing of PL 480 grain.

Amber was stunned at what she was hearing. And Ken continued his unbelievable revelations. "The big grain move began in early 1972," Ken said. "That is when Kissinger, on behalf of President Nixon, sent his memorandum marked confidential to the Secretary of Agriculture on January 31, 1972, directing the USDA to prepare a negotiating scenario to serve as the template for possible grain trading with the Soviets. Amber, here is a copy of that memo that set into motion the White House's high-risk and imperatively secret wheat sale to the Soviets," Ken said.

Amber took and read the short document. "This doesn't say much at all."

"No," Ken agreed. "But when you read that document in the context of everything else, it says a lot. Its only after you read everything in context that you begin to see the pattern of how Nixon used the wheat deal to reach his settlement with North Vietnam, a settlement, not to be announced until right before his reelection bid." Ken paused here for awhile to continue marveling at Amber's beauty, then continued, "The principal players and authors of Kissinger's negotiating scenario were Assistant Secretary of Agriculture, Clarence Palmby, and his working staff, one of whom was me."

"Do you want to go out to get lunch?" Amber asked.
"All of this has been so interesting." She was having a hard
time getting over the enormous windfall of information she
had discovered, and she was wanting to just take the packet
home and study it on her own.

"I'll just fix lunch if you would like, then maybe we
can take a little break."

"That's fine," Amber quickly answered, expecting that
after lunch, the two of them would be back in bed for more
sex, but this time, she was looking forward to having sex with
the man she had just met. She did not have any emotional
attraction toward the man, it was just sex. It was like her
catching up on what she had been missing while waiting for
RJ to get back home. But now he would never be coming
home, and in her mind, that made it Ok, that she was having
sex with a stranger.

Three hours later, Amber suggested to Ken that she
take his documents home with her to give herself time to study
them. She then added that they could meet again next Friday
at the same time and place. After just having sex with such a
beautiful woman and thinking about next Friday for more of
the same, Ken quickly agreed. He let Amber take the
documents he had worked so hard to accumulate. Ken was
fearful to deny Amber's request, thinking that if he did not let
her take the documents, he might not ever see her again. So,
after he carefully repackaged the documents, Amber took
them and headed home, not too far from Ken's apartment, but

far enough.

After getting home, she was too tired to work on the documents. So she took a long hot shower and just rested, and as she rested, she decided to make two copies of the documents. She also decided to fly down to Atlanta and get a hotel and start her careful study of all this new evidence, including Ken's written comments and explanations. After checking into the Atlanta hotel, Amber spent the afternoon visiting with RJ's mom and dad, as if she needed to do this as some sort of cleansing process for having sex with a stranger. Amber had grown close to RJ's parents and she found comfort in talking about the fond memories of RJ, they all had and cherished. They all remembered just how remarkable RJ was and what a loss they had suffered. Then after dinner, Amber returned to the hotel and turned her mind to Richard Nixon and all the documents she had obtained from Ken Downing.

These valuable documents show Nixon's effective use of American grown wheat to leverage some kind of settlement in Vietnam, the settlement that North Vietnam's premier had announced on October 21, 1972. With Ken's documents and the information she had gathered from the Canadians, the union officials, and other sources, Amber began making sense out of Nixon's plan for peace. It actually made so much sense to her. As she was putting together all the information she had gathered while isolated in the Atlanta hotel, she could not help but reflect back to Henry Kissinger's denial to her that he ever had prior knowledge of the wheat deal with the Soviets. It was all a private commercial transaction, Kissinger had

claimed.   But Kissinger's denial, tested against all the
information she had accumulated, could no longer stand.
Then, she thought, why didn't Congress challenge these
claims of denial by Kissinger and Secretary Butz?   Amber
thought long and hard on that question, but came up with no
answer.   Maybe Ken and Joshua will be able to help me
answer that question.

Amber, as she studied the documents, became
convinced that it had all started with Henry Kissinger. He was
the person within the Nixon administration who stood at the
center of the design and implementation of the secret plan to
trade American grown wheat for a settlement in Vietnam. He
was the architect, the engineer and the skilled diplomat who
carefully took the pieces and brokered them into a new day in
Vietnam.   Two weeks after his first confidential memo,
Kissinger sent his more pointed directive that put the wheat
deal on a fast-track.   On February 14, Kissinger called for
completion of the negotiating scenario no later than February
28, and in this memo he gave specific instructions on the
content of the negotiating scenario.

The negotiating scenario must include, Kissinger
insisted, a specification that the proposed grain deal would be
handled exclusively through private grain exporters.   Amber
found in Ken's documents, the identification of the private
grain exporters participating in Kissinger's wheat for peace
plan: Continental Grain, Cargill Incorporated, Bunge
Corporation, Garnac Grain, Louis Dreyfus Corporation, and
Cook Industries.   With Assistant Secretary Clarence Palmby's

extensive experience working with the grain trade, the negotiating scenario was completed three days ahead of schedule, and placed in the hands of Henry Kissinger on February 25, 1972.

Amber reasoned from all the evidence she now had, disclosing the fact that the Soviets would be required to buy the wheat through private exporters instead of buying directly from the Nixon administration, the negotiating scenario seemed to be intended to serve an important diversion for protection of the White House. With this diversion, Kissinger and Secretary Butz could claim their lack of personal knowledge of the Soviet wheat deal, and claim that it was purely a private transaction. The visible structure established by Kissinger's negotiating scenario effectively shifted the most visible responsibility from the CCC to the private companies. As so skillfully drafted, Kissinger's negotiating scenario served to take the transaction out of the open corridors of government in open view of the public, and place them into the secret back channels of privately-held businesses, beyond the direct reach of any Congressional oversight and public scrutiny. But, Amber became convinced from all the documents she reviewed that the Soviet wheat deal was a government transaction, carried out by private grain exporters, serving as surrogates of the USDA, and Nixon Administration.

On Thursday, Amber flew back to Washington, armed with questions for Ken, her new highly important insider-source for information. The next day, at the appointed time, she met Ken at the C & O Bar and Grill in Georgetown. This time, it was Ken who was a little early, sitting at the same table. After exchanging general greetings, they ordered drinks, and after the first drink, he suggested they go on down to his apartment. It had been a week, and he could not wait to get her back in bed, this time, while they were still sober. Amber was willing, thinking that it would still give them time to discuss the documents and the questions she had. She would also be sober enough to go home to her own bed. She did not want to spend the night with Ken.

When they arrived at his apartment, Ken said nothing, and led Amber into his bedroom, as if he knew this was the payoff. It was in a sense. Amber allowed Ken to be in charge because of all the information he possessed. But, she too was a willing partner in sex. The two were soon engaged in passionate sex. That's how Amber saw it! It was sex for information! And, in her mind, that was ok. After Ken satisfied his needs, they got up, showered and went into the kitchen. Amber suggested they stick with coffee that night so they could keep a clear head. Another reason, Amber wanted to go home that night. So they sat at the kitchen table and talked. It did not take long for Ken to realize that Amber had thoroughly read and digested all the information contained in the packet of documents, he had allowed her to borrow.

"Thanks for the use of the documents," Amber told Ken. "I read and summarized all of them as well as your annotations. They helped me immensely to understand what was going on with the Soviet wheat deal."

"Your welcome," Ken said. "You didn't copy them did you?"

"No!" Amber asserted in somewhat of a defensive tone, not thinking of why she thought it necessary to lie about this. Maybe, it was the way Ken asked the question, in such a leading manner. She gave the answer she thought he wanted to hear, the answer that gave him more control over her. But now, with this lie, she would have to remember she had denied copying the documents.

"Good!" Ken responded.

"Ken, I have some questions."

"Shoot!"

"Well, it's a dual question. Is it possible that the White House and Secretary Butz did not know the full details of the Soviets' intentions to buy all the wheat they could get?" And, is it possible that this was purely a private commercial transaction?"

"No!" Ken shot back in rapid response, "to both questions. Let me tell you why. For one thing, the private grain exporters, considered collectively, simply did not possess the resources that would have given them the capability of handling such a mammoth transaction. The wheat sales to the Soviets during the summer of 1972 were simply too big for the private exporters to handle." Ken paused here and thought for a moment. "Let me modify that statement. At least, the private exporters were not big enough to profitably handle such an enormous wheat transaction. Only the United States government had the financial resources and actually owned enough wheat to responsibly manage the gigantic sale made to the Soviets." Ken paused again, and then added, "That was all part of the plan!"

"What do you mean, 'all part of the plan'?" Amber asked.

"You have to remember," Ken began, "that the object of the plan was to complete a wheat deal with the Soviets, favorable enough that the Soviets in turn would be willing to pressure its ally, North Vietnam, into bringing to an end all U.S. involvement in Vietnam. If this highly sensitive plan were to work, all the pieces had to be carefully interlinked with not a single part missing, just like a jigsaw puzzle. This meant it could only be   a government-to-government transaction, with the private exporters serving the important role of shielding details of the transaction from the farmers and the public."

"OK, but why did the details of the transaction have to be shielded from the wheat farmers?"

"Well, let me see if I can explain this to you. Kissinger's plan for peace dictated everything about the Soviet wheat deal, from its very inception to its final conclusion. When we traveled to Moscow in April 1972, to complete negotiations with the Soviets," Ken explained, "we knew the wheat farmers had to be convinced to sell their 1972 wheat harvest at the lowest price possible. This was needed for the plan to work. Kissinger's master plan called for the Soviets to purchase the wheat at a fixed price that was far, far below cost. This below cost price was part of the concessions Kissinger made to the Soviets for their help in dealing with North Vietnam." Ken stopped to let what he had said sink in with Amber, then he added, "Now this is the harder part of the master plan. Under the plan, the private grain exporters had to be convinced to sell wheat to the Soviets at a fixed price that was below what they had to pay for the wheat.   They were selling the grain at a loss."

"What!" Amber exclaimed. "That is unbelievable! It goes squarely against the private exporters' economic self-interest. How could they stay in business by selling to the Soviets, wheat they did not own, at a price that was below the market price? They would have gone out of business!"

"I know," Ken agreed, "that is basic economics; but price was only part of the plan. Putting it into play was the harder part. For this Continental Grain served as the intercessor for Kissinger's Vietnam plan, and individually assumed the task of negotiating with representatives of the Soviet Union. Through Continental Grain's negotiations, specific terms and conditions of the projected wheat sales were worked out and finalized not only for Continental, but for the entire group of Kissinger's private exporters. All the other private exporters were expected to accept and conform to the terms and conditions negotiated by Continental. Without a doubt, it was a complex plan."

"I know Continental Grain actually negotiated a multi-year contract selling wheat to the Soviets at a fixed price that was below cost," Amber commented.

"Amber, I know I keep repeating myself, but it was all part of a master plan to bring the war in Vietnam to a halt. And each part of the plan had a purpose and objective."

"But how," Amber inquired, "did the USDA keep all the information about the Soviet wheat deal away from the public and the farmers? I would think the market would somehow pick-up on the information."

"You would think," Ken replied. "The market did pick-up on it, but not until most of the farmers had already sold their 1972 wheat harvest on the open market. Then it was too late for them. Once the farmers had sold-off their 1972 harvest at the lowest price, that was all the White House needed for the wheat deal to advance."

"I call this market manipulation in its purest form, with the farmers taking the brunt of the sacrifice!" Amber asserted.

"So! Everybody involved in the Soviet wheat deal knew that for 1972, the farmers had to be sacrificed. It was all part of the big plan. Such was unavoidable. I know President Nixon had personally endorsed this part of the plan, as early as May of 1971. During one of our sessions in the White House, Nixon proudly made the point that he was taking the farmer out of his own selfish little role to make him play a big role in the world. That big role in the world was in helping to bring to an end the Vietnam war by improving U. S. relations with the Soviet Union."

"Wow!" That's all Amber could say. "But still," Amber began slowly, "how was the silence maintained and how was the information kept from the farmers?" Before Ken could answer this question, Amber added, "Keeping that much secrecy would require a lot of unbroken commitment, and close cooperation."

"Secrecy was imperative by all involved: the White House, the USDA, the private grain exporters, and the unions. You might find it hard to believe just how close the administration and the private grain exporters had worked to maintain this secrecy. We did whatever we had to do, knowing that if we failed in keeping a tight lid on the flow of information, the Soviet wheat deal for peace could have been put in serious jeopardy. So, toward preserving this secrecy, those of us working on the deal had to be willing to lie and to falsify information distributed to the farmers." Ken paused again to examine one of his documents and to think, then began, "While we were in Moscow during the first part of April, 1972, finalizing the wheat deal, the private exporters were meeting secretly in Kansas City at the Board of Trade. The financial scheme kept widening."

Ken then expanded on his explanation. "Everybody involved in making the Soviet wheat deal successful understood the imperative for secrecy. It was this need that compelled the USDA to falsify the February and May issues of the 1972 *Wheat Situation*. The object of that falsification of information was to prevent the farmers from discovering the facts of Nixon's historic sale of wheat to the Soviets. Had they known, the farmers could and may well have blocked the whole deal and, with that, Kissinger's Vietnam settlement plans. So, the need for secrecy was centerpiece and permeated the entire process toward bringing peace to Vietnam.

"From the beginning of our mission in Moscow, it was understood that Palmby would succeed in finalizing the negotiations and reaching an initial understanding with the Soviets. Traveling with Assistant Secretary Palmby, we arrived in Moscow on April 8, and had three days to wait before the negotiations were scheduled to begin. While waiting, we were treated as honored guests by the Soviets, as if we were their savior. In a sense, we were," Ken added with emphasis. "We brought them wheat they needed so badly, wheat that was available only from the storerooms of the United States. They had reason to celebrate, they were getting wheat, a scarce commodity in 1972 at a depressed price. Everybody in Moscow involved in the negotiations, the U. S. team members and the Soviets, knew the United States held a worldwide wheat monopoly. Everybody also knew just how desperate the Soviets needed this reliable source of wheat."

"So, what did all this mean?" Amber asked.

"It meant," Ken began explaining, "that in bargaining terms, the grain negotiations in Moscow were setting the stage for Kissinger's political component. Holding monopoly power in the wheat market translated into power for the United States, power to dictate terms and conditions of the sale of wheat, though we all knew Kissinger had been overly generous toward the Soviets with the concession he had made. Of course, we were not there to question anything. In Moscow, our part was simply to carry out plans of the White House, to literally surrender our worldwide wheat monopoly and allow the Soviets to purchase all the wheat owned by the United States government at a fixed price, substantially below cost."

"Unbelievable!" Amber interjected. "I still marvel at how such a gigantic financial thing could ever have taken place without a break in secrecy."

"I marvel at that myself," Ken said. "But while we were still in Moscow, Palmby did receive a directive from the White House that upon our arrival back in Washington, he needed to be prepared to convince the press and thereby the public that our negotiations with the Soviets had met with failure. The White House instructed Palmby to say whatever he had to say to deceive the press in believing his disappointing failure in Moscow. I saw the White House's written instruction to him," Ken stress. "It read: 'If asked by the press, it is important that no hopes be raised as a result of your talks but rather that there be disappointment at the lack of success.'"

"It doesn't seem to have an ending," Amber commented. "The Nixon administration lied to the wheat farmers through the use of falsified market data, published in the February and May issues of the USDA *Wheat Situation*. Now, you say that Palmby was directed to lie to the press. And, Kissinger and Secretary Butz both told me they had no personal knowledge of the Soviets' intent to buy so much wheat. Where does the lying end?"

"It couldn't then and it can't now," Ken insisted. "There was too much riding on that wheat deal."

Since Ken and Amber started talking, time had slipped by, it seemed so quickly, it was almost 9:00 p.m. So Amber suggested that they take a short break and have one drink. Ken agreed, and made two scotch and waters. Then, they got back to their talk about the wheat deal. "Ken, going back to the secret meetings of the private grain exporters in Kansas City, during the time the Palmby-team was in Moscow, what was all that about?"

"The first secret meeting was held in Kansas City in April, 1972, at the same time the Palmby-team was in Moscow. These super important meetings, and I attended all but this first one, brought together representatives of the six private grain exporters , USDA representatives and railroad executives on rail lines expected to be involved in the transportation of the wheat that would be sold to the Soviets. Wheat needed to be moved from the country elevators scattered around wheat country to the seaports from which the wheat would be loaded by union members on Soviet ships." After another of his pauses, Ken added, "Can you imagine the logistics alone in transporting from the United States to the Soviet Union, 400 million bushels of wheat?"

"I can't imagine it," Amber admitted. "Explain it."

"Because the wheat was sold over a three year period at a fixed price below cost, the risks facing these private exporters increased with every transportation delay. These secret meetings, therefore, were an essential forerunner to the private exporters' willingness to commit themselves to selling so much wheat to the Soviets at such a fixed ridiculously low price. Therefore, before making any commitment to act so contrary to their economic self-interest, these private exporters had to make certain that transportation would not get bogged down, thereby creating additional risk. The big wheat and grain sales to the Soviets, finalized by Palmby's team in Moscow on April 12, were expected to create a huge burden on America's rail system. Therefore, the White House needed for all the participants to meet secretly to design a new procedure that could most efficiently move the 400 million bushels of wheat from the inland grain elevators to the Gulf ports, ready for export to the Soviet Union. Such transportation logistics were incredibly complex. Everything had to fall in place to insure the success of Kissinger's master plan for peace."

"That makes sense," Amber added. "How many of these secret meeting were held?"

"I can't recall the exact number," Ken responded, "but the meetings continued throughout the spring and summer of 1972. With representatives of the USDA, the railroads, and the private exporters coming together, we discussed the basic logistics of efficiently moving the 400 million bushels of wheat, Kissinger had committed to the Soviet Union. We were preparing for the most complex transportation problems. In fact, out of these meeting, the transportation system then being followed by the CCC was substantially modified."

"Ken, would you agree, based on all the documents you have shown me, that the President and Henry Kissinger were both fully aware of every detail about the big Soviet wheat deal?"

"Absolutely," Ken announced in his authoritative voice. "There can be no doubt in this. In fact, shortly after we arrived back in Washington, Kissinger left for Moscow with full knowledge of our successful wheat negotiations. He went to Moscow to make the linkage between the wheat deal and a guaranteed closure to the Vietnam war. During this political segment, it was expected that Kissinger would obtain Moscow's firm commitment to pressure North Vietnam into accepting the settlement terms for a cease fire in Vietnam that allowed Nixon enough room to claim that his was an honorable exit. It was expected, that when Nixon attended his Moscow summit in May of '72, he would finalize the deal. And, with the deal finalized, Nixon would hold in his hands the power to announce a settlement to the U. S. involvement in Vietnam, on his own personal timetable."

"Ken, can you pinpoint exactly when Nixon and Kissinger first began considering the trade of wheat for peace in Vietnam?"

"From the first moment the idea was raised," Ken repeated the question, "I would say it was early in 1971, after the Republican Party's political fiasco during the midterm elections."

For Amber, all the pieces were coming together. She

just needed one more piece of firm evidence, she thought, to confirm the linkage between the wheat deal and Kissinger's settlement in Vietnam. She asked Ken whether he had ever seen such a written document that made that linkage. "Amber," he began slowly, not wanting to give her the document right then, "I have seen such a document, but I have not yet had a chance to make copies. I will try to get it for you."

"Can we meet next Friday again, this time maybe at the C&O?"

That was what Ken wanted to hear. He wanted to extend his meetings with Amber just as long as possible, knowing they were not permanent. It wasn't in the cards he kept telling himself. He understood that this beautiful woman was having sex with him only because he had information she needed. With that thought on his mind, he did not tell her that he had already made copies of the document that, in his mind, was surely a barn burner or smoking gun. With another meeting set for next Friday, Amber went home, confident she would soon have the missing piece of information. So, while waiting for the week to pass, she continued working on the sequence of events, and putting her final touches on a couple of newspaper articles that were about due. She began getting anxious to see the document Ken had referred to as a "smoking gun. When Friday came on that spring-like day in April, 1973, Amber arrived at C & O's about 6:15. Ken was already at their table, having ordered two scotch and waters. "Hey Ken," Amber said as she approached the table.

"Hey."

"You been here long?"

"Not too long. You look good Amber," Ken said, as he stared, it seemed for the longest time, at this gorgeous woman he had gone to bed with. "Uh, uh," Ken sounded in almost a stutter, "glad to see you. Have you had a good week?"

The conversation went back and forth as they slowly sipped on their drinks. Then, after about thirty minutes of talking, Ken pulled out the copy of a document that appeared to be a transcript of one of Kissinger's telephone conversations. He handed it to Amber. "I made this copy for you."

"Thank you," she said in an excited voice. Amber began reading the transcript of the call that came in on June 27, 1972, at 12:02 p.m. It was a call to Kissinger from Soviet Ambassador Anatoly Dobrynin, informing him that their wheat deal was underway. He told Kissinger that the Soviet grain buying team had arrived to complete the grain purchases as they had agreed in large quantities. According to the transcript, the team was prepared to pay $150 million in cash for grain immediately, and up to $700 million on credit for more. The document contained a margin notation made by Ken that this message had been conveyed to the President, and that with this, Kissinger was telling the President that they were now free to move immediately toward ending the Vietnam war. When she finished reading the document, Amber's excitement was clearly visible in her face, as she sat there in stone-silence. Ken and Amber were saying nothing as they finished their first drink and then ordered their second. Finally, Amber's reasoning returned, as she began reflecting on the value of the document Ken had just handed her. "Based on that document," she reasoned, "it is now undisputed that Nixon and Kissinger were fully aware of the big wheat deal with the Soviets; that the wheat deal was a tradeoff with the Soviets for a peace agreement in Vietnam; and that they could right then, on that very day, have announced a settlement to the Vietnam war."

"I agree!" Ken commented. "I thought you would like that document."

"I owe you," Amber said, as her face still glowed with excitement. "Let's have another drink and go to your place."

Ken was happy to hear those words.

• • • •

It had been a long time since Amber had met with her closest friend, Josh, so she called him and they met at their favorite piano bar. They talked about everything in general but nothing specific. But, with the start of their second drink, Amber could not hold back on her latest discovery as she began telling Josh the full story of Nixon's wheat for peace exchange. Finally, she asked, more in a rhetorically tone than a point of inquiry, How can Butz and Kissinger keep denying personal knowledge about what was going on with the wheat deal?

After hearing her story, Josh remained totally silent with his mouth open, with no words coming out. "What!" he finally exclaimed. "What!" he repeated. "Amber," he said in such a low voice it was almost inaudible, "where did you get all that information? How did you get that information? How?" Josh repeated. Then he added, "This must be why I have not heard from you for such a long time."

"Yeah," Amber murmured, "I have been busy."

"Where, where, did you get that information?" Josh asked.

"You don't want to know!" Amber said softly. Her sources were confidential, something she never breached. But here she had another reason for keeping her source confidential. She did not want Josh to ever know what she had been willing to do to get the information. She was not ashamed, but it was her secret, and she wanted to keep it secret forever.

There was more silence on the part of Josh as he tried to find something to say. Finally, the words came, "Let's order another drink."

Amber could tell that her good friend was finding it hard to find the right words, so they just sat there in silence, listening to music, with Amber smiling, and Josh, still with his bewildered look. They ordered one more drink, and Amber then suggested that they walk to her apartment and enjoy the evening breeze. During their walk, neither spoke until they arrived at Amber's home. "Let's go sit on the patio," Amber suggested.

Still not saying a word, Josh followed Amber to the patio and they sat there looking into the spring-time sky with scattered clouds moving slowly from West to East. Josh finally spoke, "Where, how did you get all that information?"

"Josh, you know I can't tell you where or how I got all that information, but I will tell you that I got it honestly. And, I will also tell you that I now hold documentary evidence of the entire story of Nixon's exchange of wheat for peace in Vietnam."

"Well, I know you can't tell me." Josh then said in proud voice, "I knew if anyone could collect this information, it would be you. That is outstanding work. Congratulations."

"Thanks Josh," Amber said. "That's important coming from you."

"So, now, what are you going to do with all that information?"

"Do you agree that the information is accurate?" Amber asked.

"If you have documents that support the story, then I have no reason to deny any part of the story that does put Kissinger and Butz in a bind, if you go public with the information."

"Why wouldn't I go public with the information? At the right time, I will publish the information in news articles, but I don't want to do that until I make my final report to my farmer-clients," Amber explained.

"That's considerate of your farmers and your profession as a journalist," Josh commented. "But, you know

Amber, what you have told me is only part of the story, and if you publish your data too quickly, you might find it harder to collect the information of the second half of the historic saga."

"Don't tell me that," Amber said in a pleading voice. Right then, Josh went in to go to bed and Amber remained on the patio and began pondering over what Josh had just said. She thought, this is only part of the story? Josh just expanded the story beyond what she had discovered with the help of her insider source. Amber thought in her mind: what parts of the story remain to be discovered? As the question hung in the air, she went to bed.

The next morning, Amber fixed breakfast. Then, after cleaning the kitchen, she and Josh took their coffee back to the patio. "Josh, before you went to bed last night, you dropped a bombshell when you told me that the information I had gathered was only half the story. What did you mean?"

"You must look at the bigger picture," Josh responded. "You already know that the Soviet wheat deal was part of a bigger plan, a plan for achieving peace in Vietnam. You also know that because the strategy toward achieving this desired conclusion required serious deviation from the norms of international relations, the role played by the Nixon administration had to be shrouded in absolute secrecy. Such secrecy became the imperative to protect the international reputation of the United States, and for the more domestic imperative of avoiding possible criminal and civil entanglement."

"Criminal and civil entanglement?" Amber questioned.

"Yeah!" Josh confirmed. "Ask yourself these questions, Amber. Why would private grain exporters be willing to sell large quantities of wheat to the Soviets at a fixed price below cost? And, how could they have afforded making such sales below cost? Think about it!"

"The bigger picture will in time emerge," Amber added with confidence. "It was Nixon's peace plan that had multiple parts. But one thing I find hard to understand is how the administration was able to so effectively and so totally preserve the secrecy about the trade of wheat for peace in Vietnam."

"That is a puzzle, even to me" Josh admitted. "But, I think there is a simple answer to the puzzle."

"Josh, you are a true optimist! You always see a simply answer to even the most complex problems. For me, it is unbelievable that the President of the United States allowed the USDA to so materially distort information going to the wheat farmers."

"Just keep remembering Amber," Josh cautioned her. "It was all part of a bigger picture that might give the distortion some moral justification."

"Can official government distortion ever be justified?" Amber inquired.

"Well, you be the judge!" Josh then picked up on his story. "The White House's engineered claims of a depressed wheat market served as part of Nixon's strategy of concealment of the truth that was so essential to the success Kissinger's wheat exchange for peace. That it was all about ending the war in Vietnam, at least in my view, justified the distortion."

"I am beginning to understand," Amber admitted.

Josh then continued his version of the story that further confirmed what Amber had put together from her own investigation and from what she had learned from Ken. "Clarence Palmby, the Assistant Secretary of Agriculture, took his highly qualified team to Moscow to finalize the grain deal, while at the same time, the private exporters were meeting with railroad and government officials to prepare for the transportation of the wheat the Soviets were expected to buy. With that part of the plan firmly in place, Henry Kissinger then traveled to Moscow to translate the power of wheat into a firm and definite commitment by Moscow to force North Vietnam into accepting terms of a peace settlement with the Nixon administration."

At this point, Josh stopped to get another cup of coffee, and then continued with his story that was adding the deeper confirmation Amber needed and wanted. "Amber, there is a comical part to Kissinger's secret mission to Moscow," Josh said, as he began laughing. "Toward this task, Kissinger left on his highly secret trip to Moscow, six days after Palmby and his team of experts arrived back in Washington. On board the Presidential aircraft, Kissinger was accompanied by Soviet Ambassador Anatoly Dobrynin, and they departed Washington for talks with the top Soviet officials."

Josh paused here then continued, "Total secrecy surrounded Kissinger's Moscow mission, with that secrecy preserved by one of the strangest ruses ever perpetrated on the American press. The plan was for the White House to simply deny that Kissinger had even left the Washington area. Haldeman handled the details of the cover-up of Kissinger's mission by putting out a fictitious story for the press that the President and Kissinger, with several of the top White House officials, had locked themselves in at Camp David for the purpose of conducting top-secret policy discussions. There they remained literally locked-in as virtual prisoners for the duration of Kissinger's secret mission to Moscow. Few outside the small White House circle had any idea of what was going on. On April 24, 1972, Kissinger returned from his secret trip to Moscow, arriving at Camp David at about 8:00 p.m., thus bringing the interlude to an end. Upon his arrival, the President met with Kissinger, Haldeman and General Haig for about an hour, and then boarded his helicopter, finally able and anxious to return to the White House."

"Why do you find that story so funny?" Amber asked.

"Don't you?" Josh asked. "Think of the image of President Nixon being held virtual prisoner at Camp David, with the press being so deceived. I find that funny," Josh repeated. "The White House had worked so hard to keep all this so secret, and you, an independent journalist, have independently collected all this information. Your articles are already being noticed at the White House, and your name is being batted around quite frequently. I don't think Kissinger really likes you. I can't imagine what he will say when you finally release your blockbuster."

"I take that as a compliment," Amber said with a big smile. For a journalist, particularly a freelance reporter, there could be no better news. Getting your name recognized in any circle is good news – but at the White House? "Wow," she thought and whispered. "Does anyone at the White House know we are friends?" Amber did not want to get Josh in trouble or fired. He was too good a friend.

"I don't think anybody knows what I do outside the White House or who I know," Josh assured Amber. "You're not getting your information from me, so I have no control. And, I don't even know where you have been getting the information. But, listen to me Amber, don't be surprised after you publish the full story that someone starts an investigation to identify your source, and if they identify a person, that person could face serious trouble. So be careful."

"I will. But my concern is with you and our association which they already know about."

"I am not worried," Josh assured her. "I don't hold a high enough position, though I do keep my eyes and ears open. Anyway, I don't plan to remain at the White House much longer. I recently got a good job offer from a company back in Birmingham which I might take. That will get me back closer to home."

"Congratulations, I guess, but I will miss you if you leave Washington."

"Well, with your travels, you can always stop by my place for a visit when you come to Birmingham," Josh told her. "And, we can drive back to Clanton together, for a visit."

"And, we will," Amber softly said. They had been talking all day and toward mid-afternoon, she went into the apartment and got them a glass of wine. When she returned, she invited Josh to stay on for dinner."

"Thanks, Amber. Look at those clouds!" Josh said in an excited voice. The clouds were dark gray and churning in a display of enormous power with a distinct smell of rain to come. Josh sensed that a big storm was about to hit.

Amber sat down next to him and looked up into the sky. She too loved the storms, and began reflecting back to the Grimes wheat farm in Oklahoma and their three green chairs, the spot they used to watch the storms come in. That visit to Oklahoma had given Amber a greater appreciation of the sky. Now, she was back in Washington, D. C., sitting on her patio with her friend Josh. As they sat there looking up into the clouds, time no longer mattered. Josh finally broke the silence. "It was all about Nixon's efforts to end the Vietnam war," Josh said softly, "and he should be applauded for that. He found the way by exchanging American grown wheat for peace, a brilliant strategy in my opinion and he took it."

Once he started on the subject, Josh could not stop talking. He felt a need to defend his President, whom he respected greatly. "Amber," he began, "you need to understand that Nixon was facing serious political problems, and it was just by chance that wheat suddenly entered the equation for his political survival. Nixon had discovered that drought and harsh winter conditions had severely damaged the

Soviets' wheat crop, creating a dire need for wheat." Josh paused for a moment and then continued. "They desperately needed to buy large quantities of wheat to feed their people, and in 1972, the United States was the only country in the world that possessed wheat in huge quantities. I know I am repeating myself, but the United States literally held an absolute monopoly in the wheat market in 1972."

Joshua continued explaining the dynamics of the plan in great detail, though Amber had heard the story before. Still, she wanted him to keep talking for it provided her additional confirmation. "Nixon agreed to let the Soviets buy this country's entire wheat surplus – 400 million bushels, but only if the Soviets agreed to pressure North Vietnam into agreeing to a settlement." Amber did not mind the repetition. And after Josh had again paused, this time for the longest moment as if he wanted to wait for some dramatic finish, he began to tell Amber about the incident, occurring on June 27, 1972, as if that was the day when it all came together.

"What was that date again?" Amber asked. She already knew all the details about that date. But hearing it mentioned by Josh made it different: June 27, 1972, was the big day when the Soviet wheat deal actually moved into motion. This became the day when Nixon most certainly held the absolute power to announce an "honorable" end to the Vietnam war. This was the day when all the killing could have stopped. Everything came together on that date. It was a day when Kissinger could and wanted to make the announcement of the end to the Vietnam war, but Nixon refused to allow him to publicly announce the arrival of peace. Still, the circles were interlinking: the wheat farmers' circle, with all the risks and burdens of bringing in the harvest, and the political circle, with the risks and burden of returning peace to America and to the world. Ordinarily, the circles functioned independently of each other, but in 1971, they began moving closer together with the two independent circles eventually fading into one. Wheat had become the vehicle for peace in Vietnam! Wheat had provided a force far more powerful than all the guns and bombs used in Vietnam for so many years without accomplishing any military victory.

"What was that date again?" Amber again inquired, this time in a more saddened voice.

"June 27, 1972!" Josh said more emphatically, not yet sensing that something was bothering Amber. "That was the day, Nixon could have immediately halted all hostilities and killings in Vietnam."

Amber began to cry, almost uncontrollably.

"What's wrong?" Josh wanted to know, forgetting the significance of that date. "What's wrong, Amber? What's wrong?"

"RJ was killed on June 28, 1972, one day after Nixon could have stopped the war."

"Oh, my god," Josh said, "I forgot the date when RJ was shot down. I am so sorry, Amber!"

"With the wheat deal in place as early as the Fall of 1971, Nixon could have ended the Vietnam war even back then," Amber said, as she kept sobbing. "But on June 27,

1972, he clearly could!   That is what Kissinger was telling him. RJ did not have to die!"

CHAPTER EIGHT

*A*mber Nicole Highlander collected volumes of information from all her highly reliable sources, and from that data she became convinced that American grown wheat had been used to effectively bring an end to the Vietnam war. Now, sorting through all that data, she began summarizing her findings in preparation of her final report to the wheat farmers. In a real sense, she thought, America's wheat farmers had helped bring peace to Vietnam. Yet, these farmers received no credit whatsoever, not even an honorable mention.

Using the power of American grown wheat in '72 for ending a war that had come to haunt most Americans, take the lives of thousands, and cripple thousands more, was a wonderful, simplistic idea, she thought. But, though that exchange may have been a simple idea, converting it into the reality of providing the wheat to the Soviet Union, as Amber discovered, was highly complex and risky. Foremost among the complexities were the legal restrictions preventing the

Nixon administration from directly effecting such an exchange
with the Soviets. So, if President Nixon were to succeed in
ending the war before he once again stood before the voters in
judgment, he needed to find a way around strict legal
restrictions on government grain sales.

All legal restrictions standing in the way of the Soviet
wheat deal had to be overcome in a way that would effectively
erase the White House from the official visible picture. The
White House needed a diversion that served to shift the focus
on to the private grain companies. For this, the White House
needed to find a way to convince six private grain exporters to
sell 400 million bushels of wheat to the Soviets in their
corporate names, at a fixed price substantially below cost.
Achieving such a task would in itself be an extraordinary fete,
with measured risks to the White House as well as to the
private exporters. Possible consequences facing the exporters'
selling such large volumes of wheat below cost, was
bankruptcy. What they were asked to do by the White House
was so far outside their own economic self-interest, at least on
the surface. Despite the apparent conflict in economic terms,
as Amber discovered, the private exporters, acting against
their economic self- interest joined together to turn Kissinger's
Soviet wheat deal into a success. Under Kissinger's plan for
peace, the Soviets would be allowed to buy 400 million
bushels of American grown wheat, all the wheat the
government owned and held in storage at the time. They
would buy this wheat through the private grain exporters at a
fixed price substantially below cost, with deferred delivery

over a three-year period.

The return for such enormous economic concessions, probably measuring in the billions of dollars, was peace in Vietnam. For this wheat, so badly needed, the Soviets pressured North Vietnam into accepting settlement terms that at least created an illusion that President Nixon had achieved an honorable exit from Vietnam. The reality was that Nixon bought his way out of Vietnam, just in time for his reelection. When it was all over, Henry Kissinger's skillful and diplomatic negotiations with North Vietnam received the credit, with no mention of the incredible role the wheat farmers played in this great peace exchange.

Out of Kissinger's bartering with Moscow, Nixon avoided the need to admit defeat at the hands of the Communists. Even if this were only an illusion, Kissinger's agreement served to appease Nixon's political base. Illusions are important in politics. With the illusion to lean upon, Nixon could say, as he did, that he didn't lose the war to the Communists. Once Nixon finally accepted the plan, the agreement for peace was placed within his easy reach, at least as early as May of 1971, the month of the President's political rebirth and celebration. Amber had discovered that the exchange of wheat for peace was an event that began taking shape in early 1971, maybe as early as February or March. It was all over by May 18, 1971. On that day, Nixon began celebrating the reality of Kissinger's success in gaining a peace agreement with North Vietnam. The President and his inner-circle celebrated onboard the presidential yacht, the

Sequoia.

Josh had told Amber that based on his own personal observation, Nixon's celebration on the Sequoia on May 18, marked the point in time when the confidence level within the White House took a quantum jump. Nixon rebounded from the lowest point in his first term as President, to a high point of near certainty of reelection to a second term. Whatever the risk there might have been in achieving this new, positive level of political confidence, the end seemed to justify the means, at least in the mind of Richard Nixon. Nixon's low point in office during the first months of 1971, was marked by his Republican Party's miserable showing in the midterm elections. But, within a few months, President Nixon was celebrating his new found confidence, a proud moment for the President. And, on this proud day, he hosted a private dinner party onboard the "Sequoia."

Nixon was celebrating Kissinger's stunning successes in international relations that increased his confidence of being reelected to a second term. The only thing that could squarely block his serving a second term as President was Vietnam. But, once the wheat deal commitment was in place, Nixon knew he would be able to announce an end to that war, at any moment he so chose. Kissinger had assured him of this after he succeeded in working out the plans to exchange wheat for peace. But, for it all to work, the White House needed to keep the wheat deal on track. And, as the festivities continued onboard the Sequoia on that May 18, Nixon knew right then that he held the power to designate the precise moment he would announce a settlement with North Vietnam. Without a doubt, Amber thought, this achievement by Kissinger truly gave them something to celebrate, and if they all wanted to get drunk, peace in Vietnam seemed like a justifiable reason.

Josh had told Amber that only the President's closest and most trusted assistants had been invited to the private celebration onboard the Sequoia, and he was not one of them. Those invited, included: Henry Kissinger, H.R. Haldeman, John Ehrlichman, Charles Colson and John Mitchell. With this small group in high spirits, and without public fanfare, the "Sequoia" left Pier I with the President's party for a two-hour dinner cruise to Mt Vernon. As they pulled away from the dock, the Presidential party relaxed on the top deck enjoying drinks -- scotch and soda for Nixon, Kissinger and Colson, and ginger ale for Haldeman and Ehrlichman. As the stately vessel churned through the muddy waters of the Potomac, history was being made. Reaching Mt. Vernon at 8:00 p.m., the President and his party went to the foredeck to participate in the flag-lowering ceremony, a tradition followed by all Naval vessels to render proper respect when passing Mt. Vernon. Then dinner was served below-deck in the main cabin, New York strip steaks, fresh corn on the cob and more scotch.

• • • •

As they strolled down the National Mall toward the Washington Monument, Amber and Joshua Walker were enjoying the beautiful day in April, when they spotted the street vendor. They stopped as they always did unless it was raining. This day was sunny and mild with a light breeze. Each ordered a hotdog and a cold R C cola from the street vendor, then grabbed a bench facing the Mall, and had one of their favorite lunches.   Joshua, as always, ordered a second hotdog. One was enough for Amber on that day, though there were days when she had as many as three. It was something special about street vendor-hotdogs, always eaten with a cold RC cola.

Amber and Joshua, both from the small town of Clanton, Alabama, loved the city of Washington, the nation's capitol, for its beauty and livability. It was the center of power within our universe. It was a city of politicians who held the power to wage war or to offer peace. It was a city of transplants from different states and countries. It was a city of power brokers. And, it was a city of tourists. On any given day, one could see or imagine all the things that form a composite of Washington. One need only take the time to sit on a bench on the National Mall, eating a hot dog and drinking a RC Cola. Viewing the surface is enough for most people, but not Amber, who as a journalist was always looking for hidden meaning. As they sat on the bench, not in a hurry to move, Amber turned to her friend and asked, "Josh, when did you first learn that Kissinger might have reached some agreement with Moscow on his exchange of wheat for peace?"

There was a moment of silence before Joshua spoke, "I heard talk about it in early spring of 1971, may be even as early as February or March. But it was all hush-hush stuff. Most clearly though, it was definitely confirmed on June 27, 1972, when Kissinger received word that the Russians' grain buying team had arrived in America."

"Did the wheat farmers know about the exchange?" Amber asked in a rhetorical manner.

"Oh my god, No! It wouldn't have worked if they had learned about Kissinger's agreement with the Soviets. As you already know, President Nixon understood that the wheat farmers had to be sacrificed with respect to their 1972 wheat harvest, for the good of the nation and for his reelection." Josh paused to take a big swig of his RC Cola and to get another hotdog. He then started into one of his long explanations that Amber liked. "You have to understand Amber that Nixon truly wanted to find a way to settle the Vietnam war, not only because of politics but for his lasting image in history. He wanted to go down in history as a man of peace. So when the wheat deal came along, he thought that peace in Vietnam justified deception of the farmers and the public."

"According to Senator Henry Bellmon of Oklahoma, " Amber chimed in, "the Nixon administration had been sacrificing the farmers from day-one. That the White House had shown little or no concern about farmers who were for the most part simply taken for granted politically. I once heard Senator Bellmon charge that President Nixon had shown no interest in the farmers, and hadn't set foot on a farm, since he took office."

"I know about Bellmon's charge," Joshua added. "In fact, Bellman's public criticism of a fellow Republican shocked the White House, and Nixon wanted to know, 'what the hell got into Henry.' One White House assistant suggested that 'Henry must have eaten too much loco weed.'" Joshua, seeing a lot of humor in this, paused, and then added. "Nixon's interest in the farmers, particularly the wheat farmers, picked up only after the Republicans suffered their bitter loss in the mid-term elections. Following that terrible political loss, the White House in early 1971, began showing a keen interest in the production and harvest of the hard red winter wheat, the type of wheat grown in Oklahoma. President Nixon had discovered the power of wheat as an effective tool in his international negotiating arena. And, he was proven correct on June 27."

"You mean, Nixon gained an interest in wheat when it became politically expedient and necessary?" Amber asked, rhetorically.

"That's politics! That's the way it was, and even then, Nixon could not do anything openly. The deal made by Kissinger was allowing the Soviets to buy wheat at a price below cost. For this to work, the White House needed the farmers to sell their 1972 wheat crop on the open market at depressed market prices," Josh explained. "And to keep the market prices depressed," he continued," the White House had to make sure the information supplied the farmers was sufficiently negative to convince them not to expect wheat prices to materially increase any time soon. This made it unavoidable that falsified market information would be published in the 1972 February and May issues of the *Wheat Situation.* "

"How did he justify that deception?" Amber asked.

"Well, at least privately, Nixon thought the farmers had a duty to accept their sacrifice during the 1972 harvest," Josh explained. "At the time, I thought that this was a wise decision. The farmers were assigned a big role in the world of participating in the exchange of the wheat they raised and harvested for peace in Vietnam. And," Josh added, "the sacrifice was for only the 1972 crop year." He then again emphasized his own personal viewpoint, "Personally, I think the farmers make a magnificent contribution to America and to the world. What could be greater than achieving peace in Vietnam? They should be proud of their role as peacemakers and for serving as the determining instrument for finally bringing that dreaded Vietnam war to an end, before another American soldier died."

"Maybe so," Amber replied, "but shouldn't the farmers have been given a voice in the plan?"

"I don't see how it could have worked! If the farmers had been made aware of what was going on, they might have held their wheat off the market for their own selfish reasons. After all Amber, you must remember, it was all in the name of peace. So one year of sacrifice doesn't seem like a heavy price for peace in Vietnam, not to me at least."

Amber couldn't really disagree. She knew that if the Russians were to be permitted to buy American grown wheat in substantial quantities and at significant price concessions, the White House probably had no choice but to sacrifice the wheat farmers.   If the Soviets were to receive price concessions, the White House needed the farmers to sell their 1972 wheat crop at the lowest possible price. Kissinger's Soviet wheat sale had to follow the harvest, with enough time after that, to give the farmers time to sell-off their 1972 wheat crop. In the major wheat states, wheat harvest begins in late May and runs through the month of June and into early July, moving from South to North. So, as the 1972 wheat harvest concluded and the farmers had sold their wheat as expected, the Russian grain buying team arrived in Washington on June 27, to begin talks with the Nixon administration and the private grain exporters. All the pieces were coming together, but it could not be over until the Soviets completed their secret deal-making with the private exporters, during the months of July and August.

After carefully reading and studying the documents she got from Ken, Amber summarized the final steps in Kissinger's Soviet wheat deal.   According to these documents, it had been preplanned that the Russians would first contact Continental Grain Company, through which all the details of an agreement in terms of price, terms and other conditions would be negotiated. Continental's negotiated agreement would then serve as the template for all the other private grain exporters. Continental Grain's first negotiating session with the Soviets opened on Independence Day, July 4, 1972, with the negotiations conducted by Continental Grain's most experienced, qualified, and responsible people in its worldwide grain empire. After all, these negotiations were for the entire industry. Continental Grain's negotiations were held at a neutral venue at the New York Regency hotel. Several rooms had been reserved for small caucus meetings, private joint meeting areas, and working space for support personnel. Continental Grain's support group provided technical assistance to the negotiating team, but the support staff did not attend the negotiating sessions, limited solely to its three top negotiators and the Russians.

After hours of serious negotiations, Continental reached agreement with the Soviets on July 5, setting price, quantity, and terms and conditions of delivery of the wheat and grain. On July 5, a memorandum of understanding was signed by both parties, legally committing   Continental Grain to deliver to the Soviets 130 million bushels of hard red winter wheat, from three U.S. crop years: 1971/1972, 1972/1973, and 1973/1974, at the fixed price of $1.62 a bushel FOB U.S. Gulf ports: Beaumont, Brownsville, Corpus Christi, Galveston, Port Arthur, and Houston in Texas; Mobile, Alabama; Pascagoula, Mississippi and the Mississippi River ports, and Baton Rouge, Louisiana. Three days later, the White House announced its official three-year government to government grain credit agreement between the United States and Russia, that complimented Continental Grain's negotiated contract terms.

On July 8, the official agreement committed the United States government to an extension of credit through the

USDA's Commodity Credit Corporation (CCC), up to a total amount of $750 million, for financing the sales of US grown grains sold to the Soviets by the private exporters. Once this official credit agreement was signed by the two governments, the Soviets' grain buying team would be free to complete the planned acquisition of wheat from the other private exporters. The price and terms negotiated by Continental Grain would become incorporated in the contracts of the other exporters. The Soviet's grain buying team would remain in this country until it had purchased through the six private grain exporters, all the wheat owned by the United States government, 400 million bushels. With this, the United States' wheat position moved from its most favorable monopoly position with a large surplus on hand to a position of a severe wheat shortage, and with this American citizens began to pay higher prices for bread and other bakery items.

Amber found it comical when she compared the negotiating strategies of all the private grain exporters. Toward gaining their full commitment promised by Kissinger as part of the Vietnam settlement plan, the Soviets, after completing negotiations with Continental Grain, set up headquarters at the New York Hilton. When they were ready, the Soviets began parading the other private exporters through their hotel suite, buying up wheat without any serious negotiations. No serious negotiations were really required of the private exporters other than Continental, except in an effort to show enough independence to avoid possible antitrust charges of conspiracy against them. That no serious negotiations were necessary was confirmed by the fact that the price and contract terms agreed to by all the other exporters, over a period of a month, were identical to those negotiated by Continental Grain on July 4 and 5. One thing that did stand markedly different between the negotiations by Continental Grain and the other exporters was the level of sophistication of the negotiations.

Continental Grain's negotiations were highly professional with a level of unmatched sophistication that extended over many hours. Not so with the other five private exporters. Negotiations by these other five grain merchants, stood as spectacles of unmatched crudity. Yet, even with this extreme disparity in the levels of negotiations, there was contract uniformity in the contract terms and conditions, as to price and other terms and condition, including delivery terms and ports of departure. Such uniformity in price and terms of multiple wheat contracts entered into on different dates and times, spanning a period of two months, stands as a strange twist in terms of commodity market economics. Amber discussed the fact of this parallel behavior among these purportedly independent competitors with well known economists and commodity market traders, who had made clear to her that such uniformity is almost conclusive evidence that the private exporters were acting in concert, or maybe a conspiracy to fix the market price for wheat, with the farmers being the big losers in the deal.

These commodity and economic experts, willing to openly talk with Amber, were convinced that the private exporters were working closely with Nixon's Department of Agriculture which in turn was working with Henry Kissinger who was working closely with Soviet officials. The experts became more convinced of the presence of some pattern of concerted activity when they learned Continental Grain, had agreed to sell the wheat to the Soviets at a fixed price below cost, with the other five private exporters following this lead. Amber was smart enough to know, and now the experts were confirming her conclusion, that six independent grain exporters would have never departed from acceptable business-economic norms unless it was in close concert with the government with a necessary level of guaranteed protection.

Measured in terms of economics, nothing about the Soviet wheat deal made sense to Amber's economic experts. She observed from her extensive discovery of evidence that by the time the Soviets ended their buying spree on August 9, 1972, the six private grain exporters had entered into legally binding contractual commitments to sell to the Soviets a total of 400 million bushels of wheat at the fixed price of $1.62 a bushel. Delivery of the wheat was spread over a period of three crop years, a specification that added additional problems to the management and logistics of the international grain agreement. Much more serious was the fact that the private exporters had all sold wheat to the Soviets they did not own. And, because the transaction was so sensitive, these exporters admitted they could not go into the open market to buy the wheat needed to satisfy their contractual commitments. As strange as it might seem on the surface, the private exporters did nothing to cover their sales, another unanswered departure from economic norms. They made gigantic sales of wheat to the Soviets, and then stayed out of the market despite the fact that market prices continued escalating each day and each moment. How could they do such a thing? Amber wondered.

Amber Highlander who was investigating the Soviet wheat deal for the wheat farmers of Noble County, Oklahoma, found the underlying dynamics so fascinating. It mattered not to her that she could make no sense out of what she was seeing as an irreconcilable conflict with basic rules of economics' supply and demand order. She concluded, and her experts agreed, that these private exporters were able to stay out of the market only because the Nixon administration had somehow secretly guaranteed to them, a source of wheat in sufficient quantities to cover their 400 million bushel sale to the Soviets. After Amber had told the wheat story to her friend, Josh suggested that she go talk with the head of the Commodity Exchange Authority.

"Commodity Exchange Authority? I never thought of that," Amber commented to Josh. Not knowing what to expect from the CEA, she first carefully studied material on that Agency, including the Congressional hearing reports. She then sought and received an interview of the CEA administrator, Alec C. Caldwell, who had already offered testimony before the Congressional Committee. Out of all this, Amber was personally startled, unusual perhaps for a journalist. She had discovered that the same pattern of parallel behavior present within the grain industry in contract negotiations, was also present within the non-compliance level of CEA rules. All the private exporters in parallel fashion had filed falsified government reports on their grain positions with the Commodity Exchange Authority. Each of the six private exporters failed to disclose wheat sold to the Soviets. There was additional parallel behavior in their explanation of why the information had been omitted. Caldwell, who was so willing to talk with Amber, told her these false reports had served to conceal from the public and the farmers the full scope of the grain sales to the Soviets.

What surprised Amber the most was that the Congressional Committee, investigating the wheat deal, seemed to discount the testimony of Caldwell, the guy in charge of the CEA, and simply accepted the storyline offered by the private exporters. The Committee blindly accepted the explanation offered by the private grain exporters, and expressed criticism of the CEA Administrator as if it did not want the truth to emerge. From Amber's field of vision, it appeared to her that the Congressional Committee was simply going along with the White House. And, it got stranger still, Amber discovered. Alec Caldwell, decided to bypass the Congressional Committee by referring the matter to the FBI and Justice Department for criminal prosecution of the private grain exporters for their filing falsified, required government reports.

However, as Amber discovered, the Justice Department did nothing except rebuff Director Caldwell. Nixon's Attorney General Richard Kleindienst declined to prosecute the private exporters, reasoning that the private exporters simply made an innocent mistake. Amber reminded herself that Caldwell had not been the only grain investigator rebuffed by the Nixon administration. She remembered Ken mentioning the name Will Griffin, and began to see this as some part of Kissinger's Soviet wheat deal for peace. The puzzle in her mind became even more jumbled when she discovered that the private exporters, even by selling wheat below cost, still got super-rich at a time when all the public evidence was showing they should have been showing signs of bankruptcy. The more Amber searched for answers, the stranger the scene grew.

CHAPTER NINE

*L*abor Day fell on Monday, September 3, 1973, and for that day, Amber joined her friends at the Maritime Union for celebration. She joined in a march for working people and later published an article on what Labor Day meant. Then, she returned home and decided to relax, pouring a big glass of iced tea, and then going out to her patio and just sitting back, looking into the blueness of the sky, with only a few small floating clouds. Looking into the sky brought peace to Amber's mind, and as she followed the few clouds, she drifted off into a deep but short sleep. But the relaxation did not last long as her mind seemed to be driven by all the unanswered questions. One question that kept haunting her was how these six private exporters, selling 400 million bushels of wheat to the Soviets at less than what it cost, could still stay in business?

Basic economics, she thought, would support the conclusion that selling wheat at the quantities sold and at prices substantially below cost should have forced the private exporters out of business. Amber needed to find an answer to this question before returning to Billings in time for the 1974 wheat harvest. The farmers will want to know, and they deserve to know. Mentally stuck, Amber decided to call Ken Downing for help, knowing what he would be expecting of her in return. She could not get this thought our of her mind, that she was exchanging sex for information. It had been that way from the beginning. That was the price! And as degrading as this might be to some, it was a price Amber was willing to pay to get to the truth behind the Soviet wheat deal and Watergate.

• • • •

In the past, Ken had already helped her a lot. He held a position high enough at the USDA to have access to the most sensitive information. When he got the call, Ken was excited to be hearing from Amber even knowing that she was calling because she needed more information. But this didn't matter to him. He was excited and couldn't wait to see her. They met on Friday at the C & O Bar & Grill in Georgetown. Ordering drinks first, Amber wasted no time with her pointed question: Ken, how could the private grain exporters sell so much wheat to the Soviets at a price below cost and still stay in business?"

"They probably couldn't!"

"But, they did and they stayed in business," Amber responded.

"They didn't lose money," Ken stated.

"What? I know they sold wheat to the Soviets below cost."

"They didn't lose money," Ken repeated. "Quite the contrary, these private grain exporters profited beyond the level of economic imagination. They all became super-rich, selling wheat below cost."

Hearing this brought complete silence that extended for a long moment until finally Amber spoke, "This makes no sense to me. Ken, make me understand the math."

"Well, obviously, these six private grain exporters with dealings around the world were smart enough not to put themselves in a financially threatening position. From the very beginning, they had anticipated that by participating in Kissinger's Soviet wheat deal, they would record huge profits. This anticipation is confirmed by the fact that in the Fall of 1971, these same private exporters working with the White House and the Treasury Department sought an indefinite deferral of income taxes on half the profits made on the 1972 sales."

"What? Unbelievable!" Amber exclaimed. "What the hell was going on?"

"It was a well planned financial operation," Ken boasted, "at the highest level and measured in value, maybe even over a billion dollars."

"A billion dollars!" For Amber, the mystery only deepened. How can you sell something below cost and still make money?   In search for an answer, she knew she needed to get some actual profit data, if possible. But, for now she wanted to get what information she could from Ken. She spent the evening with him and agreed to meet with him the next Friday when he was going to give her more information on Agent Griffin's fraud investigation that had gotten shot down. Amber went home at about 11:00 p. m. The next day Josh was coming over for dinner.

Early the next morning, Amber began studying the documents and working to complete an article that was due. Then in the afternoon, she put a pork roast in the oven and took a long shower to relax. She was feeling content with her progress and was confident she would have all the answers before time to travel back to Oklahoma next May to talk with her farmer friends. She had scheduled that trip for May of 1974, to coincide with the start of the wheat harvest. While waiting for Josh, she settled into a seat on her patio, shifting from tea to beer. The October air was crisp.

Josh got there at about 4:30, took a beer and joined Amber on the patio, both looking at the sky and pushing aside all worries. Amber's patio was a perfect urban spot to watch the sky with all the cloud formations and power displays of energy. After dinner, they would head to their favorite neighborhood pub to listen to music. For that evening, Amber was pushing aside the puzzling Soviet wheat deal to just relax with her close friend.

"What's for dinner?" Josh boldly asked, only because they were such good friends.

"My specialty," Amber said in a most cheerful voice.

"We are having a salad, then a pork roast, sweet potatoes, and green beans. How's that sound?"

"Makes me hungry, and reminds me of our hometown."

"It will be ready at about 6:00. You need another beer?"

"Thanks, I am fine for now. Can I do something to help?"

"No, just relax."

Dinner was perfect, Amber thought and Joshua agreed. After dinner, she cleaned the kitchen with Josh's help. Then, they took a walk to enjoy the cool evening breeze as they headed to the pub for an evening of piano music. They were able to get their favorite table and ordered drinks. The evening was relaxing , and after about two and a half hours of music, they left and headed back to Amber's Georgetown apartment, with a slight diversion to walk along the C&O Canal. Back at her apartment, Amber fixed a pot of coffee and they sat at the kitchen table and talked.

"I'll be leaving the White House soon," Josh told Amber, "I decided to take that job in Birmingham, and I am looking forward to the challenge. I am also excited about getting back home."

"Washington will not be the same with my friend gone," Amber said with her genuine smile. "I am not unhappy Josh with your decision, because I know you will be happy, and I will be happy for you." She paused, then wanted Josh to tell her about his new job. "What will you be doing?"

"Its going to be an exciting and unique job," Josh explained. "Interestingly, it is a type lobbying job for environmental interests, from our main office in Birmingham, with only a satellite office in Washington. Much of our work is done with local groups around the country, lobbying state legislatures and municipalities to adopt stricter environmental regulations."

"That sounds challenging, rewarding and interesting," Amber remarked. "Maybe, I can get a story out of it sometime."

They kept talking until they both faded and went to sleep. They next morning, they went out for breakfast and took another long walk. When they arrived at their favorite breakfast spot, they took a table near the window, and as she looked out, Amber knew this was going to be a wonderful day. After breakfast, they headed back to Amber's apartment and Josh left for home. He needed to go to work to complete a project assigned to him. Amber then returned to her patio and turned her eyes toward the sky. It was a wonderful day.

During the next several days, Amber worked on different, smaller projects she needed to get out article-projects that gave her some distraction from the wheat deal. But, as always, she was anxious to return her focus back to all the hanging issues. The big question still in her mind was how the private exporters could make such high profits, when, she thought, they should have been going out of business. She kept asking the same question. How could six private grain companies sell 400 million bushels of wheat at a substantial financial loss and still make historic profits?   That one question just kept churning in her mind, haunting her, with no answers springing fourth.

Hopefully, she would get the answers she needed from Ken Downing when they meet on Friday. She had marked it on her calendar. That Friday, they arrived at the C & O at about the same time and ordered a couple of scotch and waters and talked about different things. Amber had previously discovered that Ken was a highly intelligent and knowledgeable person who knew a lot of people. He graduated from Purdue University with a degree in Agricultural Science and went on to earn his Ph.D. from that same university. After a couple of drinks, they had dinner, then to Ken's apartment. It was about 9:30 when they got to his place.

As they sat in his den, Amber looked straight into Ken's eyes and almost pleaded, "Help me out Ken," she pleaded. "How could these exporters sell so much wheat below cost and still make historic profits?"

Ken sensed the frustration in Amber's voice. "Amber, it gets highly complex, and comes in three separate parts. First, the exporters were paid illegal export subsidy payments to offset the heavy financial loss they all faced or did not face."

"Why do you say the subsidy payments were illegal?" Amber inquired.

"Well," Ken began, "during 1972, the White House knew the United States held a worldwide wheat monopoly, and in view of this, American grain faced no international competition. That alone made the export subsidy payments illegal."

"I confirmed that with the Canadian Wheat Board," Amber added.

"Yeah, the CWB had sent Secretary Butz a letter, alerting him that the U. S. held this commanding position in the wheat market."

"I know! I've got a copy of that letter," Amber boasted.

"Amber, you have been busy," Ken commented. Then he explained, "Inside the USDA, we justified the continuation of the export subsidy payments by claiming lack of knowledge that the United States had a monopoly. Secretary Butz told Congress and the press that had we known about the Soviets' intention to buy so much wheat, we would not have approved payment of the export subsidy payments."

"Was that not a lie?" Amber offered.

"In a way, maybe. But it had to be."

"How much was paid out in these illegal export subsidy payments?" Amber asked.

"Approximately $300 million."

"How were the subsidy payments calculated?"

"At first, the subsidy payments were calculated on the basis of the difference between the $1.62 price the Soviets paid for the wheat and the domestic wheat price at the time of the actual export," Ken explained.

"My goodness," Amber reacted. "The exporters sold to the Soviets 400 million bushels of wheat for $1.62 a bushel, and then the Nixon administration paid them $300 million more! Can, you believe that?" Amber asked rhetorically.

"It doesn't matter what we might believe or not believe," Ken explained. "The reality is that the subsidy payments were part of the bigger plan, and without them, the private exporters could not have afforded to cooperate."

"But." Amber interjected, "didn't a big dispute develop about the increasing levels of wheat subsidy payments? I know the press had picked up on that and began criticizing the wheat subsidy payments going to the private exporters."

"That's right," Ken confirmed. "The Office of Management and Budget began complaining to the White House that the subsidy payments were creating a serious budgetary problem for the country. With pressure mounting," Ken explained, "the USDA was finally forced into terminating all wheat subsidy payments, with one exception. Payments going to the private exporters on their sales to the Soviets, were allowed to continue."

Amber then added, "I attended the meeting at the USDA where the subsidy policy was scheduled to be discussed with representatives of the private exporters. I remember that before getting the subject of the subsidy policy change, Assistant Secretary Carroll Brunthaver asked all us news people to leave the room so he could speak confidentially to the private exporters. Can you believe that? A public official telling a bunch of journalists to leave the room?"

"I remember that well," Ken said with his slight smile.

"It did not go over too well," Amber confirmed, with her slight laugh, as she repeated herself. "Can you imagine a public agency telling members of the press to leave the room so the public officials could hold a private meeting with the private grain exporters? Obviously, we refused to leave! So Secretary Brunthaver, declined to proceed. He simply adjourned the meeting, with an announcement that proposed changes in the subsidy policy would be released later in the day."

"I remember Brunthaver's confrontation with the press," Ken commented. "When it occurred, the White House became overly concerned that their important plan might be coming undone. The general view at the White House was that members of the press were meddling in matters they knew nothing about, and that, unless they stayed out of this matter, they could seriously damage Kissinger's efforts to end the Vietnam war."

Amber stood fast and unbending in her defense of the freedom of the press. "Meddling is what we are supposed to do when it comes to keeping tabs on decisions made by public officials. Now, as I look back at all that transpired in the White House's total atmosphere of secrecy, it was all about the high-risk plan of exchanging wheat for peace in Vietnam. Why did I not see this from the beginning?"

"The cover was too good," Ken insisted. "Consider all the work you have done in sorting out the truth."

"Had some members of the press discovered the plan, would they not have had a duty to inform the public and the American wheat farmers?" Amber queried.

"You have to answer that yourself, you are the journalist! But, think about this. With his mammoth wheat deal, President Nixon did not set out to cheat anyone. It was all part of the plan to bring an end to the Vietnam war. If the story had broken too quickly, Nixon's entire peace plan could have been placed in jeopardy. Let me ask you, weren't all the deviations from the economic norm justified, if the final result was peace in Vietnam?" Ken then added one more comment: "Amber, the plan to exchange wheat for peace had to remain and could only survive in an atmosphere of absolute secrecy. The White House could not allow the plan to advance without unconditional assurance that total secrecy had not been compromised. So, for it to work, the American press needed to stay out of it. Personally, considering the circumstances, I don't believe that represented any serious breach in our fundamental freedom of the press. Your getting the story; it's just coming later."

"Ken, I hear you advocating restrictions on our free press, but, at the same time you aren't." Amber was trying to reconcile what she was hearing. "What I'm hearing you say," she slowly explained, "is that you would not support any official restriction on the freedom of the press."

"That part is correct," Ken accepted.

"But you might support restrictions on news reporting when those restrictions were actually self imposed by the media, and when that secrecy might be needed to support some noble objective, like peace in Vietnam."

"I can accept that too."

"And then, as I understand your view," Amber continued, "you would support the administration's decision, to intentionally withhold material information from members of the press and thereby the public, when it is justified."

"I can accept your interpretation of my view only conditionally," Ken said cautiously. "My views on restrictions on the press are limited strictly to the secret dealings within the White House to get the Vietnam war settled. That's the reason private grain exporters had to be so firmly protected. Even after it was determined that the export subsidies had to be terminated, the USDA had to carve out a special exception for Kissinger's six private grain exporters." Then, before Amber could add her comments, Ken suggested they quit for the night and go to bed.

Amber agreed and the two went to Ken's bedroom. She was beginning to find comfort in having sex with Ken, but there was still no feeling of love. They slept until past 8:30, showered and then Ken fixed another of his magnificent breakfasts. After breakfast, they cleaned the kitchen and then sat at the kitchen table where their conversation continued. With Ken's help, Amber continued putting the pieces together into her own panoramic version. It began to make sense to her. As long as the objective of peace in Vietnam was kept at the center of the universe, the wheat deal made more sense, at least in her mind.

The Office of Management and Budget had pressured the USDA to terminate export subsidy payments on wheat. But the USDA was firmly locked-in to continuing the protection of the six private grain exporters by a specification that the termination of the subsidies would apply to those export sales occurring after August 24, 1972. That date of August 24 conveniently served to protect Kissinger's six exporters' sales of wheat to the Soviets by the fact that all the sales to the Soviets all occurred prior to August 24. That fixed date shielded the six private grain exporters from losing their subsidy payments on wheat they sold to the Soviets. Nonetheless, the prior subsidy policy, though not terminated, was modified by eliminating the variable subsidy rate for calculating export subsidy payments. This variable rate that was creating the serious budgetary problems was replaced by a fixed subsidy payment of forty-seven cents per bushel.

After Ken offered his summary, Amber asked, "How did the USDA settle on the fixed subsidy payment of forty-seven cents per bushel? Was that just an arbitrary figure?"

"No!" Ken stated in his firm voice. "Amber, to completely answer your question, we need to go to the second prong of the three-part plan. After a lot of private talk with the exporters, the fixed rate export subsidy payment was linked to a guaranteed source of government owned wheat, made available to the exporters at a protected fixed price. It had all been worked out to protect the private exporters against catastrophic losses on the wheat sold to the Soviets at the fixed price below cost."

"So, in reality, the wheat sold to the Soviets was a government to government transaction, correct?"

"Yes, all the way!" Ken blurted out with firmness. "It had to be. The private exporters were simply not big enough to handle the transaction alone."

"Well," Amber began slowly, "tell me how the private exporters, even under the modified subsidy policy, were able to make so much money. As I see it," she reasoned, "the new fixed rate subsidy could only protect them against losses, with no guarantee of riches." Learning about this linkage between guaranteed wheat subsidy payments and a guaranteed supply of CCC wheat, Amber better understood how the private exporters were being protected by the White House against serious financial losses. Her remaining nagging problem was finding an understandable explanation of how they were able to make so much money. "From where did the money come?"

"Amber, your last question triggers the third part of the equation that led to Nixon's success in bringing the war to a conclusion. Have you ever heard of PL 480, America's international humanitarian program?" Ken asked.

"No," Amber said. "What does that have to do with anything?"

"Everything," he suggested. "You need to understand the PL 480 program to really grasp the full plan of Kissinger's

exodus from Vietnam," Ken added. "America's food for peace
program was once hailed by many around the world as the
greatest humanitarian venture ever conceived by government.
It is a program that grew out of the Agricultural Trade
Development and Assistance Act passed by Congress in 1954,
Public Law 480.   It is a law enacted during the
Eisenhower/Nixon administration, with support of USDA
Secretary Benson, who saw an added benefit of disposing of
huge grain surpluses. Over the years, the PL 480 program
became the cornerstone of America's efforts to address
malnutrition and hunger throughout the world."

Ken paused here to give Amber a chance to ask
questions, but she just wanted him to continue the story.
"Congress authorized two types of food assistance under PL
480," he explained. "Title I authorized the President to
negotiate and carry out agreements with friendly nations to
sell them surplus agricultural commodities, under highly
favorable terms. Title II assistance enabled the President to
make outright gifts to countries suffering from famine or in
need of urgent relief. Under the law, the Commodity Credit
Corporation was required to make available to the President
such surplus agricultural commodities as he might request."
Ken stopped a moment, then explained, "The PL 480
Congressional mandate authorized President Nixon to order
the CCC to increase the surplus grain designated for transport
to eligible countries."

Amber interrupted to ask, "How did this foreign aid
program help the private exporters get rich?"

Ken paused a long time before responding, then he spoke, "Amber, let me be blunt here, these exporters were given a license to steal a portion of the PL 480 grain, destined for some poor, eligible country."

"What! Are you saying that the administration actually sanctioned the stealing of grain that had been committed to some famine stricken country to feed the hungry children of the world?"

"That's exactly what I am saying! It had to be. It was all part of the plan for peace in Vietnam."

"God, how could the President of the United states support such illegal activity?" Amber pressed.

"God might have been on his side," Ken responded. "It depends on how you view it. If allowing the massive stealing to occur resulted in bringing an end to the war in Vietnam, would the stealing then be justified? I say yes, even recognizing the dire effects on the starving children. These children stood as part of the necessary sacrifice. Don't you agree that it was arguably justifiable if it brought us peace in Vietnam?" he asked Amber.

"I don't know," she hesitantly said, "maybe, probably yes. Tell me how it worked."

Ken was willing to keep talking because he knew that when he stopped, Amber would leave. He wanted her to owe him. "Here is how it worked, Amber," Ken began. "Under the PL 480 program, USDA distributed vast quantities of grain and other commodities it owned to feed the hungry people of the world. In its beginning, the program had been advanced

by Congress as a way of reducing commodity surpluses that
were so costly to maintain and store. It was out of these
surpluses, that the great international humanitarian program
evolved. Then when the Soviet wheat deal arose in 1971, this
PL 480 program offered a convenient, workable, way to
compensate the private exporters for their participation in
Kissinger's wheat for peace exchange.

"The USDA administered the PL 480 program," Ken
emphasized and then continued his explanation. "With
approval of the President, PL 480 assistance could be
extended to eligible countries. This grain came out of the
USDA's grain surplus. Logistically, the private grain
exporters contracted with the CCC to handle the transportation
and accounting of the grain to PL 480 eligible country. Once
an eligible foreign government received approval from the
USDA for receipt of a certain quantity and grade of grain, one
of the private exporters was then given authorization to
transport the commodity to the designated foreign country's
port." After a short pause, Ken said, "Amber, I collected and
copied a number of documents about how the PL 480 program
worked that I think will surely help you. But for now, it's
nearly 4:00 and I need to go back to the office, so why don't
we stop here and meet later to complete this review. He told
Amber he had to leave on another trip that would take him out
of the country for a few months. "But I'll be back."

"That's fine," Amber agreed. She too was ready to
quit for the day and get back home. "Ken, I do appreciate all
your help and I think this will give me time to study the

documents. Have a good trip."

During Ken's absence, Amber turned her attention to Cook Industries's profit picture. On Monday, October 8, 1973, she headed to the offices of the Securities Exchange Commission, knowing that Cook Industries was the one private grain exporter which was a public corporation, legally obligated to file with the SEC, its annual financial reports. These financial reports were freely accessible to her. She expected the SEC documents to reflect a huge loss in view of the fact that Cook had sold huge quantities of wheat to the Soviets for less than the market price. What she found, however, for the company's fiscal year ending May 31, 1973, a huge jump in Cook's income. The year before Cook's sale of wheat to the Soviets, the company recorded a profit of $665,000. One year into the historic sale of wheat, Cook recorded profits of $34 million for the year ending May 31, 1973. Such high increase in profits stood as a mystery, particularly in view of the fact that Cook Industries operated only from a single export grain terminal.

So that these numbers could sink in, Amber put them on a big board in her home office and stared at them, thinking and hoping that some message would spring forth that might help explain the inner conflict. But, even after studying the figures for the longest time, she remained puzzled, wondering how it could be. She then went back to her patio, looking for answers in the clouds. Amber knew that establishing an accurate and reliable expanded profit profile for the entire grain industry would be less probable, maybe impossible. The five other grain exporters, unlike Cook, were closely held private corporations, with no legal obligation to file financial reports with the SEC. But with Ken's vast quantity of information, Amber now understood from where the profits came – thievery. Suddenly, the fraudulent and illegal component of the wheat deal loomed as a huge financial mystery of the Nixon Administration.

Fall was turning into winter when Ken returned home from his extended trip on Wednesday, December 19. It was about 9:00 a.m. when she arrived at his apartment, and, after their brief greetings, Amber suggested they go to bed. It had been a long time since she had had sex and she also wanted to get past Ken's lusting stage, so they could more clearly focus on the subject that brought her over. They had been spellbound in passion for two full hours, and after they showered, they went out for lunch. Only then was the subject of the wheat deal finally raised by Amber.

"Ken, let me ask you, how big was the PL 480 humanitarian program?"

"Well, let's see," Ken began, "in 1972, that's when all this got underway, Nixon reported to Congress that over one hundred countries throughout the world had benefitted from PL 480, with millions of people receiving food from the humanitarian programs. Continuing with his annual report, the President informed Congress that the food for peace shipments had meant life itself for the millions of victims of famine and other natural and man-made disasters."

"Refresh my memory Ken on how the program

worked."

"Well," Ken began. "Assume for a moment that the USDA's Commodity Credit Corporation authorizes a private exporter to transport a certain quantity and grade of a specific type grain: wheat, oats, corn or other. That exporter then became responsible for loading the grain on to a transport vessel just as specified in the authorization. For proof that the private exporter had in fact loaded the grade and quantity of grain as specified in the authorization, the exporter was required to present certification before receiving payment from the government. This certification of weight and grade was obtained from one of the USDA licensed inspectors at the grain export terminal. The licensed inspectors' certification system was designed and intended to verify that the exporter remained honest and did not cheat. Upon completion of the transportation of the grain to the eligible country, the private grain exporter is then paid by the USDA's Commodity Credit Corporation, based on that weight and grade certificate." Ken paused for a long moment. "Amber, this is the critical part of the story. During the loading stage of the PL 480 shipments was the point when the private exporters stole a portion of the grain legally committed to some poor country. With this stealing, the exporters, materially deviated from the official specifications. In other words, they stole a share of the grain that had been committed to a PL 480 eligible country."

"How did they steal the grain if it had been certified as accurate by a licensed inspector? Amber inquired.

"That is the interesting part," Ken began cautiously,

"some of the licensed inspectors took bribes to look away, as the exporters took a portion of the grain. Then, there were the highly skilled workers inside the export grain terminals who could steal the grain right in front of the inspectors without detection. They had made stealing an art form. Two methods were used. First was the technique called misgrading, that is if the CCC specification called for No. 2 grade grain, the private exporter might send No. 3 grade. The second method was called short weighing, where the exporters simply sent less grain than the quantity authorized. For example, if the CCC authorized one million bushels of wheat to a PL 480 eligible country, the exporter might transport only 900,000 bushels.

"Was an estimate ever made on the total, expected level of this stealing by the private grain exporters?" Amber queried.

"Yeah!" Ken exclaimed. "It was conservatively estimated to have been in the hundreds of millions, with the anticipated total perhaps surpassing a billion dollars."

"Unbelievable," Amber stammered. "Unbelievable. Hundreds of millions of dollars! A billion dollars!" Amber exclaimed, almost gagging on the words.

"You heard me right," Ken confirmed. "This was the big "financial thing" the White House could never talk about it. No other illegal financial thing, occurring during the Nixon administration, came even close to equaling the Soviet wheat deal, illegal payoffs."

"Tell me again, at what stage in the delivery process did the stealing take place?" Amber asked.

"The highly sophisticated stealing scheme took place at the point of loading the grain on ocean transport ships. But I'm not the person most qualified to give you a detailed answer to your question. There is this one guy, if he will talk to you, who can fully educate you on the industry techniques of stealing PL 480 grain."

"Who?"

"His name is Billy Hall. He works or did work at Cook Industries."

"I'll try to locate him," Amber confidently said.

"I can get his address for you," Ken quickly added.

"Thanks," Amber said. "Ken, why don't we stop here and go for lunch."

"Sounds good."

It was a beautiful afternoon for walking. The air was crisp and a light snow was falling, with about six inches already accumulated on the ground. They walked slowly and soon reached the restaurant Ken wanted to try. They took a table near the window so they could continue watching the first snow of '74. After lunch, they headed back to Ken's apartment, stopping on the way at a local pub where they had one drink. Back at his apartment, Amber asked Ken to tell her more about Will Griffin and Billy Hall.

"I told you a little bit about my good friend, Will," Ken began. So some of this might be repetitious."

"That's OK," Amber assured him. "Repetition might help me. Everything seems so complex."

Ken sat back in his easy chair facing the fireplace, and

for a long spell, he remained silent as if contemplating on what to say.   Then he spoke, "It was shortly after those midterm elections that I overheard talk about the White House blocking some grain fraud investigation by one of our investigators. That early probe in 1971 had been initiated by USDA's Special Agent Willard W. Griffin, a good friend of mine, and his fellow-agent Joel Gibson. These two agents worked out of the Department of Agriculture's Office of Inspector General. They had discovered evidence of the grain fraud at Cook Industries' Bayside elevator, at Reserve, Louisiana, during one of their routine inspections during late 1970 and early 1971. Griffin became convinced they had discovered serious and criminal fraudulent practices at Bayside, and notified the administration of the fraud, with a recommendation that criminal and civil legal action be taken against the private exporters. At first, things seemed to be moving quietly, as if heading in the direction of criminal prosecution of Cook Industries." Ken paused again to take a deep breath, and then continued, not wanting to leave anything out. "Before Will's recommendation of criminal prosecution could advance," Ken explained, "Department officials stepped in and blocked all further action. I remember so clearly how disappointed my friend was."

"I can understand the disappointment he must have experienced," Amber said with belief in her voice.

Ken's voice began trailing as if he too was disappointed in the outcome of the Cook investigation. "They blocked Griffin's efforts to expand the inquiry into the alleged corruption in the grain trade, and even ordered him to halt his probe and turn his attention to other matters. When he persisted, he was rebuffed and called a 'scandal monger.' He was told to stop rocking the boat and to back off from his probe," Ken concluded in a soft almost inaudible voice. "I was personally saddened by how they treated Will. He had worked so hard, only to get a slap in the face. But," Ken hesitated a moment, "I later learned that Will's rebuff may have become necessary. Had he been allowed to continue his investigation, the private exporters, so essential to the success of Kissinger's deal making with Moscow, would surely have backed out of the deal. And with that, the peace deal may have been delayed."

"Did Cook Industries do anything to blunt Griffin's investigation?" Amber asked.

"Yes, Yes, Yes!" Ken emphasized. "They were busy, to say the least, doing their part toward blocking any extension or additional official inquiry into the grain fraud at Bayside. After Special Agent Griffin's early 1971 investigative entry, two top executives at Cook led an imperative need to purge the company files of all incriminating evidence. Phillip H. McCaull and John Finlayson hurriedly met to plan this strategy to remove all incriminating evidence from company files and then to remove that evidence from company property. Finlayson was placed in charge of the purging-detail. Given that assignment, he immediately assembled the company's clerical and operational personnel, and told them they would be working all night if necessary to extract all evidence from the vessel files. Impressed with the urgency of the situation, Cook's employees finished their assignment by 10:00 that night. They had extracted from the files and boxed up all the incriminating evidence and took it to Finlayson's house in Memphis, out of the reach of Special Agent Griffin."

"What a wonderful story," Amber murmured.

"Wonderful?" Ken retorted. "Purging business records of incriminating evidence? That's illegal, I think."

"Maybe," Amber responded. "But it's still a beautiful story of employee loyalty to Cook Industries."

"Well, in any case, Griffin's and all future investigations were blocked, thus freeing the private grain exporters to continue down their path of stealing, even increasing the stealing to a higher level. Billy Hall can fill you in on all this. In my opinion, nobody knows more about what was going on with the short weighing of PL 480 grain in the grain export elevators than the workers who made it all happen. Billy Hall was one of those workers."

After getting Hall's address from Ken, it did not take long for Amber to find Billy Hall in Mobile, Alabama, where he had first started working in the grain business, in December 1959. He was twenty-three years of age at the time. His first employer was Continental Grain, but, during the years, he worked for other grain companies as well. He was hired to work at Cook's new Bayside Grain Elevator in October 1968. Quite literally, he brought to Cook's new export elevator a high level of expertise in the technique of stealing PL 480 grain through the techniques of short-weighing and misgrading.   As a new entry into the export grain industry, Cook needed Billy Hall's skills at stealing, as it tried to catch up with the other private grain exporters.

It was on February 6, 1974, when Hall, agreed to meet with Amber at a local diner in Mobile, near the waterfront. This had been at Hall's request. He was more comfortable on the waterfront. When they came face to face, Amber was surprised that he was so willing to talk with her. He even began boasting about his art of stealing. "While working at Cook's Bayside Elevator, I stole for the company and I stole for myself," he told Amber.

"How much did you steal for the company?" Amber asked.

Pausing as if making a mental calculation, Hall responded, "My reasonable estimate now is that sixty to seventy percent of all export vessels loaded out of Bayside, or fifty percent of all the grain handled from that facility, was short-weighed."   Then Hall added, "An even higher percentage of this grain was misgraded."

"How much did you steal for yourself?"

When Billy Hall heard this question, his face seemed to glow with a feeling of pride. "During the time I worked at Bayside," he began, with a big smile on his face, " I personally stole seven or eight barges of grain or a total of some 300,000 bushels of grain."

"What was that worth at the time?" Amber asked.

"Probably, close to a million dollars."

"Mr. Hall, why are you so willing to tell me about all

the stealing you did for yourself?
 Aren't you fearful of getting arrested and criminally charged?
I'm not going to tell anyone. My sources are confidential."

Another big smile came on Hall's face. "I am smarter
than most. I feel free to talk with you without fear of arrest
because I was given complete and absolute personal immunity
from criminal prosecution on all matters arising out of the
grain stealing scheme at Bayside."

"Why would the government grant you immunity?"
Amber, now so curious, wanted to know.

"They needed me! It was a tradeoff," Hall told her.
"During my years at Cook's Bayside Elevator, I had collected
and saved all the incriminating written evidence of the stealing
scheme going on at the company. I took all this evidence
home for my own self protection. Since I was stealing grain
for myself as well as the company, I figured I might need this
evidence one day. And sure enough, I did. After the FBI
entered the scene of the industry-wide scam of stealing PL 480
grain, my lawyer traded my evidentiary treasure trove to the
government for complete immunity. The only condition was
that I tell them the complete story of the grain fraud going on
at Cook Industries as well as the grain industry."

"Will you tell me that story?"

"Sure!" Hall volunteered as if he wanted everybody to
know. "After Cook began operating its new Bayside export
grain terminal at Reserve, Louisiana, top officials of the
company, I believe it was in June of '69, met secretly in a
Memphis public park behind the Rivermont Hotel, to discuss

plans to introduce the illegal practices of short weighing and misgrading of PL 480 grain shipments. The small park where they met, overlooking the Mississippi River, was the perfect spot to get away from the ears of the office and Ned Cook, the head man who would never have gone along with the plan."

"Was Ned Cook that honest?" Amber interjected.

"He was either that honest or naive," Hall answered.

"OK, sorry to interrupt. Go on with your story."

Hall then began his story that had earned him complete immunity. "Well, after that meeting in the park, the fraudulent grain practices began at full scale."

"What do you mean, full scale?" Amber interjected.

As I told you before, sixty to seventy percent of all export vessels loaded out of Bayside was targeted to be short-weighed."

"I remember now," Amber said. "I agree that that is full scale. Go on with your explanation, please," she said as she smiled at her new source of information.

"Let's see," Hall said, as he paused a moment. "The top company officials, after getting word from the USDA of PL 480 grain shipments, notified the grain elevator manager of these shipments with the identity of the transport ships, designated for transporting the PL 480 grain. The elevator manager would then hand me a slip of paper identifying the ships destined for certain PL 480 designated foreign ports, with a notation of how much to short weigh and misgrade. Each time this occurred, almost daily, I was always told by the manager to destroy the slips of paper after the ship was short weighed. But, instead of destroying these slips of paper, I took them home and later traded them for immunity."

"Mr. Hall, I have heard it explained before, but would you explain the practices of short weighing and misgrading?"

"Sure!" Hall again paused a moment to think of the best way to explain the terms to a reporter who probably had never been around wheat. "Short weighing," Hall began, "is when the amount of grain actually transported is less than the amount certified as being shipped. With PL 480 shipments, the USDA would authorize a specified quantity and grade of grain for shipment to some PL 480 recipient country. The grain would come from USDA inventory. Most of the poor countries receiving PL 480 grain did not have the technology needed to verify the quantity and grade of grain received on their dock. They were happy just to be getting the food product needed so badly to feed the people. They simply relied upon the weight and inspection certificates issued by U.S. inspectors, licensed by the Department of Agriculture."

"Wow!" Amber exclaimed. "These poor countries were easy targets."

"Countries suffering from famine were inclined to accept whatever was unloaded onto their docks without taking the time to test or weigh the grain. The private grain exporters depended on this inattention. As the exporter begins loading the grain from the elevator to the transport vessel, the short weighing take place," Hall explained. "Take me, for example. As the operator at Cook's elevator, I operated a highly mechanized system of moving the grain from the elevator to the ship. After the grain inspector measured the quantity of grain loaded to make sure it matched the USDA authorization, I could then divert the flow of that grain back into the elevator without the inspector's awareness. The Company had the technology, and I had the skill. So the end effect was that ships transporting PL 480 grain never contained the actual amount of grain the USDA had promised the PL 480 recipient country."

"That's short weighing," Amber noted. "Now what about misgrading of the PL 480 grain?"

"When the USDA approved a shipment of grain to a PL 480 recipient country, it specified the grade of grain to be transported to the country, like number 2 grade, number 3 grade etc. So, if a ship designated as a target by my supervisor, called for number 2 grade I reduced the grade of grain actually being loaded on the ship; that is "misgrading." Misgrading of grain had also become highly automated in the 1970s, as if the corporate grain exporters had been planning for this historic period of stealing. The skilled elevator operator could blend the grain entirely by buttons and levers located in the grain elevator's control room." Hall paused to order another cup of coffee, then continued. "When grain arrived at Bayside, it was first cleaned of all foreign matter, dirt, trash, glass, metal parts, and this trash is discarded. Next, the full grain kernels are separated from broken grain kernels, with the broken kernels and dust, the by-products known as "screenings," retained in the elevator."

"Why are the screenings not discarded?," Amber

asked.

"These screenings are retained and stored separately. They are super valuable. When filling an order for export, the operator at the elevator, determines the grade level to be transported by first mixing different grades of grain and then blending in a quantity of screenings which lowers the grade of grain loaded on the ship. For regular buyers, such as the Soviets, the screenings are blended in only to bring the grain grade to the level specified in the contract. But with PL 480 shipments, the "screenings" were blended in to reduce the grade to a level below than that specified in the USDA contract."

"That is super interesting," Amber said, "Such sophistication. But let me ask you a question. How did the exporters profit on the short weighing and misgrading of the grain?"

"They profited in two ways," Hall explained. "First, they profited by filing false claims with the USDA for payment on the PL 480 grain shipments they handled for the Department. They were paid for the full quantity authorized for transport, as supported by the official weight and grade certificates. But that total quantity was never shipped. So, they were paid for grain not shipped. The second way they profited was selling the grain they had stolen through the short weighing process for full market value."

"Do you have any idea of how much the private exporters were making from these illegal grain practices?" Amber asked.

"I don't know," Hall replied. "I don't think anybody knows, but it was a hell of a lot. Remember what I told you earlier. Cook owned only one export elevator, the one at Bayside, and from there, I personally stole 300,000 bushels, worth upward to a million dollars. Now imagine what Cook made from its share of the short weighing. Profits from these illegal practices were staggering. If Cook Industries made millions by illegal means within its single export elevator, imagine what Continental Grain and Cargill Incorporated must of made from their illegal operation. They both operated multiple grain export elevators. They were the big operators in the industry."

"You know Billy, as I listen to you describe the technique and quantity of the stealing of grain, it seemed to me that the whole operation was so easily detectible. Wouldn't the short weighing of grain show up as an overage in inventory?"

"I am impressed with your keen observation as a reporter," Hall told Amber. "You're exactly right! The exporters, engaging in this fraudulent practice of short weighing, would in fact have shown huge overages in grain inventory, amounts equal to the quantities they stole. This is how Special Agent Griffin discovered the evidence of the short-weighing of PL 480 grain at Cook's Bayside elevator."

"Well, how did the exporters explain the inventory overage?" Amber asked.

"Cook and probably all the other private exporters accounted for the inventory overage with a simple falsified accounting adjustment. It was a paper transaction to account for the excess grain inventory; they simply created record receipts of fictitious or phantom barge loads of grain equaling the amount of grain they stole."

"Unbelievable!" Amber said. "Unbelievable. This is what the Nixon administration was protecting?" Amber stated rhetorically. "Billy I appreciate all your help and information."

"Your most welcome," Hall said, and the two went their separate ways.

Back at the hotel, Amber stopped at the lobby bar for a drink, scotch and water, and sat back to think about what Billy Hall had told her. She understood, she thought, how the White House may not have had any real choice but to protect the private exporters. Protecting the stealing may have been the only way to compensate the private exporters for taking part in the critically important scheme. How else could the exporters have been paid off? Amber thought. And Nixon did succeed in ending the Vietnam war. So, maybe it was all justified. But, after the operations became fixed, Nixon probably had no choice but to continue the protection of the private exporters, as their stealing continued.

When she got back to Washington, Amber could not wait to tell her story to Josh She called him and they met at their favorite piano bar. She wanted to tell him about her conversation with Billy Hall. At first, they talked about different things, including Josh's plans to move back to Birmingham. Then after ordering a second drink, Amber started telling him about her interview of Billy Hall. "It was weird!" she told Josh, "but exciting."

"That's an interesting story, Amber," Josh said, displaying an expression of concern on his face. He then offered a caution, "Amber, if it were ever disclosed that the White House was deeply involved in this illegal financial operation of fraudulent short-weighing and misgrading of PL 480 grain, albeit in the name of peace, the reputation of the United States in the community of nations could be seriously and irreparably tarnished. Imagine the discovery that the United States government was engaging in illegal payoffs to gain some international commitment. If you can imagine this, as you seem to be doing, you know how damaging the truth would be. Had the truth ever been discovered, it might have been difficult for the United States in the future to continue its honored place in the world, of providing international leadership through honest diplomatic negotiations. The Country's international trust level would be placed in serious jeopardy."

"What are you suggesting, Josh?" Amber sounded an alarm.

"Nothing. I am only making an observation."

"It might be an observation," Amber suggested, "but I am hearing a suggestion that I not write a story about the billion dollar grain fraud perpetrated by Nixon's White House. Is this what you are suggesting to me?"

"Amber, I know better. How long have we known each other? Whether you write an article disclosing this financial thing, you must trust your own judgment. And I will fully respect your decision. I only share with you my views on the possible consequences to America's reputation within the international community."

"I can see where disclosure of such an enormous financial fraud sponsored by the President of the United States could be harmful to the reputation of the Country," Amber reasoned. "Kissinger's deal making with Moscow could, in fact, be viewed as a form of international bribery."

"I agree," Josh asserted. "And this could harm our reputation as a reliable international trading partner," he repeated.

"Maybe," Amber admitted. "But, there is a bigger issue here!"

"What?"

"The right of Americans to know, freedom of the press!" Amber almost shouted. "The freedom of the press is a centerpiece of our Nation and our Constitution. Under this charter of freedom, do I not have a moral responsibility to disclose such matters of public importance?"

"Only you can answer that," Josh said softly with his genuine smile to let Amber know he supported her.

"I guess."

CHAPTER TEN

$\mathscr{I}$t was a Monday, May 27, 1974, when Amber Highlander headed back to Oklahoma to make her final report to the wheat farmers. She had been looking forward to getting back to Oklahoma, and arrived two days before the wheat harvest was scheduled to begin. Tyler had promised to give her a chance to drive a grain combine during this trip. She had been invited to once again stay with the Grimes family, an invitation she quickly accepted. She was still hoping to get another opportunity to learn firsthand the progress Michael might have made since her last visit.

Arriving at the airport in Oklahoma City, Amber, by choice, rented a car to drive to the Grimes' farm. On that short trip, she wanted to take her time, driving leisurely through the countryside, not missing anything. She was particularly anxious to see the ripened wheat crop, that, she had been told, flowed like fields of gold. And sure enough, when she came to the first open field, there it was, just as it has been described. With the sun shining brightly, it was quite literally a field of gold. For the first time, she could see the image they saw - it was indeed an impressive sight as she gazed over the expansive fields. As she drove through the countryside toward Billings, staying on the back-roads, Amber was amazed from the moment she came to the first wheat field. Looking out over these fields, spreading their reach from both sides of the road and extending outward to the point where the fields touch the sky, it was like magic. For Amber, the sight was breathtaking. It was just as she had been told, but never believed, the wheat fields indeed appeared golden and the fields flowed with the rhythm of the wind.

As she drove toward the farm, Amber stopped frequently to take pictures, knowing at the time that no photograph could truly capture the actual beauty of the wheat fields. These fields moved like waves of the sea, flowing with the gentle breeze, creating an appearance that all the earth was swaying. The scene she was experiencing would never be erased from her mind. Reaching the Grimes wheat farm, she stopped at the mail box to take more pictures to preserve this one scene out of Michael's past. Then she turned onto the dirt road leading to the house, remembering that this was the stretch of dirt road that had played a role in Michael's young life. As she drove up the dirt road from the mail box, Bessie, who was looking out the window, spotted her, and she and Tyler came out to greet her and take her luggage to the guest room.

Once in the house, it did not take Amber long to get settled. She did not want to waste a moment during her five day visit. When she came into the kitchen, where everything started each day on the Grimes farm, Bessie offered her a glass of iced sun tea. Then after a moment of casual chitchat, Amber asked if they could go outside and sit in the green chairs while they drank their tea.

"Sure," Tyler said. "Those green chairs haven't been used at all since Michael returned from Vietnam."

"This would be a nice time to go out," Bessie added. "Do you need a refill on your tea?" Without waiting for an answer, Bessie said, "Oh, I'll just bring the pitcher." Bessie always made sun tea in a gallon jug during spring and summer. She thought that was the only way to make the tea taste like tea, and everybody liked it, so she kept it up.

When they reached the chairs that had never been moved, Amber sat in the middle one, the one used by Michael when he sat there listening to his grandpa. The sun was still high in the sky at about 4:00 o'clock, and as the bright beams of sunlight touched the wheat so gently, it made Amber more certain of the power of wheat that could end wars. The fields as far as her eyes could see, did look like gold, with the sun adding to the brightness. As she gazed out over these fields, Amber could better appreciate her discovery that it was wheat from Oklahoma's fertile fields and America's prairie that had been used by President Nixon to finally bring peace to Vietnam. After settling into the three green chairs, Amber turned to Bessie and asked her about Michael. The question at first brought a moment of silence that lasted, it seemed forever.

Bessie sat there in silence as tears came to her eyes, then she spoke in a low, soft voice, almost a whisper that exposed the depth of her sadness, "He is still not doing very well. We are all getting so discouraged. We don't know what else to do. More and more, I get so angry just thinking about Vietnam and how that damn war destroyed our son. Thank God, it is over. Maybe now, American mothers will not have to go through what we are still experiencing and what we might be experiencing the rest of our lives." Bessie paused again, then added, "Amber, you ought to write about the lingering effects of the Vietnam war and how it destroyed the productive lives of so many young men."

• • • •

"We were given the details," Tyler spoke. "His unit had been on a search and destroy mission when they came under heavy artillery fire, when a round exploded nearby, hitting Michael's young body with shrapnel. Then, as he laid on the ground bleeding, Communist forces kept firing on the unit, preventing Michael from being lifted out. Finally, one American helicopter came in with rockets and cleared a path through the Communist line. The nameless pilot was able to land his helicopter long enough to evacuate Michael and one other seriously wounded soldier."

Listening to this scene being described caused tears to roll down Amber's cheek, as she remembered her fiancé.

"Excuse me," Amber said, trying to keep her

composure, as she hurried back into the house to the guest room, closed the door and started crying."

Tyler and Bessie had sensed that something was bothering Amber, so they followed her into the house, and could hear her crying."

Bessie knocked on the door, and asked Amber if she were alright. There was no response, as the crying continued. So, Bessie opened the door and walked in and put her hand on Amber's back. "Amber what is wrong?" Finally Amber's crying turned to sobs, and as she looked into Bessie's eyes, finally telling her the story about her fiancé, who had been a helicopter pilot in Vietnam. His name was Robert Jefferies and we called RJ. He was later shot down and killed."

"I am so sorry," Bessie said in her comforting voice. "It might help if we go back out and sit in the green chairs."

"OK," Amber said.

When they came out of the bedroom, Tyler was still in the kitchen and asked if anything was wrong. Bessie told him the story and Tyler too tried to comfort their guest. They then all returned to the three green chairs, and just sat in silence, drinking Bessie's sun iced tea. It was Amber who finally broke the silence. "As you do, I now know how the Vietnam war has squandered the productive lives of so many young men. My fiancee, lost his young life in Vietnam when his helicopter was shot out of the sky. We had gone to the University of Alabama together. He majored in aeronautical engineering, making straight As during his entire college. RJ had dreamed of having a career in aviation, designing aircraft.

And we had dreamed of a life together."

Amber returned to her silence as she gazed out over the fields of wheat. No words were spoken for a long time, with the only sounds being the sounds of nature, and Bessie, refilling the ice tea classes. Amber once again broke the silence, "I plan to write a series of articles on the suffering of Vietnam veterans and their families. She then told Bessie, "I think it would be a story that might help many families. For now," Amber told Tyler and Bessie, "you might find it interesting to know that the Vietnam war was finally brought to an end by President Nixon on the power of American grown wheat. Wheat had been discovered by the White House as having more power than all the bombs dropped on North Vietnam. I came to realize this through my investigation into the Soviet wheat deal, but that's what I will be talking about in my presentation to the farmers. Quite simply, President Nixon, through the work of Henry Kissinger, worked out an exchange of American grown wheat for peace in Vietnam."

"If only this could have been carried out before our son Michael, who had dreamed with his grandpa of becoming a wheat farmer, had been sent to Vietnam," Tyler pleaded. "I would have been willing to contribute all our wheat if it could have brought peace to Vietnam and saved the lives of our soldiers, including my son and your RJ." Tyler's comments had brought on another long period of silence.

Finally, the silence was broken again when Bessie asked, "You want more tea?"

"Please," Tyler answered.

"Me to," Amber said.

Bessie then told Tyler and Amber that she was going in to start dinner. She had been looking forward to Amber's visit and their talks about Michael and about living on a wheat farm. She remembered that Amber was so easy to talk with. She headed for the kitchen, as the sun dropped closer to the horizon, sending forth different glows cast over the wheat fields. Amber discovered that sitting in the green chairs seemed to magically, bringing forth a sense of being, without any consciousness of time. That was something all the Grimes had long accepted. For them, it was the present. Tyler learned from his pa and came to believe there is little need to think in a time frame other than the one in which one has the power to do something about. There was nothing one can do at the present moment to alter the past or dictate the future. For Tyler, it was the present, when the wheat crop occupied his attention. If only Michael would come back to the three green chairs, he too might be liberated and find peace, Tyler thought. For now, he hoped, maybe Amber will experience that healing from her loss.

As the sun began to set, it was spellbinding for Amber to gaze out into the extended wheat fields within her easy reach, just a few feet from the green chairs. "Amber," Tyler said in breaking her spell, "would you like to take a walk through the wheat fields and feel and touch the wheat?"

Without hesitation, Amber jumped to her feet as the image of walking through a wheat field flashed before to her mind. She was ready to take that walk through the fields of gold. "Do we just walk over to and along the field?" Amber asked.

"Don't stop there," Tyler said, as he led the way toward the nearest field. "Walk into and through the field with your hands reaching out to touch the tops of the wheat." Amber followed the directions and started walking through the field, listening to the rustling sound that helps tell the farmers that the crop is close to harvest. Suddenly, her mind was at peace as she began experiencing tranquility as if nobody else was present, that is until she heard Tyler's voice, "Are you still planning to drive the combine when the harvest starts?"

"What?"

"Are you still planning to drive the combine day after tomorrow, when the wheat harvest starts?" Tyler repeated.

"Oh! I want to," Amber excitedly said. "I have been looking forward to that since my first visit, when you invited me to do just that. But, in a way Tyler, it will be sad to see the beauty of these fields suddenly disappearing as the combines pass through. Still, I know the scene can't last, and I have enjoyed the moment. I will be ready to climb in the combine, but, I expect you to be with me."

"I will be right next to you and will help you if you need help. But, it wouldn't surprise me if you quickly became a pro. You could then hire out to work the wheat harvests that start in Texas and move northward in sequence with the readiness of the wheat."

"I can't wait," Amber said. "But, I might not become a regular."

Well," Tyler explained, "what we are walking through today is what you will be cutting down when the harvest begins. You will see and experience the wheat operation first hand. Did you bring the right cloths?"

"I hope," Amber answered. "I brought blue jeans and running shoes, but I don't have a hat."

"We have extra hats," Tyler assured her. Then, as they ended their walk in the fields of wheat, they headed toward the kitchen. As they approached the backdoor, Tyler told Amber, "I as well as all the other farmers are looking forward to your report tomorrow."

When they got back to the house, Amber washed up and went to the kitchen to help Bessie with dinner, and Bessie's coveted conversations with Amber began. As they talked, Michael walked into the kitchen and said his first word to Amber, "Hi." But, he could not be brought into the conversation. He did listen to his mom talk about his problems and Amber's comments about the Vietnam war. He just sat there expressionless and stared at the ceiling. Michael did sit at the dinner table with his sisters, and continued listening to his mom and dad talk. But, he offered no response and showed no emotion.

"Michael," his dad said, "the wheat harvest is about to begin and Amber is going to drive the combine. Do you want to come and show her how to opcrate the machine?"

Amber picked up on what Tyler was trying to do, and added, "Michael, I would sure appreciate your coming along to help me. I have never been on a grain combine." None of this seemed to matter, as Michael remained in his own world. Then, not saying a word, he got up from the table and went to his room. After dinner, Amber helped Bessie clean the table and straighten up the kitchen. Then, the two sat at the kitchen table, drinking coffee with a little touch of brandy, as they continued talking about different subjects.

Later that evening, Tyler took Amber over to Jake's place to socially meet with some of the wheat farmers. When she walked in, she was greeted by about twenty-five farmers who surrounded her and extended their personal greetings. It was obvious she was pleased by all the attention. The group was drinking beer and telling stories about their own farm experiences, laughing and telling jokes. Amber could tell that these farmers were happy. It had been a long time since they experienced a string of two profitable years. The year after the Soviet wheat deal, market prices for wheat were the highest they could remember. And this year looks even better. The group broke up at about 10:30 p.m., and Amber told them, she would see them at the hall tomorrow night.

As they drove back to the farm, Tyler told Amber, "They all really like and respect you."

"I am glad," Amber said. "This has been one of my most interesting projects, and I appreciate the trust you and the wheat farmers placed in me."

The next night was the grange hall harvest meeting, held annually to celebrate the wheat harvest. Before the meeting started, they had their annual Barbecue and chili dinner followed with homemade ice-cream. This social gathering gave the farmers a chance to visit and to meet individually with Amber Highlander. But quickly after the socializing, things got serious after the meeting was called to order. Tyler Grimes took the floor to introduce their guest, who by now they all knew. Tyler reminded the farmers they had voted to retain Amber Nicole Highlander to investigate the 1972 Soviet wheat deal and the depressed prices at which they had sold their '72 wheat crop. "Fortunately," Tyler told the farmers, "wheat prices were much higher last year, and this year looks even better. The Soviet wheat deal eliminated all the surplus wheat, and now, wheat prices will probably stay high for a few years to come. But now let's hear what Amber Highlander has to say."

As soon as she stood and slowly approached the podium, Amber received a standing ovation as if her involvement was the cause for the uplift in farm wheat prices. Without a doubt, she loved the acclaim. After Tyler's brief introduction, Amber expressed her appreciation for the opportunity they had given her. She told the farmers that the 1972 low prices had occurred because President Nixon needed to keep wheat prices depressed, just as long as possible. Keeping these prices low was part of the secret deal the White House had made with the Soviets. Nixon had committed himself to a plan with the objective of ending the war. But, in ending the war by an exchange of wheat meant the sacrificing of the farmers for the one year. Amber explained that the President needed them to sell their wheat at the lowest price so Henry Kissinger could confidently work his deal with

Moscow. "It was nothing personal against you," she said. "It was all about finding an end to the war in Vietnam. That in a nutshell is what it was all about, and why you farmers had to be sacrificed for that one year," she explained.

After a short pause, Amber continued, "During the first two years of Nixon's first term as President, Kissinger was trying to negotiate an agreement with the Soviets to bring an end to the Vietnam war. Nothing worked! Nothing worked until the Soviets suddenly faced a dire need for wheat to feed her people. Kissinger saw this phenomenon of nature and came up with his plan for trading wheat for peace. The Soviets would be permitted to purchase American grown wheat at a low fixed price over a period of three years, in return for the Soviets' agreement to pressure North Vietnam into accepting settlement terms. Nixon had reached the point of desperation, willing to accept settlement terms with the Communists that gave him just enough room to claim his exit from the war was with honor. But it was a shallow honor, yet one without the need for him to lower his head. So, with the help of the Soviets and of course you wheat farmers, Nixon was able to say he ended the war with honor. "Quite literally," Amber emphasized, Nixon bought his way out of Vietnam with your 1972 wheat crop. And as you know, the settlement was timely announced in October 1972, right before the elections, giving Nixon a victory to a second term."

Amber paused again for a short moment with her soft smile, and told the farmers, "With all the bombing raids on North Vietnam that Nixon ordered, the Communists kept moving toward Saigon, bringing peace no closer. So, if the war were to be ended, Nixon's strategy had to change. And after becoming convinced that the bombing raids were not achieving peace, someone in the administration came up with the idea of exchanging wheat for an end to the war. As I said before, it was an exchange of wheat for peace. Your 1972 wheat harvest became Nixon's instrument of peace." Amber then added, "your wheat brought peace without the loss of additional lives."   Amber lingered a moment to place additional emphasis on her next words, "You should be proud of this! Yours was the heavy financial sacrifice in 1972. You sold your wheat at artificially depressed prices, manipulated by the USDA through its falsified market information incorporated in the February and May 1972 *Wheat Situation*. Still, on the high road, your personal, economic sacrifice opened the door to bringing peace to Vietnam and to America."

In her mind, Amber thought the wheat farmers were the true peacemakers. "By your sacrifice during your 1972 wheat harvest, you saved the lives of many American combat troops and helped bring home our American prisoners of war. But sadly, you could never be officially recognized for your contribution and sacrifice. Unfortunately, public accolades had to be limited to Henry Kissinger, who, I heard, has been nominated for the Nobel Peace Prize. All of you should acknowledge your personal sacrifice and lift a glass to toast the honor of all your fellow farmers. I personally salute you," Amber said with pride. With this, the farmers erupted in

cheers and applause. They were feeling good and so was
Amber. Then after going through her entire report, a copy of
which she left for the grange president, Amber again thanked
the farmers and opened it up for questions. "If any of you
have questions, I will be happy to try answering them," she
said confidently.

"Ms Highlander, I want to know how they could sell
wheat to the Soviets at a price below cost and then agree to
keep that low fixed price in place for a period of three years?"

"That's a good question," Amber acknowledged. "I
asked myself that same question at least twenty times before I
settled on the answer." Then she thought, without saying
anything before adding, "it was the government that in fact
sold the wheat below cost. The wheat sold to the Soviets was
wheat surplus the government owned. So, the private grain
exporters, while publicly selling the wheat to the Soviets, were
simply delivering the wheat. But, I have to add here, these
private exporters still assumed enormous risks."

Another farmer then leaped to his feet, "I understand
what you are saying Ms Highlander about where the wheat
came from, but I don't understand how they could sell wheat
at such a big loss and still make a profit."

Amber listened closely to that question and then
paused, not wanting to misspeak. She thought carefully on
what she needed to say, and then spoke. "Quite frankly, the
exporters did in fact make enormous, unheard of profits, how
much, nobody but them knows. Except for one of the
companies, Cook Industries, all the grain exporters taking part

in Kissinger's wheat deal are private corporations with no obligation to file financial reports with the Securities Exchange Commission.   But, I was able to examine the financial records of Cook Industries, and I know that company made huge profits during the year after its sale of wheat to the Soviets.   These profits," Amber explained, came from a sanctioned stealing scheme, that according to estimates involved the illegal taking of hundreds of millions of dollars, maybe even more than a billion dollars.

"Did Nixon take a share of those millions of dollars?" another farmer asked.

"I don't think so," Amber responded.   "I found no evidence that President Nixon or anyone in the Nixon White House ever personally enriched themselves from the Soviet wheat deal. The only thing President Nixon wanted to achieve was peace in Vietnam, and for this, he personally accepted a heavy burden on himself, as he placed a heavy burden on your shoulders, for one year."

Amber took several more questions, and was willing to keep going, but, the grange president stepped in and called it quits, thanking Amber for her great service. She then received another standing ovation, and the meeting was adjourned. After the meeting, many of the farmers came up and thanked her personally. She had truly impressed them.   Back in the truck, heading home, Tyler personally expressed his thanks, and told her how she had solidified the grange membership. Then he suggested they go celebrate at Jake's Place, without telling her the true reason for wanting to go there.

When they got to Jake's, only a few people were in the place. They ordered a beer and started talking about life in Washington. Then a couple of more farmers came in and joined them and the number continued to climb as the farmers kept arriving. Finally, Scott Weaver, the grange president, came in and joined the group and ordered a beer. Then with all the farmers holding up their beer, and Jake joining the group, Weaver offered a toast to Amber Nicole Highlander, and the group let out a cheer. He then handed Amber an envelope which she opened in front of the farmers and found a check for $35,000. She was speechless. The farmers had voted to add $10,000 to the second half of her retainer. Amber's mouth opened, but no words came out. Finally, she spoke, but her only words were, "Thank you." That was it and the farmers gave her another cheer, and then ordered another beer.

On the way back to the Grimes farm, Amber told Tyler how she was still so overwhelmed by the generosity of the farmers. "When we have a good year," Tyler explained, "we can be generous. But," Tyler, adding emphasis, said "those guys were generous to you because they were so impressed by your representation of their interest. If you want to we can visit a few of them to express your appreciation."

"That would be great," Amber said, "but maybe not tonight."

Tyler laughed, then suggested, "Maybe before you leave."

It was getting late when they got home, but Bessie was

still up. When Tyler explained what went on, Bessie knew Amber was not ready to go to bed. She suggested to Tyler that they take Amber back to the green chairs to let her see what a sky full of stars looks like. He thought that was a great idea. The sky was clear that night and the stars were filling the universe. Settling into the three green chairs, they gazed into the night and up to the stars. The evening air was cool, it was a moonless night and the stars and the milky-way shone their brilliance. "I bet you do not see skies like this in Washington," Tyler offered.

"No, we don't," Amber admitted. "It is so peaceful and humbling to look up at such natural beauty and peacefulness found in a star-filled sky."

As they sat, looking into the heavens, Tyler told Amber that his pa loved sitting out here. "He wanted me to love the sky as much as he. More than once, he told me, 'When you sit outside and watch the sky, you begin to think in color instead of black and white.' And then he would add, 'this gives everything deeper meaning.' And it does!"

"That's a beautiful thought," Amber said, "it's one I'll remember for a long time. My problem though is that back in Washington, we can't see all the stars you can see from these magical green chairs."

"If you can see one, you can imagine the rest. They are there, but beyond the vision of humans because of humans."

The next day, Amber would experience the working life of a wheat farmer. Watching the process from the cab of the combine, she would see the wheat stems cut by the front blades of the combine and move into the machine that collected the grain, depositing it in the holding bin, until transferred to the trucks for delivery to the farm grain elevator or local coop. Amber had watched carefully as Tyler so skillfully operated the combine, and now it was her time to take the controls. She quickly learned that it was not the same as driving a car.

In operating the combine, Amber had to learn how to use the gears and controls inside the cab. So after a detailed lesson from Tyler, she was ready. As it turned out, she was a natural, but she wasn't ready to quit her day job. Tyler allowed her to stay in control of the combine until she had cut enough wheat to fill the bin. As the wheat was transferred from the combine to the grain truck, Tyler suggested that she get in the truck and go to the co-op to add that part of the operation to her experience. During her two days working the wheat harvest, Amber got to perform every task involved. For a short while, but more than a moment, Amber was a wheat farmer, bringing in her harvest. It was exciting to this journalist.

But now it was time for her to head back home to D.C., and back to the sky with few stars. She left on June 2, a Sunday. After a big breakfast and another long visit with Bessie, Amber headed to the airport, carrying with her a new appreciation for America's farmers, particularly those farmers in Noble County, Oklahoma. She appreciated the confidence they had placed in her, and she was grateful for their generosity. This $35,000 would allow her to continue her investigation into the Soviet wheat deal, something she was committed to continuing, for as long as it took. She wanted to get the full story. The big questions left in her mind were those raised by the farmers during her grange hall presentation. And, in her own mind, there were still a lot more of her own questions she wanted to explore.

On her way back to Washington, Amber stopped over in Birmingham, Alabama to visit her friend Joshua Walker. She had called him before leaving Oklahoma. When she arrived, Josh was happy his friend had come for a visit. He picked her up at the airport and they headed back to his apartment located on top of Red Mountain, not far from the mighty statue of Vulcan, the largest cast iron statue in the world, and the symbol of Birmingham's once leading position in the iron and steel industry.

When they got to his apartment, Josh poured them a cup of coffee and took Amber out to his patio looking out over the panorama of the City and a view of Vulcan, as their guardian. This view was the thing that sold him on this apartment after he returned to Birmingham. Coming from Clanton and going to school at Alabama, Amber also considered Birmingham as her second hometown. Josh had taken off work a few days while Amber was in town and during her visit, these two old friends made the rounds to all their favorite spots. They drove down to their hometown of Clanton, and spent time on the University of Alabama campus in Tuscaloosa, about sixty miles west of Birmingham. During her three day visit, they talked about everything except the Soviet wheat deal. For the most part, they talked about their old days at Alabama and about Joshua's new job and life in Birmingham.

At the end of her three day visit, Amber left for Washington, ready to get home and excited about getting her wheat pictures developed to prove to her Georgetown friends that she had driven one of the big wheat combines. She also wanted to get back to work, and the many stories she wanted to write. With all her work as an investigative journalist on the Soviet wheat deal, Amber, a perfectionist, was not satisfied she had yet discovered the full story.

CHAPTER ELEVEN

*A*mber returned to Washington on June 6, having fulfilled her obligation to the farmers who had shown their satisfaction by way of a generous bonus. Now, she could take some time off before continuing her investigation into the Soviet wheat deal. She was committed to finding answers to the remaining questions about Nixon and Kissinger's exchange of wheat for peace. But, for now, she wanted to just relax. She decided to call Ken and meet him for drinks and dinner, and go from there. Ken was surprised to hear from her but did not hesitate to meet. They met at their regular spot, the C & O Bar & Grill. Ken was more surprised that she was not seeking information. This was her first time for that. After a few drinks and dinner, they went to Ken's apartment and soon were in bed together. The next morning, Ken fixed one of his gourmet breakfasts. Amber remembered he was a good cook; he had a way with food and wine. After breakfast, they took their coffee and went to the patio, where they talked about different things, different people, and different places, but no business talk.

Ken then told Amber he was going to Paris for a week of good food and wine and long walks during the day while waiting for the night scene. He was scheduled to leave in two days. He then looked into Amber's blue eyes and invited her to go with him, if she had the time. At that moment, time is what Amber did have. She had no deadlines facing her. And a week in Paris, she thought, how could she go wrong? It was one of her favorite cities. She had been going there since her second year at the University of Alabama, where she minored in French. So, on that spur of the moment, she accepted Ken's invitation and decided to go with him for a week of relaxation, good food, wine, and sex.

It will be wonderful for Amber to be back in the City of love, and to watch the mastery of Ken in his selection of food and wine. He too spoke French. During that week, nothing was said about Kissinger's Soviet wheat deal, at least not until the last day. Then, with only one day left, when she began thinking about her return to Washington, her mind became refocused on the one big unanswered question. That question lingering in her mind is how the White House was so successful in keeping the real story of the wheat deal and its fraudulent component so secret. For Amber, as a journalist, it was so incomprehensible that the truth about this huge illegal financial thing could remain secret for so long. Secrets in government are not ever supposed to last. Someone seems always ready to leak the most confidential of information.

"How?" she asked Ken. "My god, the White House was secretly sanctioning a PL 480 stealing scheme that allowed six private grain exporters to steal hundreds of millions of dollars of public funds. Maybe it even exceeded a billion dollars. Without a doubt, this was probably the biggest illegal financial thing in the history of America. It dwarfed by many times the old standard-bearer of public scandals, the 1921 Teapot Dome oil scandal that had rocked the administration of President Warren G. Harding," Amber elaborated. "How were Nixon's secrets preserved for so long?"

"You have raised the right question," Ken said. "But finding the full answer is going to be harder. I am not sure I have the answers to that. You might need to rely on some of your other sources."

"How did the White House prevent J. Edgar Hoover from cracking down on this illegal grain activity? Was the Director of the FBI involved in this illegal PL 480 practice?"

"No way!" Ken insisted in a firm voice. "I knew Hoover, and I know he was no saint. Had he discovered the billion-dollar, White House sanctioned stealing scheme, he would have held an inordinate level of political leverage over the President, as long as he preserved the secrets."

"That does fit Hoover's reputation," Amber put in.

"Yeah!"

"Ken, I know the FBI served as a centerpiece for White House security during Nixon's first two years. I also know the FBI was monitoring the wiretapped White House telephone conversations of selected staff members. So, from this, I would think the FBI would have discovered the White

House's involvement in this giant illegal financial thing. I don't know how the White House avoided this dichotomy. Tell me," Amber pleaded.

"Amber, before trying to respond to your loaded statement, let's take a break and walk down to our favorite street café for a glass of wine."

"Fine."

Sitting at their preferred table, with the glass of wine selected by Ken, he got back to Amber's question. "Amber, this might sound weird to you, but ..."

Interrupting, Amber interjected, "Everything and nothing seems weird to me in this case. Not anymore! Sorry for the interruption."

"Well, what I was saying about it sounding weird, the White House's efforts and needs to maintain total secrecy required that they find a way to eliminate or neutralize the Hoover factor, before Kissinger's wheat deal could be allowed to advance. That was a powerful challenge for the White House. And knowing Hoover," Ken stressed, "he would have challenged every effort to bypass him and his FBI. Amber, I think you need to accept as a supposition that the White House's active involvement in the wheat deal and the illegal payoffs to the private exporters made it impossible for the White House to continue its reliance on the FBI for security. A good chronology might help you find some interaction between the wheat deal and the White House's imperative for a new security system designed to operate independently of the FBI. From the moment the White House first conceived the idea of exchanging American grown wheat for peace in Vietnam, serious security problems emerged. Realizing from the beginning that such a plan would generate special and serious security problems, Hoover and his FBI had to be first neutralized, even removed from the scene of White House security. I know I am repeating myself, but let me stress one thing. That for the secrets of the wheat deal and illegal payoffs to remain intact, the White House had to find a way to literally take the FBI out of all White House internal security matters."

"That is a weird predicament for the White House," she admitted. "But Ken, I don't see how Nixon, as powerful as he was as President, could effectively push aside the authoritative and commanding power of J. Edgar Hoover from his security details in the White House. From the moment Nixon took office, he and Kissinger had relied on the FBI to install wiretaps on certain White House individuals who had access to sensitive information. And, after the wiretaps were installed, FBI agents closely monitored the intercepted telephone communications and prepared logs of the conversations. From these daily monitoring logs, FBI agents summarized the discussions and forwarded them to FBI Director Hoover for transmittal to the President and Dr. Kissinger. Quite clearly then, under Nixon's wiretap program, the FBI held an important and critical place at the very center of White House security, with open access to the most sensitive information. And remember this," Amber continued, " FBI Director J. Edgar Hoover had served eight Presidents and eighteen attorneys general, during his forty-eight years in office. He had developed a highly disciplined and efficient law enforcement agency within the Department of Justice. Under his leadership, the FBI evolved into a highly sophisticated law enforcement operation with an elaborate surveillance system, operated by highly disciplined undercover agents and paid informers. How could even the White House push aside such power as that?"

"Whatever," Ken responded. "That is exactly what they had to do for success of Kissinger's wheat for peace exchange."

"So, how?" Amber pressed.

"I don't know," Ken admitted. "I know it got done because the wheat deal was allowed to advance. But how it was accomplished, I don't know. Do you have any contact inside the White House who might have the answer?"

"I'm not sure right now that I even know what I'm looking for." Amber did not tell Ken about her friend Josh who had worked at the White House and had been a reliable source of information, up to a point.

"I am confident you will find the answer, and I will read about it in one of your future articles," Ken confirmed. "But, let me repeat: what you need for comparison are tight parallel chronologies of the wheat deal and the evolving White House security. I can help you a little bit with this, but you will need a lot more information."

"Well that will be my project when we get back home. For now though, let's just enjoy our last day in Paris. Ken, I am glad I came with you. It's been a good trip."

"I have certainly enjoyed it."

Back in Washington, Amber was ready to tackle the one big open question. Toward this objective, she first summarized and recorded everything Ken had told her. Then she began visiting and revisiting her contact sources of information. After about a month of talking and studying documents, Amber called her friend Josh. She was thinking about flying down to Birmingham to see what help he might provide. But, when she called, she got a surprise. Josh told her he was coming into Washington the next day and wanted to know if he could stay at her place in Georgetown. "Absolutely," Amber said, not even trying to conceal her excitement. What timing, she thought. "I will even cook you dinner."

Josh arrived the next day and Amber met him at the airport, and drove back to her apartment. That afternoon, they just hung-out as two old friends and talked about everything except work. Then, early in the evening, they walked to their favorite piano bar and continued reminiscing, as they listened to the music. After dinner at a nearby restaurant, they headed back to Amber's apartment. He was going to be in Washington for four days, so Amber did not raise her project with him during his first day. But the next morning after Amber fixed breakfast, they took their coffee and went to the patio, and there, Amber got to her point. She summarized all the information she had gathered and then raised that one big open question she was now trying to solve.

"Amber, where in the world did you get all that highly confidential information?"

"I would rather not say," she responded.

"That's Ok," Josh said. "I respect that. I am not sure I want to know. But, I am dumbfounded at what you have discovered. Still, I always had confidence that if the truth were to be discovered, it would be you who discovered it." Josh paused for a moment, then asked, "Did anyone tell you about Nixon's February order, calling for the creation of a White House internal security unit?"

"No!"

"Well let me hand you a copy of Nixon's order," Josh said. "I brought it with me after you told me where you had brought the story. I was surprised when I first read that document, and I made a copy of it before leaving the White House. According to the information, Nixon met for two hours with the Attorney General and Haldeman, discussing the increasing need for creating an internal security unit that would operate with complete independence from Hoover and the FBI. After that two-hour meeting, President Nixon directed Attorney General John Mitchell to go ahead with his implementation of the internal security operations, despite Hoover's objections."

"I can't wait to read that document," Amber excitedly commented. "Why did you ever make a copy of the document? And why are you now willing to give it to me? In the past, you have been so careful not to give me any highly classified, insider information. Creation of that internal security unit must have been something so highly secretive."

"I don't know why I copied that document," Josh said. "But I did, and I am giving it to you because I know you would eventually find it on your own. You are so close to the full truth of the Nixon Administration."

"Thanks Josh. I have been working like hell since you left the White House," Amber replied. "But getting this document will help bring the loose pieces together."

"It's obvious that you have. Are you getting ready to publish all that information?"

"That's my plans."

"You might shock the world! I would love to be in White House when you do. Kissinger will be going berserk," Josh expressed his thoughts.

After Josh headed back to Birmingham on July 21, Amber began putting the pieces together in preparation of a series of articles on Vietnam and Nixon as the peacemaker. From all her highly reliable sources, Amber had found the answer to the big open questions that had haunted her for so long. How did the White House maintain the secrecy of its involvement in the biggest financial scandal in history, and how did it prevent the FBI from entering the case and shutting down the illegal operation. The answer that overwhelmingly surprised her was highly complex, but yet so simple. She was most surprised and impressed by how Nixon got rid of the immediate presence of the FBI as the centerpiece to White House security.

First came the February 4 order creating the

independent White House internal security unit. Then, on February 10, 1971, Nixon ordered the FBI to eliminate all the FBI wiretaps on White House staffers and members of the press. These two orders took the FBI completely out of White House internal security circles. Removal of these wiretaps, may have ended the prying eyes of the FBI and J. Edgar Hoover, but it created a gap in the White House security. As long as the FBI continued monitoring the wiretapped White House phones there was a check on the potential level of insider leaks by staff members. But after these FBI internal wiretaps and their monitoring were halted, a security gap was created. Just as fast, this gap was quickly closed one day later, when Nixon ordered his secret White House taping system installed and placed in operation. Installation of that system was handled by Secret Service technicians who were not permitted to listen to and monitor the recordings. With these three security measures, the FBI was effectively removed from White House internal security matters. The White House had a new security system that effectively shielded the billion dollar illegal financial scheme of paying off the private exporters.

Identifying the initial steps in the parallel chronologies of the wheat deal and White House security, Amber discovered that the idea of the wheat deal had its beginning during late 1970 and early 1971, as a reaction to the Republican midterm election-fiasco. One way Amber timed the moment the White House began showing an interest in wheat was when the administration decided to block an official grain fraud investigation of Cook Industries' export grain elevator. Ken had told her about the investigation blocked; it had been initiated by USDA Special Agent Willard W. Griffin. Right along with the White House's interest in wheat came an increased attention to White House internal security. The first step in early January 1971, was when the White House brought in E. Howard Hunt, a highly experienced retired CIA agent to perform special assignments considered very sensitive in nature. Born in 1918, in Hamburg, New York, Hunt, had twenty-one years experience in techniques of physical and electronic surveillance, photography, document forgery, and surreptitious entries into guarded premises for photography and installation of electronic devices.

As the White House began seeking its security independence from the FBI and J. Edgar Hoover, Hunt offered the White House the security expertise lost with the removal of the FBI from the security scene. He had attended the same college as Charles Colson, and the two men became acquainted during Brown University alumni activities. During the fall of 1968, Colson began discussing with Hunt, his intelligence activities at the CIA. On May 1, 1970, Hunt retired from the CIA and joined a private CIA front organization with close ties to the White House. Hunt's presence for special assignments gave the White House a level of security expertise that permitted it to more quickly gain security autonomy from the FBI. Amber had collected all this information from different sources. She was now summarizing the information stored in her mind.

　　　The dominant step in establishing the needed White House security autonomy was President Nixon's creation of an independent White House internal security unit on February 4, 1971, by presidential order. On that day, Amber summed up, Nixon directed Attorney General John Mitchell to implement the internal security operations. He called for Attorney General Mitchell to set up and take total charge over operations of the White House internal security unit, with Haldeman serving as second in command. Amber also discovered that this security centerpiece was followed by two other factors: first the removal of all FBI internal wiretaps, and second the installation of Nixon's secret taping system. By the end of February 1971, the White House had in place its organized, widespread, internal security unit, with the expertise of spotting potential treats of information leaks. This ISU had to be dependable enough to confidently allow Kissinger's Soviet wheat deal to advance, with complete reliable knowledge that no information had been leaked, particularly to the Democratic Party. There was no room for error. Nixon's new ISU had to be secure enough to assure the private exporters they could safely continue their PL 480 grain stealing scheme. One slipup could be fatal.

　　　With Nixon's White House internal security unit firmly in place, it did not take long for the new security unit to serve its intended purpose, and justify its creation and existence. Amber had heard this from several sources, but she did not have the details of what kind of threat they faced.

So, she called Josh again, hoping for a bailout. "Josh, after the internal security unit was created in February 1971, are you aware of any serious information leaks that potentially threatened the Soviet wheat deal?

"Yeah," he said. "For one thing, Nixon's enemies list had been created, and did serve to identify one very real serious threat. This threat was discovered when the name of one of the top officials of the private grain exporters suddenly appeared on Nixon's enemies list.   That official was Gerard Louis-Dreyfus, president of the Louis Dreyfus Grain Corporation, a person fully knowledgeable of all the details of Kissinger's Soviet wheat deal. He could not be ignored." Josh paused a moment and then continued, "the seriousness of the threat was closely monitored. A White House memo, marked in   all   caps,   'PERSONAL   AND   EXTREMELY CONFIDENTIAL,' alerted Haldeman of the serious risk Gerard Louis-Dreyfus, president of the Louis Dreyfus Corporation, represented to the President.   Haldeman was warned that this was a serious risk, and that it represented real trouble for the White House.   According to the new internal security network, it had been discovered that Gerard, at the same time he was participating in the wheat deal, had contributed $1,500.00 to George McGovern's campaign for president. That is what caused him to be prominently placed on Nixon's enemies list."

"Was it only his financial contribution to McGovern that made him such a threat to the White House?" Amber inquired.

"No, not by a long shot. That was probably the least part of it," Josh replied. "The bigger threat was more his philosophical bent. It had been discovered that Gerard had a known reputation within the grain industry of being an unpredictable individualist who just happened to have come from a long family line of grain dynasties, such as the Bunge Corporation and the Louis Dreyfus Corp. He was a maverick within the grain industry who was supporting the Democratic antiwar candidate McGovern. And now from his high corporate position, he knew all the secrets that, if released, could have seriously damaged the President."

"With his being an active participant in the grain fraud, how serious was the risk that he would actually leak information to the Democrats?" Amber asked.

"Actually," Josh replied, "the risk was probably relatively shallow. But, whether the risk was real or not and regardless of how it might be analyzed, the Gerard factor stood as a potential threat to President Nixon and Kissinger's Soviet wheat deal. It was real enough not be ignored," Josh emphasized. "In fact, considering the seriousness of the risk, the White House could take no chances that Gerard might go off on some tangent, as part of his social crusade, disregarding the fact that his own company was making big profits from the Soviet wheat deal. "

"He sounds like an interesting person," Amber observed.

"He was, I have read up on him," Josh began. "William Gerard Louis-Dreyfus earned his B.A. and law

degrees at Duke University in North Carolina.   After law
school, he joined Dewey, Ballantine, Bushby, Palmer &
Wood, a prestigious New York law firm which represented the
American division of the family grain company, the Louis
Dreyfus Company.   Practicing as a corporate lawyer for seven
years, Gerard got bored or something and deserted the legal
profession.   From being a lawyer, he became a journalist in
Raleigh, North Carolina, and as a journalist during the early
1960s, he was active in the American civil rights movement,
with his idealism tinged with questionable pragmatism.   He
once admitted that as a journalist, writing about civil rights, if
he couldn't find the right black family to illustrate a point, he
simple made them up."

    "I would like to meet this guy," Amber noted.

    "Yeah," Josh continued with his review. "I am sure
you will one of these days. He was interesting, but the White
House saw no humor in it, and was concerned about him, as a
threat.   Gerard had not joined the family grain business until
he was 30, but then, after six years with the American division
of the Louis Dreyfus Company, he was named one of eight
vice presidents. A year and one half later, he was appointed to
the board of directors and then named president of the
American division. He had assumed the top leadership role at
the company just as Kissinger's Soviet Wheat Sale began to
unfold."

    "Other than putting him on Nixon's enemies list, what
could the White House do to counter the Gerard factor?"
Amber asked.

"That was the problem facing the White House. There was not much the White House could do had Gerard personally decided to leak information to the Democrats," Josh replied.

"I can see where the White House was in a real pickle," Amber said. "What could, or better yet, what was done to address the Gerard risk factor?"

"Had he leaked information about the wheat deal, the illegal payoffs to the private exporters and the fraudulent component, it could have resulted in untold damage. I would not even want to speculate about this," Josh cautioned.

"So, what had to be done as the most practical solution?"

"As I see it, the White House was limited to preventative measures!" Josh exclaimed in his firm voice.

"What does that mean?" Amber asked.

Josh did not answer for the longest moment, then he explained. "A workable preventive measure would have to be something that gave the White House immediate notice of any information leak and with enough time to react to any leak discovered."

"Explain that a little more," Amber asked.

"Well," began Josh, "before allowing the Soviet wheat deal to advance beyond the point of no return, the White House had to gain a level of certainty of knowing whether Gerard or any other person had leaked material information about the Soviet wheat deal to the Democrats or anyone else."

"That seemed like a super challenge," Amber inserted.

"Maybe so, but it was a challenge that had to be met successfully," Josh explained. "The White House needed to reserve its ability to withdraw or scratch the wheat deal, if it were discovered that information had been leaked. But, for this part of the plan to work," Josh continued, "the White House needed to know immediately if information about the wheat deal had been leaked to the Democrats, and the White House needed to gain this knowledge in time to take whatever action was considered necessary, even withdrawing the plan before the wheat deal had become too firmly committed."

"Was that accomplished?"

"In a sense, it was," Josh said in a soft voice. "The choices available to the White House were few. Considering the extraordinary risk, perceived or in fact, of the Gerard factor, the most rational option considered was some surreptitious entry into the Democratic National Committee to examine or copying of DNC records and files, and to plant wiretaps to allow interception of conversations within the DNC. If successful, the White House would have a working monitoring system within the DNC, with the capability of placing the White House on immediate notice of any leak of information about the wheat deal. If an information leak had been discovered, the White House could then back off from the wheat deal. But, after monitoring DNC conversations for a period of time, about two week, and no leaks of information were overheard, the White House could more confidently allow Kissinger's wheat deal to continue, knowing that with this there would be peace in Vietnam."

"My god, you're talking about Watergate," Amber exclaimed in a startled voice. "What a risky plan. I can't believe it. I just can't believe it."

"But with the war continuing, it seemed like a good risk at the time," Josh added. "That is what I kept hearing while at the White House."

"Who came up with the plan for making an entry into the DNC to install the wiretaps?"

"I don't know," Josh told her. "But, remember what I told you about Nixon's creation of the White House Internal Security Unit. Logically it was this unit that Nixon had created back in February of 1971."

"I remember," Amber echoed. "I remember the exact date; it was February 4 of 1971."

"Good memory!"

"Well, I have been living and relieving this story for a long time."

"You have," Josh added with a big smile that conveyed his pride for his friend. "Do you also remember when the White House in early January 1971, brought in E. Howard Hunt to perform special assignments considered very sensitive in nature."

"I remember that too," Amber said in a voice that showed her pride. "Hunt was the highly experienced, retired CIA agent, who had over twenty years experience in techniques of physical and electronic surveillance, photography, and the installation of electronic devices." She paused a moment, then added, "Josh, it's all coming together, thanks to you."

"No thanks to me," Josh insisted, "this is your project, and what you have already done to bring forth the truth has been masterful."

In her continuing construct of the parallel chronologies of the wheat deal and White House internal security, Amber ran though a mental inventory of what she already knew. She had already determined that Kissinger's wheat deal had been allowed to advance as the private exporters continued down their path of stealing grain from the poorest countries of the world. This alone, she thought, served as a positive indicator that Nixon's new security system was firmly in place and working. She knew the wheat deal that had led us to peace in Vietnam had its operational beginning when Kissinger issued his call on January 31, 1972, for the USDA to prepare the negotiating scenario for the grain trade with the Soviets. On the security side of her chronologies, Kissinger's negotiating scenario was delivered three days before G. Gordon Liddy stood ready to make his presentation to Attorney General Mitchell of his "Gemstone" security operation, the plan that would lead to the necessary surreptitious entry into the DNC. It was this operation that would tell the White House whether the Soviet wheat deal could safely proceed.

Based on Liddy's far reaching security operation called, "Gemstone" that he presented to the Attorney General, Amber was convinced that Liddy had not been fully aware of the underlying objective of the security operation. At his meeting with John Mitchell, Liddy came fully prepared for a full scale security operation, far exceeding the needs of the White House.   His "Gemstone" plan covered the entire political Democratic universe. He was prepared to wrap his security tentacles around all aspects of Democratic operations and political campaigns. Armed with a series of three-feet-by-four-feet, commercially prepared, multi-color charts, Liddy spelled-out in crystal detail his proposed new security operation. Attorney General Mitchell and John Dean would listen to the plan in disbelief.

Each separate operational arm of Liddy's "Gemstone" was identified by the name of a precious or semiprecious stone.   "Diamond" designated the counter-demonstration operational arm; "Ruby" referred to the use of political spies infiltrated into the Democratic camps; "Emeralds" identified the use of chase planes to eavesdrop on the Democratic candidate's aircraft; "Quartz" was the operational arm involving microwave interception of telephone traffic; "Crystal" covered electronic surveillance; and "Sapphire" identified the use of prostitutes. Other operational segments of the "Gemstone" operation were dubbed "opals," "topaz," "turquoise," "coal," and "brick." Considering the scope of the elaborate plan, it seems obvious that Liddy had no understanding that the planned target was limited to the Democratic National Headquarters, and there but for only a narrow purpose.

After two rejections, Liddy's less elaborate security plan for entry into the DNC for photographing documents and wiretapping the telephones was approved by Mitchell as head of the White House Internal Security Unit. This was all that was needed, but Liddy did not need to know this. The object of the limited security plan was to give the White House the ability to discover whether information about the planned Soviet wheat deal had been leaked to the Democrats. And if a leak had occurred, the White House would have time to react, scrapping the entire operation if necessary.

Attorney General Mitchell's approval came three days after Secretary Butz sent to the President the final version of Kissinger's grain negotiating scenario with the Soviets. He approved "Gemstone III" with a limited budget of $250,000, for entry into the Democratic National Committee headquarters for electronic surveillance and photographing of documents. The entry needed to be carefully planned and timed to coincide with Nixon's travels to his Moscow summit, where the wheat deal was expected to be secretly finalized. Everything was moving smoothly, just as the team had planned and carefully trained, coinciding all moves to the political moves of the President.

On Saturday, May 20, at 9:27 a.m., the President's entourage left Washington for the historic Moscow summit aboard the "Spirit of 76," arriving two days later. Right at that point-in-time, as if carefully synchronized, the "Gemstone" break-in team landed in Washington and registered at the Manger-Hamilton Hotel, just waiting for their next signal. The next signal the team would receive would be the target date for entry into the DNC, scheduled for May 26, two days before the scheduled signing of agreements President Nixon reached at the Moscow summit.

Meanwhile in Moscow, President Nixon and Henry Kissinger were playing their diplomatic cards, expecting to sign the grain agreement that would create a concrete sense of political victory for Nixon. Formal signing was scheduled for May 28, two days after the target date for the DNC break-in.

Preplanned to coincide with Nixon's Moscow Summit, the highly trained break-in team stood ready to move into action. Hunt's wife had booked a banquet room large enough for ten to twelve persons in the name of a fictitious company, to serve as cover. When the time approached Hunt, Liddy, and the Cuban-Americans, convened in the Continental Room of the Watergate Hotel for dinner and drinks. After everyone had been served, the hotel waiter was excused so their "board meeting" could begin. As the team went into the final steps toward their objective, sounds of the team's serious planning were deflected by a travelogue film that ran repeatedly. The team members dispersed at 10:00 p.m., moving as a team toward their target area. After two frustrated attempts, the team finally succeeded in gaining entry into the DNC. Once inside, McCord's highly skilled and disciplined team quickly and efficiently installed electronic bugging devices and photographed papers from DNC files. After their highly successful execution of their well designed and executed plan, the entry team met Hunt and Liddy at the command post for a brief victory celebration, and then headed home to Miami – "Mission Accomplished." Indeed, Amber thought, this celebration was in order, for the mission had surely been a great a success.

A priority for the White House and Kissinger's wheat for peace operation was security that rang more urgent in view of the lingering Gerard problem. Kissinger needed to know whether Gerard or someone else had leaked information to the Democratic Party. For this, the White House had a good start, now with access to all the DNC documents photographed by McCord's break-in team. From these photographed documents, the White House would be able to determine with a level of certainty whether any information about the wheat deal had previously been leaked. But this would cover only the past, but this was not enough to give the White House the security confidence needed. An equally pressing need was future possible leaks.

The White House needed a period of time to monitor the future conversations coming in and going out of the DNC offices. This was the purpose of the wire taps installed by McCord's break-in team. During the break-in, Alfred C. Baldwin, III, a former FBI agent, stood as a lookout across the street from the Democratic headquarters, at the Howard Johnson Motor Lodge. Baldwin's principal continuing assignment was to intercept the telephone conversations from the DNC phones tapped by McCord's team. He would receive these intercepted calls through his well-equipped listening post. Baldwin wold type the conversations almost verbatim, and give the logs to James McCord, the break-in team leader, who would deliver them to the White House. This was the security needed by the White House to make a reasoned calculation on whether information had been leaked to the Democrats. Through the intercepted DNC telephone calls, the White House could gain the confidence level needed to give the signal that the Soviet wheat deal could safely proceed.

As a result of the success of McCord's break-in team, the White House gained the ability to monitor and summarize the telephone conversations intercepted from the Democratic National Committee.   From the intercepted DNC calls, the White House could hear if there had been any leaks of information about Kissinger's wheat deal.   With the wiretaps, installed during the first Watergate break-in going undetected, the White House had the capacity to listen in on conversations within the DNC for three full weeks.   During this three weeks of monitoring DNC calls, the White House heard nothing that even suggested a leak of information.   Based on this knowledge, the White House could confidently give the go ahead signal for the wheat deal to begin.   As a result of the success of the DNC break-in on May 28, Kissinger's Soviet wheat for peace plan, proceeded safely and confidently.

Success of Liddy's "Gemstone" security operation had furnished the White House three weeks of uninterrupted access to DNC telephone conversations, probably more than enough time to give the White House the confidence needed to allow the wheat deal to advance. Relying on that well placed confidence, the Soviet wheat deal was in fact launched on June 27, 1972, the day Kissinger received word that the Soviet Minister of Foreign Trade and the Soviets' chief negotiator, Mikhail R. Kuzmin, had arrived in Washington to complete the grain deal. After he received this message, Kissinger, unable to control his excitement, immediately interrupted a White House meeting between the President and H.R. Haldeman to excitedly announce to them that he had settled the Vietnam war. Kissinger wanted Nixon to publicly announce this feat right then, and shout the news to the world.

But Nixon thought otherwise. For political reasons, Nixon was not ready for the peace agreement to be publicly announced. In order to restrain Kissinger from making any announcement that America's involvement in Vietnam was over on that happy day of June 27, Nixon instructed Alexander Haig to make certain that Henry's desire for a settlement does not prevail. An announcement too quickly could have changed the course of history. With Kissinger's continuing excitement over ending the war, Nixon, the politician, explained to Haldeman that ending the Vietnam war too quickly was the one way we can lose the election. Amber thought on this a long time before concluding in her mind that for one thing certain in the course of history, had Kissinger announced to the public on that June 27, that he had a Vietnam peace agreement, George McGovern would probably not have won nomination at the Democratic National Convention as the Democrats presidential candidate. Keeping alive the Vietnam issue served Nixon's political advantage. It kept the Senate Democrats on the hook for a longer period of time, and it made more probable that the Democrats would more likely nominate an anti-Vietnam candidate, someone like McGovern. Announcing the Vietnam peace agreement prior to the beginning of the Democratic National Convention would have eliminated Vietnam as a campaign issue. With Vietnam eliminated as an issue, Amber thought, who would have won the Democrats nomination?

Amber was now ready to write her series of news articles on how Nixon ended the Vietnam war. She would write about the leveraging of wheat and how this had meant the wheat farmers had to be sacrificed on the market price for wheat. She would write about Nixon's political strategy in delaying the announcement of peace until the Democrats had first nominated McGovern as their presidential candidate. And, she would write about how the wheat deal's fraudulent component had compelled the creation of the White House's internal security unit that operated independently of the FBI. Amber was ready to write, and twenty independent newspapers were committed to publish the series. This was the life of a freelance reporter.

CHAPTER TWELVE

*T*wenty-five independent newspapers, excepting the *New York Times* and the *Washington Post*, published the first part of Amber Nicole Highlander's five part wheat for peace series. As soon as these papers hit the newsstand on Sunday, July 28, 1974, her telephone began ringing with invitations to appear on radio and television talk shows. Little did Amber know that shortly after the second segment of her five-part series was published on August 4, Richard Nixon would announce his resignation from office. Josh had called her on August 8, after hearing the President's speech. "Amber, it finally happened!"

"What, finally happened? Amber blurted out, not knowing what Josh was talking about.

"Nixon resigned."

"I'm sorry I missed it, but the news will play it over and over. You weren't surprised were you?"

"No! As we talked about what Nixon faced, it is my

opinion that Nixon's resignation had long been planned by him and his legal counsel John Dean. My guess is that under the plan, the timing of President Nixon's resignation announcement was set by what the House Judiciary Committee did on the Articles of Impeachment."

"That makes sense to me," Amber said. "You know that Committee adapted three of the Articles of Impeachment toward the end of July. The last Article was voted out on July 30, 1974."

"I know," Josh acknowledged. "I am saddened by the resignation, but, I understand now that it had to be. Amber, your investigative work helped me understand why the resignation of the President of the United States had become necessary. Are you going to modify your third segment of your series of articles?"

"I don't have time to change that segment that comes out on Sunday, August 11. But I will write a separate article on the resignation."

"Are you going to claim some personal credit for Nixon's resignation," Josh asked with a grin, knowing what Amber's answer would be.

"Of course not! But the juxtaposition of the articles and the resignation is interesting. I am sure there will be comments."

After all five parts of Amber's series had been published, along with the additional articles on Nixon's resignation, the calls increased. Most of the calls and comments were confirmations, but some newspapers challenged the accuracy of the facts and conclusions stated in her articles. She was publically rebuffed by many, but she never backed down. Interestingly, though, none of the private grain exporters voiced any public criticism or challenges to her series. They simply remained silent, refusing all comments. The challenges raised against Amber's articles were based principally upon the serious and open conflicts between her articles and John Dean's testimony given before the Senate Watergate Committee back on June 25, 1973. Amber had attended every session of Dean's appearance before the Ervin Committee, when he told his version Watergate. She had listened carefully to every word, but, she also listened to what he did not say. Dean's factual omissions, she thought, were more telling than the story-line he offered. Reflecting back on his testimony and his response to the questions from Committee members, and reading and rereading everything Dean said, Amber remained confident in her articles. She was quite aware of the variances between her articles and Dean's Senate testimony. But she was confident her articles were accurate.

Her research and investigation had been too thorough; and her sources too reliable. So, why the variances? she thought. In searching for answers, she would follow the advice her friend Josh gave her, to reread Dean's Senate testimony. Her twenty-five newspapers were loving it and had complete confidence in Amber's work. In fact, more newspapers were wanting to publish her articles. Amber Nicole Highlander's name had spread across the land and had not been overlooked by her Oklahoma wheat-farmer friends. They were proud of their freelance journalist.

Amber once again carefully reviewed Dean's testimony before the Senate Watergate Committee, when he began by somberly reading his prepared 245-page statement, copies of which had been provided the Committee members and the media present. As he began reading, at about 10:10 that morning, a hush came over the hearing room, and Amber and the other reporters at the press table attentively listened, turning the pages simultaneously to keep up with the text. He did not reach the end of his prepared statement until 6:05 p.m., when Chairman Sam Ervin announced recess until the next morning, when Dean would return to the Committee to face questions.

The key point Dean stressed to the Committee was that the Watergate break-in was not something planned by the white House. It had just happened. It was like an accident or bad dream. Amber had underlined these words, thinking at the time that they were not believable to her. She began suspecting that Dean's testimony had been carefully scripted to stay within the narrow lines drawn by President Nixon, that the break-in made no sense. Amber reasoned that if the break-in made no sense, the Senate Committee, inquiring into reasons, would find no clear motive. The Committee would then accept that it was all an accident of fate, just as Dean suggested. Dean's testimony seemed to reinforce the President's version of Watergate, that there was no motive or planning behind the break-in. Amber began to think that Dean had set out to create a lasting image that the break-in was just a fluke, growing out of a pattern of pervasive conduct that included wiretapping and other covert activity. "The Watergate matter," Dean told Committee members, "was an inevitable out-growth of a climate of excessive concern over the political impact of demonstrators, excessive concern over leaks, an insatiable appetite for political intelligence, all coupled with a do-it yourself White House staff, regardless of the law." Dean made no mention of Kissinger's Soviet wheat deal, as he kept repeating, it was all "an accident of fate," and not the product of any "conscious design." It just happened!

It happened, Dean explained, after the White House's concern about information leaks took a quantum jump after the first segment of the Pentagon Papers was published by the *New York Times* on Sunday, June 13, 1971. Amber had also underlined this portion of Dean's testimony. She was impressed with this part of his testimony. He had identified a clear, visible, tangible reason that could arguably explain the timing of the break-in, the publication of the Pentagon Papers. With his testimony, he had skillfully fixed a precise date of the occurrence of that observable event that offered a rational explanation for the break-in, thereby eliminating any need to look at anything prior to that magical date of June 13. Based on that part of Dean's testimony alone, nothing occurring before that date was important or relevant. So, with that set date, Dean had no need to testify about Nixon's internal security decisions back in February, because they predated the exact date the Pentagon Papers were made public. Very clever, Amber thought.

The Pentagon Papers were a secret study of the Vietnam war. They were prepared during the Johnson administration, to document the events leading to the war. They were a complete unabridged history of that war. Until leaked to the *New York Times* by Daniel Ellsberg, the study had been considered highly confidential. Leaking these highly confidential records, Dean testified, planted the seed of paranoid mentality, that led the White House into its beginning of illegal spying and wiretapping, the creation of the White House internal security unit, later called the "Plumbers' Unit", and from there, as if inevitably, to the Watergate break-in. Amber was impressed with just how neatly all the pieces fit within the frame-work of Dean's picture of the Watergate paranoia. Dean's image presented a clear explanation of the why of the Watergate break-in.

Unbelievable, Amber thought. But even as a skeptical news reporter who questioned everything, she was impressed with how Dean had put all the parts together in a neat fit, and yet without telling the whole story. His explanation changed the entire thrust of Watergate and made the story sound plausible. But, Amber knew Dean's story-line omitted the most critical block of evidence. His version, that the break-in was merely an accident of fate, occurring by chance only as an overreaction to the *Times'* publication of the Vietnam war study, simply was not true. From all the evidence she had collected, she knew Nixon's security measures had in fact been carefully planned and fully implemented, way back in

February of '71, long before the Pentagon Papers' incident saw the light of day.   Nonetheless, Dean's skillfully crafted testimony provided protection for President Nixon and Kissinger.   It shielded them from any link to the wheat agreement with the Soviets. Had Dean identified the February 1971 security measures of the President as the start of it all, he would have lost the important causation link to the Pentagon Papers.   It would then have become necessary for him to explain why the White House was running from J. Edgar Hoover and the FBI.

Amber decided she needed to take a break from thinking about Watergate and John Dean's Senate testimony. She needed to clear her mind. So, she went outside and sat on her patio in her own green chair to liberate her mind, taking with her a glass of scotch and water. As she sat there, she gazed into the sky watching the clouds. Her patio had become her place to think or not to think, a place where time could pass so quickly or stand still.   After sitting there for the moments she needed, she decided to take a walk along the C & O Canal. Life is wonderful, she thought.

Returning to her apartment with a clearer mind, Amber once again read Dean's prepared statement, focusing on the part about how the Pentagon Papers had started it all. She was personally acquainted with Daniel Ellsberg, the person they claimed leaked the secret Vietnam study to the *Times* and *Post*, as part of his antiwar voice.   Later, Ellsberg admitted this and claimed that it was his leak of the secret Vietnam study that had caused the Watergate break-in. This, Amber thought, was a claim drawn from Dean's testimony. That idea, in fact, became the generally accepted theme of Watergate , and from there, the story would grow. Amber found the story-line fascinating, and yet, so contrary to her own findings

Dean's story-line became entrenched. That publication of the Pentagon Papers by the *Times*, had, according to the White House, been such a gross transgression of national security, it created international havoc. As the official story went, Nixon had become so concerned with the consequences of allowing Ellsberg to get away with leaking such highly classified documents to newspapers, he demanded swift action by the FBI. But, according to the emerging story-line, J. Edgar Hoover put his personal friendship with Ellsberg's father-in-law, Louis Marx, a wealthy, ultraconservative toy manufacturer, ahead of the President, in terms of priority. That, out of this friendship, according to the story, the Director of the FBI declined to give the "Pentagon Papers" more than a minimum-priority, even refusing to assign a special FBI task force to the matter. In Amber's mind, this was one of the most hilarious political scenarios being offered as an explanation for the creation of the White House's internal security unit.

Amber played the official scenario over and over in her mind, that faced with such a do-nothing attitude by Hoover, the White House decided to create its own task force. One view Amber heard was that Nixon got mad as hell about Hoover's lack of vigorous investigation into Ellsberg, and had angrily blurted out "that if nobody in this damn government is going to do anything about the serious problem of Ellsberg's unpardonable leak of classified information, then, by God, we'll do it ourselves." This part of the story-line shows Nixon ordering Ehrlichman to set up an independent White House internal security unit to stop leaks. And, according to that scenario, the White House internal security unit was established on July 17, 1971. Thus, the birth of the "Plumbers Unit."

Amber knew this part of Dean's story-line collided head-on with the compelling evidence she had collected, that Nixon had in fact created the White House internal security unit by written order, on February 4, 1971. She knew this because she held in her possession, a copy of that presidential order, directing Attorney General Mitchell and H. R. Haldeman to establish the White House internal security unit. Back in February 1971, several months before the Pentagon Papers, Nixon's object for creating the ISU, was to gain White House security independence from the FBI and J. Edgar Hoover. Nixon had determined that this security independence needed to be firmly in place before Kissinger's wheat deal with the Soviets, could be permitted to advance. There was no lingering doubt in Amber's mind that Nixon's creation of the White House internal security unit had nothing at all to do with the publication of the Pentagon Papers. The Pentagon Papers had not even been published at the time Nixon issued his order to John Mitchell. She was firmly convinced that the underlying motivation behind the creation of the internal security unit was to shield all the illegal activity behind the wheat deal, including the billion dollar stealing-scheme used to pay-off the private exporters.

Amber was confident in the accuracy of her version of the events, based on hard evidence. Her version in fact finds confirmation from Nixon himself, something John Dean left out of his Senate testimony. During a conversation between the President and Haldeman about the motivation behind the break-in, occurring a few days after the Watergate arrests, Nixon expressly admitted that the cause of the break-in had been "this financial thing." Nothing was said about the Pentagon Papers during that conversation. It was that "financial thing," Haldeman said, and Nixon agreed

This "financial thing," Amber thought, could have only had reference to the billion-dollar illegal payoffs to the private grain exporters. Standing alone, that grain deal, of such financial proportions, was a serious criminal transgression as well as a gross civil fraudulent violation. If ever made public, the White House, the USDA, and the private grain exporters could be exposed to serious legal criminal and civil consequences. Considering the potential consequences, the White House knew it could no longer afford the presence of Hoover and the FBI in its security network. Amber had determined that change was needed with respect to White House security. And change did occur. The White House's independent internal security unit was created on February 4, 1971, with the purpose being to remove Hoover from the scene of White House Security.

The story-line that the internal security unit was

created out of a reaction to Hoover's disapproval of and refutation of Nixon's call for the FBI to investigate Ellesberg's leaking of the Pentagon Papers to the *Times*, clashes squarely with the facts. Amber thought, how unreal was the story that Hoover thumbed his nose at President Nixon, by his refusal to give priority to an investigation of Ellsberg. How likely was it that Hoover ever rebuffed the President, and still kept his job? Amber decided to call her friend Joshua and pose these questions to him. When she got him on the line, she explained what she was coming up with in her review of Dean's Senate testimony. She was hoping to get his confirmation that she was on the right track. Specifically, she asked, "How likely was it that Hoover ever rebuffed President Nixon?"

Before Josh offered a direct response to Amber's question, he reminded her of a bit of Hoover history. "Amber, you need to remember that Hoover had served a term as director of the FBI for a period spanning eight Presidents." Then, he posed a rhetorical question to her, "Do you think Hoover could have survived eight presidents had he rebuffed any one of them?" Not expecting any answer to his rhetorical question, Josh added with emphasis, "Nixon demanded and received strict loyalty from everyone in the White House. Any agency-head rebuffing him would have been fired on the spot. I know from my time working at the White House as one of Haldeman's assistants, that Richard Nixon demanded and got complete loyalty from his top advisers. And this included his legal counsel." Then he paused a moment to reflect, "One good example I remember, might help you understand. It was back in 1970, when Secretary of Interior Walter J. Hickel crossed President Nixon, openly criticizing him after the Kent State campus antiwar incident on May 4, 1970. When this happened," Josh added, "all hell broke loose in the White House."

Amber broke in, "Didn't that Kent State incident involve the platoon of National Guardsmen who opened fire on a group of student demonstrators, killing four of them and wounding eight?"

"That's it," Josh said. Then he continued his story. "After Kent State, Secretary Hickel sent a letter to the President, scolding him for embracing a philosophy that showed so little respect toward student demonstrators. He might have gotten by with that," Josh speculated, "had the letter remained private and confidential to the President. But Hickel, for some personal reason, thought he had to make the letter public. He sent a copy to the *New York Times*, which published it on May 7, 1970. I remember that so well," Josh said, "and I remember that the President was so furious. He told Haldeman that Hickel had broken his pick and needed to resign, and until then, the President directed the staff and cabinet members to give Hickel 'hell' and to act extremely cold toward him."

"Did Nixon ever get Hickel to resign?" Amber asked.

"Well at first, Hickel declined to voluntarily resign, even resisting his firing. He believed he had become untouchable because he had the support of the press. Nixon, at first, showed his pragmatic side by delaying the firing until after the 1970 mid-term elections. But as soon as those elections were over, Nixon told Hickel he had to go. When Hickel inquired whether his departure would be at the first of the year, Nixon responded emphatically that it would be effective immediately." Another pause, this one a little longer, then Josh asked , "Amber do you still think J. Edgar Hoover would rebuff President Nixon?"

Hearing the story about Hickel, and Josh's rhetorical question, Amber asked, "Is it possible that J. Edgar Hoover rebuffed President Nixon?" Then, she added, "Was there a difference between Hickel and Hoover?"

"Very unlikely."

"That helps a lot. Thanks Josh, good talking to you."

"Bye Amber."

After her thirty-minute conversation with Josh, Amber poured a glass of wine and went to her patio to think more about Dean's Senate testimony. If the story about Hoover rebuffing the President cannot stand, there are probably more weaknesses in Dean's Senate testimony. Amber knew there were other conflicts that further discredited Dean's testimony. The most striking conflict, Amber thought, was with the date the internal security unit had been created. According to the scenario created through an interpretation of Dean's testimony, the internal security unit was established on July

17, 1971, in direct response to the publication of the Pentagon Papers. This conflicted with the written document, a copy of which was held by Amber, that confirmed that the creation of the unit was on February 4, 1971, long before the Pentagon Papers. Amber reminded herself that this February 4 order was only one part of a patten of internal security decisions, all made by the President during the month of February of 1971. In her mind, it was clear that Dean was not correct on the date he gave as the date when the unit was first created. She reasoned that such material variances, raise questions about the credibility of Dean's entire testimony.

Based almost solely on Dean's testimony, the dominate view of Watergate emerged that the White House internal security unit had been created out of Nixon's reaction to being rebuffed by J. Edgar Hoover on an investigation of the person suspected of leaking the Pentagon papers. As a counterpoint, Amber points to the February 4 document and other hard evidence she had collected that establishes rather compellingly that the internal security unit had been created with the object of taking Hoover and his FBI totally out of the White House security picture. Dean testified that the break-in at the DNC had not been part of any conscious design or planning. That it just happened. Amber knew this was not so! She had documented the careful planning that went into the decision to authorize the break-in. As she viewed the situation, Amber became convinced there was no reconciling or harmonizing of the stark variances existing between Dean's Senate testimony and the views she drew from the evidence –

one is right and one is wrong, she acknowledged.

In identifying the multiple conflicts between Dean's testimony and the evidence she had collected, Amber realized that John Dean, in offering his testimony before the U. S. Senate Committee, never claimed he was offering a complete factual review of the events.   For one thing, based on an agreement reached between the White House and the Watergate prosecutors and the Senate Committee, Dean was excused absolutely and unequivocally from testifying about anything relating to Kissinger's wheat deal with the Soviets. This agreement restricted the scope of Dean's testimony, and was strictly enforced by the Committee chair, Sam Ervin of North Carolina.   As a fact, there would be no testimony about Watergate in the context of Nixon's foreign policy.

Senator Sam Ervin, chair of the Senate Watergate Committee, did in fact strictly enforce the agreement that the Committee not inquire into Nixon's foreign policy.   All testimony was limited to domestic presidential politics. Amber remembered during Dean's testimony that one of the Committee members had asked him a question touching on foreign policy.   When this question was posed, the Chair immediately halted the testimony and asserted that such inquiry went beyond the limits agreed upon.   The question about Nixon's foreign policy is beyond the Committee's scope of inquiry.   Chairman Ervin announced: "The committee is anxious to avoid disclosing any matters which affect national security, which are matters defined as matters relating to national defense or relating to our relations with other nations."   This limitation on the Watergate inquiry preordained that all Nixon-Kissinger meetings involving the agreement with the Soviets to exchange wheat for peace would be excluded. This restriction then, Amber reasoned, established an evidentiary limitation that made it impossible for the Committee to ever gain the full truth about Watergate. As a consequence, she thought, the history of Watergate would long remain distorted. Now, she only hoped her series of articles would serve as a breakthrough toward allowing that truth to finally emerge.

Amber decided to go though Dean's Senate testimony once again, this time comparing it with information she had collected from different sources. She wanted to continue trying to find some way to reconcile the conflicting views, knowing she faced an improbability. She wanted to test the credibility of Dean's testimony, thinking that the most striking thing was his view that everything about Watergate was somehow linked to the *Times'* publication of the Pentagon Papers. That single incident, Dean explained, had led to the White House's wiretapping program, and the creation of the White House internal security unit on July 17, 1971. With this precise date and event, the Committee made no effort to inquire into matters occurring prior to the Pentagon Papers' publication date of June 13, 1971.

Amber saw this as a highly skilled design by Dean to keep the Watergate inquiry tightly confined to a narrow ambit of domestic presidential politics. She knew Dean's time frame had helped accomplish this by excluding all the evidence she knew was highly relevant to showing the truer underlying motivation behind the break-in. But, again, she reminded herself, Dean never said he was telling the full story of Watergate. Amber had long been convinced that John Dean may well have told the truth, but not the full truth. Comparing his testimony to the material she had collected, there were several material conflicts. It all began to make more sense to her after she realized Dean never said his testimony was complete. He did give his sworn oath that the evidence he was giving to the Senate Committee "shall be the truth, *the whole truth*, and nothing but the truth, so help me God." He would be tested on this, during the second day of his testimony, when Senator Joseph Montoya, of New Mexico, confronted him about truth-telling. During that exchange, Dean began sparring philosophically with Senator Montoya on the subject of truth.

Amber decided to call Josh again and use him as her sounding board, as she had so often done. "Josh, I listened to all of John Dean's testimony and I have now read and reread the transcripts, and I am convinced he did not tell the complete story of Watergate. He left out highly critical evidence that most likely would have changed the entire landscape of Watergate."

"Are you saying that Dean lied to the Senate Committee," Josh inquired. "You need to be careful about that!"

"I know, libel and all that," Amber acknowledged though displaying no fear that such would ever occur. "I am not saying he lied. I don't believe he did lie. He simply did not tell the whole truth. I know that Dean failed to disclose all data occurring before June 13, the date the *Times* published the first segment of the Pentagon Papers. I know that from the hard evidence I collected."

"What if he had lied?" Josh asked.

Amber did not answer for a long time. There was silence, as she continued holding the phone to her ear. Finally, she answered, "I don't know. I'll call you back." She decided she needed to talk with some philosopher to help her understand the question Josh posed. So she went to see her church pastor and asked him about the concepts of "truth" and "right and wrong." Pastor Bob, as she called him with his consent, was a wise man, educated in England and closely attuned to the politics of Washington and the world. She sat down with Pastor Bob and began talking, "Whether to tell the truth or not to tell the truth; and whether something is right or whether it is wrong seemed always to be issues during Nixon's noble but risky steps toward gaining peace in Vietnam." She stopped for a moment to think, then asked the open ended question, "What are your thoughts on this, Pastor?"

"Well, Amber, you are raising lifelong and century-old questions of mankind," Pastor Bob began. "Whether to tell the truth or not to tell the truth can be a ponderable and profound question that we all must face at different times in our lives as citizen, as doctor, lawyer, judge, corporate manager, or even as a politician and elected office holder.

Truth telling may be an essential component for effective personal and general interchange and communication. Truth telling may also be important for the confidence level we place in decisions of the professionals in whom we put our trust for medical, legal, financial or spiritual help. Yet, truth telling as a concept, standing alone as some sort of internal aspiration, is not a moral command to be defended for its own sake and without reference to some functional value. Truth, morality and integrity are quite clearly not synonymous or equivalent words, though they may frequently intersect in our personal lives as well as the diverse world of business, politics and government."

Without telling the Pastor all the details, for sake of time, Amber asked, "What if the lie and the tragic wrong had served to bring an end to the Vietnam war? Would that make the official wrong any less a wrong?"

"Was the wrong you speak of only an economic wrong?" Pastor Bob asked.

"Yes," Amber said, "but it was a billion dollar rip off of the government."

"But did that billion dollar rip off contribute to the settlement in Vietnam?"

"Yes."

"So, the question I see is whether the loss of one additional life in Vietnam is worth more or less than the billion dollars that were ripped off. For me, Amber, the decision is easy. A single life saved from needless killing is worth tenfold the billion dollar rip-off."

"That is enlightening Pastor Bob, thank you."

Amber took the words she heard from Pastor Bob and thought a lot about them and the balancing of values – a life against the billion dollar illegal payoffs to the private grain exporters who were individually and collectively responsible for the success of Kissinger's exchange of wheat for peace. Without the efforts and the risks of these private exporters, Kissinger's peace deal might not have worked and the war might have continued with the loss of more lives, even one life. Amber had listened and played over-and-over in her mind Pastor Bob's explanation, and based on what she kept hearing, she began to reason that one might well claim justification for disregarding law or ethics if the objective sought is lofty enough such as peace in Vietnam. Amber continued theorizing that Nixon may have considered peace in Vietnam as a noble enough objective to justify sacrificing the wheat farmers and allowing private grain exporters to become enriched through their stealing of PL 480 grain.

With the words of Pastor Bob now embedded in her mind, Amber turned back to the dialogue on truth telling between Senator Montoya and John Dean. During that exchange, Dean was asked by Montoya, how he could "expect to resolve the truth in this matter when you state one story . . . and the President states another story and does not appear before this committee." Dean responded with somewhat of a philosophical answer on truth, "I think this," Dean told Montoya, "I strongly believe that the truth always emerges. I do not know if it will be during these hearings; I do not know if it will be as the result of the further activities of the special prosecutor. I do not know if it will be through the processes of history. But the truth will [come] out someday." When Amber listened and thought of this philosophical answer, she began to think that he might well have been faithful in his sacred role as legal counsel to President Nixon, carefully protecting his President as a continuing loyal disciple. Amber saw Dean's testimony as creating a story-line, built upon truth that served to create a believable diversion from the full truth about Watergate.

As she studied Dean's Senate testimony more closely, she continued her focus on Senator Montoya's questions. At one point, he asked Dean, "Do you have peace of mind now about what you have done?" Dean replied, "Yes sir." Then he was asked the harder question that could not so casually be answered with an emphatic "Yes." In substance, the Senator asked whether Dean was telling the Committee everything he knew about Watergate, which clearly he was not, Amber believed. His question: *"In disclosing everything that you knew,* do you have a peace of mind and a clear conscience?" This could be viewed as a compound question on whether Dean was "disclosing everything" and whether this gave him "peace of mind." Because Dean knew he was not disclosing everything, he could not answer the question with a clear "Yes." He was testifying under oath. So he gave his noncommittal, yet highly revealing, answer: "I am not here as a sinner seeking a confessional," Dean responded, " but I have been asked to be here to tell the truth, and I had always planned at any time before any forum when asked to tell the truth." So through this exchange between Dean and Montoya, Amber thought it reasonable to conclude that in coming before the Senate Watergate Committee, Dean was *telling the truth but not the whole truth.*

Amber was beginning to suspect that Dean had come before the Senate Watergate Committee as the continuing legal servant to President Nixon. If true, Dean's goal must have been to create a diversion from the full truth of Watergate, keeping it outside the ambit of all matters relating to international relations. It was a matter of protecting the international image of America as a reliable and trusted trading partner. Had Kissinger's dealing with Moscow in making enormous wheat concessions to the Soviets become public, America's image would have surely been severely tarnished. In an effort to avoid such international tragedy, therefore, Henry Kissinger's reputation had to be protected and guarded at all cost, without regard for the real truth. Amber believed, this was John Dean's assignment. For this diversion, Dean needed to paint a picture of Watergate that kept it confined within the narrow scope of American domestic politics, with no involvement of foreign policy or commerce. And that is what Dean in fact did. He did what he had to do, and he did this skillfully and with great success.

Not to be forgotten, John Dean was President Nixon's lawyer, so why would anyone believe him? Amber thought. As Nixon's lawyer, he would be expected to construct a wall of diversion. That's what lawyers do. From the beginning, Dean faced this believability problem. So, in an effort to counter and offset his biased image, and thereby increase his personal credibility as a witness against the President and his White House colleagues, Dean needed to transform himself into a Judas type. Standing as an avowed betrayer of the President, his testimony became more credible and believable.

Dean's transformation began before he was ever scheduled to appear as a witness. Planning for the inevitable, he set out to transform himself, visibly converting his image into a betrayer of his President, just as the Disciple Judas was supposed to have betrayed Christ. At the time Dean was preparing for his transformed role, the Watergate conflagration had already totally engulfed the White House, and it was only a matter of time that President Nixon would call it quits. Toward setting the stage for his orchestrated performance before the Senate Watergate Committee, Dean to Camp David, at the President's suggestion, to escape the news hounds. His assignment was to sort out all the Watergate mess for the President. There, at Camp David, he would be secluded in a pastoral and inspirational locale, where he could think in peace.

It was there while in this peaceful setting that Dean had his "vision of truth." Amber saw a little humor in all this, but she thought Dean's version of his transformation was masterful. While walking deep in the woods surrounding the presidential retreat, he wrestled with his conscience and found the strength to tell the truth. Wow! Amber thought.

According to Dean's version, he began to inwardly engage in a self-debate over lying, taking the Fifth Amendment, or telling the truth. "Whatever else happened in the days, weeks and months ahead," he explained, "I was not going to lie for anybody, even the President. Despite what I'd done for him, I would not take that step. I might go down the drain as Watergate burst its dams, but I would hang on to one piece of myself at least."

Amber was impressed, she had to be. Nonetheless, she could not fully escape her reservations about the genuineness of Dean's crossover from being a Nixon loyalist to his standing as a Judas-type insider, ready to betray his President. Amber thought, Dean's betrayal of Nixon seemed too simple to be real, but yet understandable. His testimony did serve as part of his masterful, orchestrated cover-up. She was convinced the suspicions she had beforehand had been confirmed when she discovered that Dean's Senate testimony had actually been formally endorsed by President Nixon. This reality has been basically ignored until Amber began focusing on the subject. She realized that Dean, as Nixon's lawyer, had been allowed to testify before the Senate Committee only because Nixon had personally released him from the most restrictive attorney-client privilege as well as from Nixon's power of executive privilege. Amber was convinced, it was all a show by Dean, and a masterful one at that.

On June 19, one week before Dean was scheduled to appear before the Senate Watergate Committee, Nixon's new legal Counsel, Len Garment, delivered a letter to Dean and the

Senate Watergate Committee, formally releasing John Dean from the attorney-client privilege. In this letter, that opened the way for Dean to testify, President Nixon also waived his executive privilege. Reading the letter, Amber noted the important limitations on his release. He was released by the President to testify on matters "concerning the Watergate break-in, efforts to cover it up, or any other matters relevant to the inquiry of the Senate Select Committee." He was given the freedom to testify about all "matters relevant to the inquiry." Amber focused on these words that defined the permissible scope of Dean's clearance to testify. She noted in the President's letter, one additional exception. The letter read: "The President is not authorizing any release of legally protected national security material." This, Amber thought, would include everything about the Soviet wheat deal.

Considering the careful wording of Nixon's letter, Dean was not free to testify about things relating to foreign policy, thus excluding Kissinger's wheat for peace deal with the Soviets. Amber learned from reliable sources that Dean's testimony had in fact been planned for several months by the White House. He was not a Judas-type or a betrayer. He was a Nixon loyalist. He had recommended to Nixon that the White House needed go public with its own version of the story of Watergate. Nixon trusted his legal counsel and agreed to Dean's plan. So, in preparation for Dean's anticipated testimony, Nixon reached an agreement with Henry E. Petersen, Assistant Attorney General in charge of Watergate inquiry, limiting the scope of Dean's testimony. The prosecutors and the Senate Watergate Committee agreed that Dean would not be expected to testify about anything relating to foreign policy. It was under that agreement that Nixon could safely allow Dean to stand as a witness against him. In preparation for his testimony, Nixon had cautioned Dean against lying and the importance of telling the truth. He reminded Dean that "if you are going to lie, you go to jail for the lie rather than the crime. So believe me, don't ever lie." The truth though, coming from the lips of Dean, would , by agreement, be strictly limited to domestic matters, with no involvement in foreign policy. This arrangement made it impossible for the full truth about Watergate to ever be brought to the surface within the vision of the public.

During his testimony before the Senate Watergate Committee, Amber again raised the question in her mind, did John Dean lie to the senators? She kept mulling the question over in her mind, and became convinced, he had not lied. She was, however, accepting the difference between lying and not telling the whole truth. In the setting he was in, Dean was not free to tell the whole truth. He was Nixon's lawyer, bound by his sacred attorney-client privilege. As Amber kept thinking about that question, there was a knock on her door. It was Josh who was in Washington for an environmental conference, scheduled to begin on September 9. She was delighted and dropped everything to spend time visiting with him. "How long will you be here?" she asked.

"Four days."

"Are you going to stay here? I'd be happy to have you."

"Maybe tonight," Josh said. "But I need to stay at the hotel this time, because of the conference. There is a dinner tomorrow night at the conference, if you would like to join me."

"I will," she quickly accepted. "When does the conference start?"

"Tomorrow at noon. I came a day early, thinking I might stay over, to give us time to visit."

"Great! Did you hear the news?"

"What?" Josh responded.

"President Ford granted Nixon a complete pardon, on the very day you arrived back in Washington."

"What do you think about that, Amber?"

There was a long pause before Amber answered. "I don't know yet, but I am thinking that a pardon is something good. But I need to think more on it."

Through the afternoon, the two friends sat around Amber's apartment, and then they took a long walk along the C & O Canal, as they visited, catching up on each other's life. That evening, they went out to dinner, and then, as if as a matter of routine, they went to their favorite piano bar. The evening went by so fast. Then the next morning, Amber made coffee and fixed breakfast, and the two talked, eventually reaching the subject of the wheat deal. "Amber, I have been reading all of your articles on the wheat deal. They are getting a lot of attention around the Country.   How is the project going?"

Amber had been holding back on raising her wheat deal project, but was happy when Josh was the one raising it. "It's going good. But I still have questions. Josh, I have been analyzing Dean's testimony, and would like to get your view. In his testimony, Dean, saying it more than once, insisted that Watergate was an accident of fate and not the product of any conscious design. He insisted that there was no hidden motive behind the break-in. But, my findings show the opposite, that there had been careful, detail planning."

"The view offered by Dean that Watergate was only an accident of fate," Josh explained, " was the view that became necessary for the White House's successful cover-up.   It removed from official consideration all the security decisions Nixon had made during January and February of 1971, long before the Pentagon Papers." Joshua went on to explain, "it seemed like a chain reaction. Nixon had no choice but to end Vietnam; he needed the wheat deal to accomplish that task; risk associated with the wheat deal required special internal security consideration; and part of that broad internal security plan that began in February of 1971, inadvertently turned into the Watergate scandal."

"Why did you say that it inadvertently turned into Watergate?" Amber queried.

"I think the two break-ins at the DNC need to be separated," Josh stated. "I don't believe anyone was thinking about Watergate when the first break-in occurred, back in May of 1972. Considered in total context, that first break-in was simply part of the operation of the internal security system that had been set up in the White House in February of 1971. That highly successful entry served to clear the way for the beginning of Kissinger's wheat deal. The decision arose out of a serious, potentially damaging information security breach, when the name of one of the private exporters suddenly appeared on Nixon's enemies list, as a financial contributor to the McGovern campaign." After a moment of thought, Josh added, "If Gerard Louis-Dreyfus had leaked information about Kissinger's Soviet wheat deal to the Democrats, it would have all been over."

"That's my understanding too," Amber added.

"All the cover-up activity that became Watergate, became necessary, only after the second break-in, occurring in June, the time when the team members were arrested. Right at that moment, Nixon's future as President began to unravel, because he could not afford to defend himself." Then Josh added, "when the break-in team got arrested, that was the accident of fate."

"Ah!" Amber responded as if she had experienced a sudden breakthrough. "So to stop the unraveling, John Dean came up with his Pentagon Papers incident theory that arose on June 13, thus taking Watergate out of the time-range of the circumstances that had in fact made the break-in essential."

"It was all part of the cover-up," Josh repeated. "But Dean's testimony was more to protect America's international image than to protect President Nixon." Josh paused once again, and after a period of thought he added, "Amber, I really believe this! I believe that President Nixon was placing his country ahead of himself. Before it was all over, Nixon sacrificed himself to protect the image of American."

"So," Amber added, "In Nixon's efforts to bring an end to the Vietnam war, he allowed the White House to become deeply involved as an active participant in the illegal billion dollar grain fraud. All of this had become necessary because of the increased antiwar attitude pervading America. Pressure from the antiwar activity made Nixon more willing to take desperate chances to end the Vietnam war, even embracing the illegal grain activity.

"And," Josh interjected, "because the White House had become an active participant in the illegal grain fraud, absolute secrecy from the FBI became the imperative for the White House. It was this imperative that had compelled President Nixon, back in February of '71, to order the creation of his own independent White House internal security unit." He paused for the longest moment, then began speaking in a somber voice. "Looking back," Josh reflected, "it is sad that President Richard Nixon had to take on such a heavy burden on his own shoulders. But because he embraced such illegal activity, he could not shift the burden of security over to the FBI. And, as you know Amber, once a public official crosses the line and begins participating in illegal activity, albeit in the name of peace, the consequences mushroom into situations that sometime become uncontrollable. That's what I think happened here. It all grew out of the noble cause of peace in

Vietnam, and ended in the tragedy of Watergate and the loss of a great President."

"You think Nixon was a great President?" Amber asked.

"Why did you ask such a question, Amber? But, my answer is Yes! without any doubt or reservation in my mind. I find it sad that he elected to go down, without waging any fight, through skilled lawyers. His work days started early and he sometimes worked late into the night. He was a committed man to finding peace. He knew what needed to be done, and was willing to do whatever it took to accomplish his lofty goals, including the settlement of the Vietnam war. But, I have to admit, he was a politician."

"What I'm curious about," Amber inquired, "is whether the wheat for peace information held by Nixon and Kissinger was also known to the Senate Watergate Committee."

"I would assume, it was," Josh replied. "But I don't know. What do you think?"

"The evidence suggest to me that the Senate Watergate Committee and the full Senate had been fully, but secretly, informed of Nixon's plans to allow Kissinger to exchange wheat for peace in Vietnam."

"What evidence?" Josh asked.

"Two things, principally," Amber responded. First, I think the agreement between Nixon and the Watergate prosecutors and the Senate Committee, that placed a tight limitation on the scope of the permissible testimony of John

Dean. This to me suggested knowledge of the details. And
secondly and most convincingly, I think the wording of Senate
Resolution 60, authorizing the Senate investigation into
Watergate, supports this position. That Resolution expressly
limits the investigatory powers of the Committee to domestic
politics with no extension into Nixon's foreign policy matters.
The Senate Committee was only authorized 'to conduct an
investigation and study of the extent, if any, to which illegal,
improper, or unethical activities were engaged in by any
persons, acting either individually or in combination with
others, in the presidential election of 1972.'" Amber paused a
moment, then asked Josh, "What do you think now?"

"You make a convincing case that the Senate was fully
aware of all the facts surrounding Kissinger's exchange of
wheat for peace, and understood the imperative for secrecy."
Josh paused, then added, "The concern of the Senate probably
was the protection of the Nation's international image."

"The Nation's international image was the centerpiece
for everyone involved, including President Nixon, John Dean
and the U.S. Senate. And, out of all this commitment," Amber
concluded, "the true cause of Watergate has been covered-up."

"Yes," Josh agreed. "History had to be distorted for
the sake of America's image among the community of
nations."

CHAPTER THIRTEEN

*I*t was a cool September evening. Amber was home, sitting on her patio with a glass of wine, wishing Ken would call. But, he was out of town. So, she used the time to think and work on the puzzles remaining in her mind. Trying to figure everything out, she wanted to make sense out of what she was reading of Dean's Senate testimony. With no deadlines to meet, Amber took long walks along the C&O Canal, and in the evenings she visited her favorite piano bar for a couple of drinks. Out of all this, Amber concluded that John Dean's Senate testimony had offered a believable image of Watergate. It was an image the Senators and the public could easily accept and adopt as the settled theory of Watergate.

The image created by Dean took Nixon's White House off a highly sensitive spot, a spot they did not want to traverse. It was an image the Senators had little choice but to accept, in view of the reality that the White House had become so deeply and directly involved in a fraudulent financial thing of historic proportions that reached into the arena of America's international relationships. That it did fall within the arena of Nixon's foreign policy made it too sensitive for the Senate to even face it directly. In considering whether the U. S.

Congress had been fully aware of the Soviet wheat deal and the billion dollar illegal payoff to private exporters, Amber examined more closely the hearings on the Soviet wheat deal. From there, she became convinced that Congress's awareness became evident from the shallowness of the Congressional Committee's investigations into the Soviet wheat deal.

When exercising its duty and power to investigate the Watergate break-in, the Senate appeared to have closed all eyes to the billion dollar financial fraud that had paved the way for Nixon's exit out of Vietnam. In collectively closing their eyes, the Senators had zero concern toward protecting Richard Nixon. Their serious concern was that public disclosure of the truth could seriously damage America's international image as an honest, reliable ally and trading partner. Viewing the total picture, Kissinger had extended huge economic concessions to the Soviets, not offered to any other country, and stood ready to abandon South Vietnam. Out of those same economic concessions, the Soviets were prepared to abandon its ally, North Vietnam. Kissinger's wheat deal had opened the door to a disdained method of relationships among nations, bribery in commerce and trading nation against nation. As Amber theorized in her own mind, it was out of this concern that the U. S. Senate had lost its freedom, in a realistic sense, to truly conduct an open investigation into the Watergate matter. The Nation could not withstand the truth. If there was to be an investigation, it had to be narrowly confined to domestic matters without any touching at all into international matters. Outside this scope, President Richard Nixon could still stand as the target. The image of America was at stake, and could not withstand the revelations of the truth.

Amber Nicole Highlander had become convinced that it was out of this deep concern over the need to protect America's international image that the Senate and the Watergate prosecutors had been willing to agree with the White House to narrowly confine the investigation into the Watergate break-in.   Under terms of the agreement, the investigations would be narrowly confined to domestic, presidential politics, excluding all matters relating to Nixon's foreign policy and international relations.

Just as she was thinking about all this puzzle , Amber got a call from her friend in Birmingham.   Josh would be coming to Washington again for a business meeting on Wednesday, October 16. He called to see if he could stay at her place a few days after his meeting. It had not been very long since she last saw Josh, but she was happy he was coming, and invited him to stay at her place, during his entire visit to Washington.   They could catch up on each others' lives.   She was hoping to get his views on her current Watergate issues with which she had been struggling. Josh expected this. It wouldn't be Amber otherwise. Still, he was looking forward to his talks with her, even about Watergate. As scheduled, he arrived on Wednesday, with his meeting scheduled for Thursday. He would leave on Sunday, October 20.

When he first arrived, Amber stayed away from her project, not wanting to interfere with his getting ready for his meeting.   But after that meeting, she would not hesitate to monopolize Josh's time, if he let her. The next day, Josh headed to his meeting which lasted nearly all day but it went well for him. So, at the end of the day, he was in good spirits. That evening, Josh and Amber went to their favorite neighborhood piano bar.   They ordered drinks and took advantage of the free food the bar always provided on weekdays. They sat at their favorite table. At first, they talked about everything, then their second drink, Josh opened the door when he asked Amber about her project.

"Josh," Amber began, "I am now convinced that the U. S. Senate and the Senate Watergate Committee were fully aware of Kissinger's secret dealing with Moscow toward ending the war in Vietnam."

"I don't disagree with that," Josh interjected.

"I am also convinced that the Senate-sponsored investigation into the Watergate break-in was intentionally limited to exclude everything dealing with Kissinger's Soviet wheat deal and the billion dollar illegal payoffs to the private grain exporters."

"Yeah, it had to be," Josh insisted.

"So, the way I see this," Amber began slowly as if she were carefully choosing her words, "if we accept as a fact that the wheat deal, and the billion dollar financial thing were the real motivating factors behind Watergate; and if the Senate Committee takes all this off the table; it became impossible from the outset for the Senate Committee to ever identify the real cause of Watergate."

"That's a rather accurate statement, in my opinion. But, as I have said, that's the way it had to be," Josh said, as he smiled, "out of a need to protect America's image among the community of nations."   Then he added, "This is the reason historians have never been able to identify the real cause of Watergate. They all seem to accept John Dean's identity of the Pentagon Papers as the motivating factor." Josh paused here and then stated firmly, "The Pentagon Papers had nothing to do with Watergate."

"That makes sense," Amber offered. "But, it would make the Senate part of the coverup,"

"Clearly! But it had to be," Josh kept repeating. "Amber, think about it. The Senate and the prosecutors knew that if they fully opened the investigation into Watergate, America's image in the world as a reliable trading partner would have been severely damaged.   One Watergate prosecutor even made that observation to Seymour Hersh, saying that if they found something against Henry, the country would be in bad shape."

"I too had heard that statement," Amber said. "That statement to Hersh goes along with what Senator Edmund Muskie said on the floor of Congress. As close as I can get, paraphrasing what he said, it was essential that Kissinger be cleared of any taint of Watergate-related misdeeds, because the likely consequences for America's standing in the world could be tragic." Pausing for thought, she added, "It didn't seem to matter what level of culpability belonged to Henry Kissinger. Regardless of his fault-level in the Watergate matter, and he was at the very center, the United States Senate was committed to shielding him."

"The Senate's shielding of Kissinger was, in my opinion," Josh observed, "confirmation that Kissinger's wheat deal and billion dollar payoff to the private exporters was the real motivating factors behind the Watergate break-in. So, keeping the Watergate matter limited to domestic politics to fit Dean's testimony, helped preserve the image of America. That it also prevented the real truth of Watergate from emerging was secondary."

"Is image protecting what it was all about?" Amber asked.

"In my opinion!"

"How could all this have damaged the international image of America?" Amber asked.

"America's reputation in the community of nations has long been as an honest trader in commerce and a reliable, trustworthy partner in its relationship with other nations," Josh explained. "With the Soviet wheat deal for peace in Vietnam, the United States was transferring all the wheat it owned to the Soviet Union, at huge economic concessions, with no regard for the needs of other nations. In a sense, Kissinger, was paying a huge bribe to the Soviet Union in order to gain a commitment from Moscow to apply pressure on North Vietnam. And, one more thing, the United States was abandoning South Vietnam and to a lesser extent, the Soviets were abandoning North Vietnam. Diplomacy had been replaced by economic bribery." After a moment of reflection, Josh continued with his explanation, "The American people might well have accepted Nixon's international bartering with the Soviets in their exchange of wheat for peace. The people just wanted out of Vietnam, and if this is what it took, so be it."

"That was the mood of the people," Amber added. "So

why didn't Nixon just announce what he was doing, and then join in the celebration, that the war was over."

"No!" Josh exclaimed. "It could not be made public."

The international community would not accept this kind of international bartering as a replacement for honest diplomacy. They might find it hard to accept that the most powerful nation in the world was paying the Soviets an enormous ransom for the peace agreement, even if it were Vietnam. The international community would have found it more acceptable for the United States to have simply walked away from Vietnam with an acceptance of defeat. But this was not something Richard Nixon, the anti-Communist crusader, could ever have done. Defeat at the hands of the Communists was unthinkable. So, for the sake of preserving the international reputation of America, Nixon could not defend his actions to the American people. He had no choice but to maintain absolute secrecy to protect the private grain exporters from prosecution, with the secrecy maintained forever if possible, even if that meant he had to resign from office.

"I see that now," Amber acknowledged. "I think I now better understand what Senator Edmund Muskie was saying about the need to shield Kissinger from any fault. It was all about protecting the international reputation of this Country."

"It wasn't only Muskie saying this," Josh inserted. "The whole Senate had to go far afield to clear the name of Henry Kissinger."

"Who designed this incredible cover-up of the truth about Watergate, and the use of American grown wheat to end the Vietnam War?" Amber asked.

President Nixon made it clear that within the White House, John Dean would be his point man for handling the Watergate matter. Dean was given exclusive control of the issue to protect Nixon. Nixon told Haldeman and Ehrlichman to stay out of it and not be diverted from their own defense. And, he made it particularly clear that Charles Colson was to stay out of Dean's way. The President wanted everyone within the White House's inner circle to understand that he was putting Dean in total charge of handling Watergate. With this line of authority fixed, Nixon notified Attorney General Richard Kleindienst that Dean was the only person within the White House he should talk to other than the President himself."

"Josh, how did you, only an assistant to Haldeman, learn all this?" Amber asked.

"It was because I was an assistant to Haldeman," Josh responded. "Haldeman kept extensive notes and was keeping a daily diary on all events occurring in the White House. He intended to write a book on the Nixon presidency. And all the time I worked there, I kept my eyes and ears open."

"Josh, tell me more about John Dean's role."

"Nixon had long held and expressed complete confidence in John Dean's skills of diversion and containment. He had successfully limited the investigation by the FBI into the Soviet grain deal, after the press had pressured the President into ordering the probe. With this success behind him, I guess it was only natural for the President to look to him again when the Watergate matter heated up. Nixon knew that wheat and Watergate were interlinked. During an evening meeting with Haldeman and Dean on September 15,

1972, Nixon complimented Dean, on how he had so skillfully, put his finger in the leaks that have sprung up. On April 15, 1973, I believe Nixon was getting ready for Dean's testimony as he discussed the parameters with Henry E. Petersen, the Assistant Attorney General in charge of Watergate inquiry."

"Josh, was Dean's Senate testimony intended to serve as a cover-up to protect President Nixon."

"No! You're missing the point Amber."

"What?" Amber, astounded by Josh statement, sternly stated.

"You are missing the point!"

"Tell me how."

"With his Senate testimony, Dean was not creating a cover-up to protect Nixon. To the contrary, the burdens of Watergate would be placed squarely on Nixon's shoulders for him to endure alone. The cover-up, designed so skillfully by Nixon and Dean, was meant only to protect America's world image by giving the Senate Committee something tangible enough to allow that body a way out of the investigation without damaging the international reputation of the Country. But, out of all this planning, Nixon would have to go. He would have to resign. That was a necessary part of the plan. Like I said, Nixon chose to personally bear the burden by surrendering the office he loved."

"Oh, my goodness!" Amber exclaimed in disbelief. "Are you telling me or suggesting that Nixon's ouster was all part of the plan, engineered by the President himself and John Dean?"

"I don't know this as a fact," Josh stated. "It's my

opinion! But that opinion is based on my reading a lot of White House internal documents that I had been instructed by Haldeman to summarize and file. And, I believe my opinion is consistent with what you are finding from Dean's Senate testimony."

"How do you get rid of a President?" Amber posed. "So, why did he run for reelection if the plan was for him to be ousted."

"That's simple. Nixon, at first, could not accept any notion that he would be unable to ride out the storm. At the time of his reelection, the Senate had not even authorized an investigation into Watergate. The need for him to exit his office as president was not finally reached until after his landslide reelection over McGovern."

"How was Nixon supposed to exit?"

"There was only two ways for this: impeachment or resignation."

"Oh, I see," Amber inserted. "If the plan was to shut down all investigation into Watergate and the Soviet wheat deal, it would seem to me that Nixon could not take a chance with impeachment. So, once the House of Representatives voted to impeach, Nixon's only option was to resign, with the resignation serving the function of shutting down all investigations."

"I don't disagree with that! But, as to how he would in fact exit his office, Nixon had to wait until the vote on the Articles of Impeachment. Had all the Articles been rejected, Nixon would have been able to weather the storm. The key was held by the House Judiciary Committee and the votes on the Articles of Impeachment. Once the Committee voted for impeachment, Nixon's time as President was effectively over."

"It is ironic that Henry Kissinger was going to survive, while the President of the United States was expected to fall on his own sword. It's sort of sad to me, a Shakespearian tragedy of sorts," Amber murmured.

"John Dean had set the stage," Josh began, "and from the circumstances of protecting America's international image, there was no other option. Kissinger had to be sheltered, protected, exonerated and even sanctified, while President Nixon had to fall."

"I understand. Why don't we take a break here," Amber suggested, "and order burgers." During dinner, the subject of conversation shifted over to Josh's new job and his adventures in Birmingham. He did consider his new job, working to improve the environment, an adventure. Josh's face shone when talking about his job and the nation's environment. He had become an advocate for clean air and water. After, dinner, they ordered one more drink and got back to their discussion about the task of saving Kissinger over the President of the United States. "I recall the exact words of historian Stephen Ambrose," Amber said. "He wrote: 'Thank God we have Henry, let's confirm him so he can run foreign policy while we get after Nixon for Watergate.' Interestingly," she observed, "those words tell the story. Imagine," she continued, "President Nixon was more expendable than Kissinger, because his duties covered both domestic and foreign policy matters. Unlike Kissinger, the President could be taken down without involving international relations and foreign policy, just as long as the Watergate investigation remained strictly and narrowly confined to domestic presidential politics.   As for Henry Kissinger, Congress would be risking serious damage to the international integrity of America within the community of nations had he not been protected. He was Nixon's foreign policy and had to be protected."

"That's an interesting view," Josh offered. "Do you know how Kissinger could be protected, when he was so deeply involved ?"

"Lie! Create a new face for Watergate! Actually, it's very interesting and, at the same time, very comical how they set out to accomplish this," Amber observed.   "Its what Senator Muskie had said about the need to protect Kissinger. Following the call to protect Kissinger, the U. S. Senate quickly encircled Nixon's Secretary of State, with an impenetrable protective shield."   Amber paused, then explained, "From my examination of the Congressional Record, thirty-nine senators signed a formal resolution officially exonerating Kissinger from all taints of Watergate. The Senators set out to certify Kissinger as a man of integrity. Senator Allen led off the group in their campaign to glorify the man, by speaking in favor of the resolution that Dr. Henry Kissinger had worked so hard to bring lasting peace throughout the world. Allen then spoke of Dr. Kissinger's and in his integrity, his ability, and his veracity. After Allen read his remarks into the official Record of Congress, individual Senators then began taking the floor to hail Kissinger as some sort of savior beyond the reach of accusatory fingers." Amber stopped here and suggested that they head back to her apartment.

The short walk back to her apartment was peaceful, though it was a little hot. When, they got to her place, Amber fixed glasses of iced tea, as they continued talking. She acknowledged her fascination with all these U. S. Senators offering personal glorification to the man who was probably most responsible for the exchange of wheat for peace in Vietnam, the financial payoffs to the private exporters, and thereby Watergate. She told Josh that her favorite of all the speeches given in defense of Kissinger was delivered by the Senator from South Carolina.   She thought Senator Strom Thurmond, with his southern drawl, added perhaps the most color, drama and urgency to the tribute. "Josh, would you mind if I read Thurmond's remarks to you. Paraphrasing won't do it justice"

"No," Josh answered her. He was now anxious to hear them.

Amber excused herself and went to her home file and pulled Thurmond's remarks. "Are you ready Josh?"

"Sure."

"Here is what Senator Thurmond said, and I quote from the Senate record," 'Mr. President, it is outrageous that Secretary of State Henry Kissinger who has achieved such diplomatic successes under very difficult circumstances must now carry the extra burden of serious and misleading innuendo being leveled against him. The leaks of information about him are scurrilous, dangerous and damaging to our foreign policy. Secretary Kissinger is a man of truth whose standing both at home and abroad needs no defense. The circulation of anonymous reports challenging his truthfulness about [the] wiretaps is typical of so many derogatory insinuations which get general distribution in our national life today.   It is unfortunate, to say the least, that leaks of misleading information can exist in our Government and gain not only national but international circulation.'"   Amber then paused to place emphasis on the Senator Thurmond's warning, "'These whispered assaults on his honor; which gain gross amplification in the echo, must be stopped.'"   Pausing once again to take a break and another sip of tea, Amber added her own editorializing. "Now Josh, is that not a flip. Henry Kissinger is free to stretch his international powers while his own President who appointed him Secretary of State continued under relentless attack. Where is the justice?"

"It was never a question of justice," Josh pressed. "Remember, everybody was on the same page with this. Each person was playing his own part.   President Nixon and his loyal legal counsel John Dean, as well as the Senate were all in this together.   It was a carefully orchestrated drama, carefully designed to help preserve the international integrity of their beloved Country, accepting as an unavoidable component, the need for the personal sacrifice of the President." Josh stopped here, then added, "You know, Amber, "you have had a front row seat in all this, unlike any other person. You have had the rare opportunity to watch this great tragedy of sacrifice and survival unfold. For the sake of America's international image, Henry Kissinger had to be allowed to survive, without any regard to his culpability, as Richard Nixon, President of the United States, prepared himself to be sacrificed. As part of the unfolding of this drama, the six private grain exporters participating in Kissinger's plan for peace also needed to be protected."

"I have watched the dynamics," Amber observed, "and can truly say that it is one strange tragic scenario." Nodding her head in bewilderment, Amber asked, "Do you think President Nixon ever accepted the reality that he was the one who had to be sacrificed for the good of America's reputation?"

"Yes! I have no doubt," Josh answered in a firm confident voice. "That was the only way it would have worked. It was his own idea, that came out of his love for America. In my opinion, Richard Nixon clearly put the Country ahead of self. Even if he had to lie about how the war in Vietnam was ended to protect the image and reputation of America, he was willing. That is how much he truly loved America."

"Wow," Amber reacted. "You do have faith in Nixon. Do you have any evidence that Nixon made such a sacrifice? Isn't it just as plausible that he tucked his tail between his legs as simply a disgraced politician?"

"Amber, what do you think? You have collected the evidence, and better than most if not all, you are in the best position to say whether we should see Nixon as a disgraced politician or as an honorable statesman, willing to take the fall for the good of the nation."

"Josh, I am beginning to lean your way, but I would like to keep the question open until I consider the hard evidence, you say you have."

"Well, that's fair. The clearest evidence, in my mind, is the fact that President Nixon, faced with all the charges and hatred directed toward him, never put up any personal defense. I believe," Josh explained, " that President Nixon's failure to raise any serious defense for himself was not out of any feeling of guilty, but rather out of his recognition of the importance of preserving the international integrity of America. If the international integrity of America were to be preserved, Nixon could not defend himself. The truth in his defense would have made it necessary to disclose the harmful, even destructive, matter that could damage the country's international reputation. Personally, I don't think President Nixon ever thought about raising any personal defense in any of the matters," Josh stressed with a lot of emphasis, revealing his continuing respect for President Nixon.

"Did anyone urge President Nixon to go out and hire the best lawyer available?" Amber asked. "I would imagine that many lawyers would have come running to offer to represent the President, particularly if they had learned that everything Nixon had done was aimed at bringing an end to the Vietnam war. And, had he put up that defense, I don't believe any jury would have ever convicted him."

"I agree with that statement," Josh said. "Nixon had been urged to retain independent counsel to fight the charges being leveled against him, but he ignored all the calls, even as the White House began to crumble under the weight and the flames of Watergate. Leonard Garment, who had replaced John Dean as White House counsel, strongly urged Nixon to hire an experienced outside attorney to represent him in all the Watergate proceedings, including the House of Representatives' impeachment hearings. Alexander Haig made the same suggestion, recommending that Nixon hire the best lawyer available. But out of all this urging, Nixon said no," Josh concluded.

"Why did he say no?" Amber asked. "Why didn't he accept legal representation?"

"Remember, Nixon was a skilled lawyer, and knew quite well that turning his defense over to an expert independent outside attorney would surely have threatened his need to protect the international reputation of the United States," Josh explained. "As a lawyer himself, Nixon understood that an independent attorney would be ethically bound, subject to disciplinary consequences, to competently and zealously represent him without regard for any predicament the defense might have had on the international reputation and integrity of the United States. An independent lawyer would have had no other choice but to vigorously defend Richard Nixon, raising every defense and justification for the break-ins, including Nixon's efforts to end the Vietnam war. And out of all of that, America's image in the world would have been tarnished. "So," Josh concluded, "President Nixon, as a man of integrity, had no choice."

"I understand," Amber acknowledged.

"One other thing," Josh added, "self preservation did not seem to be Nixon's primary interest. He was driven during this period of his tenure by love of country, and his deep respect for the international reputation of America. It was this love and respect for country that had made it impossible for him to defend himself. Remember Amber, Nixon was a trained and highly skilled lawyer, yet he still offered no defense. If he had so chosen, he could have, in my opinion, justified his actions as being necessary to achieve peace in Vietnam. But he did not offer these justifications because of the certain damage that would be done to

America's image among the community of nations."

"What I'm hearing," Amber summarized, "is that Nixon would never allow America's image to become tarnished even if this required him to resign from office as President. I am just speculating here, but the safest course of action for Nixon might well be for him to resign, and then maintain his silence on the subject of wheat for peace for the balance of his life. I am not sure, however, that he could surrender the power of the office of president."

"That would be a big decision on his part," Josh offered. "Let me ask you this Amber. When you published your wheat for peace series of articles, disclosing all the things Nixon saw a need to keep secret, did you give any consideration to the possible impact of your articles on America's international reputation?"

"No! At the time, I did not."

"Should you have?"

"If, in the beginning of all this wheat for peace exchange, the White House had told me off the record what was going on with Kissinger's efforts to end the Vietnam war, I probably would have kept the secret. I would not want to report any news that could extend the Vietnam war. But, after the war was declared over and with the passage of enough time, the damaging impact of the news would be lessened. With the passage of time, facts begin to fade into history, and then they can be viewed as part of the history of the Nixon administration.

CHAPTER FOURTEEN

As detached as she needed to remain as a journalist, Amber could not help but experience deep intrigue whenever she thought about the success of John Dean's enduring cover-up of the true cause of Watergate. Because of his personal skills, John Dean had been placed fully in charge of keeping the Watergate investigation within acceptable bounds. Acceptable bounds meant that there would be no investigation into Nixon and Kissinger's foreign policy with regard to the Soviets, China and Vietnam. Dean had a visible, tested track record within the White House, as he had earlier kept the FBI investigation into the Soviet wheat deal, narrowly confined.

After the wheat deal first broke into the news, the media began pounding the White House about what was being viewed as a historic scandal. Facing this media pressure, President Nixon finally ordered an FBI investigation into the grain deal, but, the truth is that Nixon had no desire for an open investigation. Right then, John Dean was called in to make sure the FBI probe remained harmless. Specifically, Nixon did not want the wheat deal from ever being linked to Kissinger's settlement of Vietnam, or to the Watergate break-in. Dean's assignment was to monitor every step of the FBI probe on a daily basis. For this, he received frequent status reports on the probe from the Bureau. Not surprisingly then, the White House knew the outcome of the investigation even before the FBI concluded its probe.

Having demonstrated his extraordinary skills in keeping the FBI from drifting away from the limited direction set, Dean was later entrusted by the President to keep the Watergate scandal from building into the danger point of threatening the levies. From the moment he took charge, Dean did a masterful job in keeping the Watergate scandal narrowly confined to domestic presidential politics, preventing it from spilling over into Nixon's foreign policy arena. He faced one of his biggest challenges toward keeping the wheat scandals from being linked to Watergate, and Watergate then from being linked to Vietnam.

Amber had gone home to Clanton to spend time with her parents for the Christmas holidays. She arrived in Clanton on December 21, a Saturday, and planned to stay away from Washington until after New Years of 1975. Josh knew she was going home and was able to take some time off from work to visit his parents, who still lived in the same house in Clanton. During the holidays, Josh and Amber spend a lot of time together. When they got together, Amber could not help getting on the subject of Nixon and Watergate. She had committed herself to writing a series of articles about the skills of John Dean. Thinking through all the accomplishments of Dean in creating such an effective diversion of the real truth of Watergate, Amber asked Josh, "Why didn't some news media recognize what was going on?"

"That's an interesting question," Josh replied. "Well, you are the press, so what is the answer? Why did you not report Watergate as an incident arising out of Nixon's foreign policy arena? Why did you not report that the wheat deal had been used to leverage an end to the Vietnam war, and that out of that the Watergate break-in had become necessary?" Josh was slamming Amber with questions.

"That's several separate questions," Amber said, without offering any answers. "Josh, what do you think? Did we journalists simply overlook this linkage?"

"I don't know how much independent journalistic efforts ever went into the reporting on Watergate, other than what the two young reporters at the *Washington Post* were doing. Nobody seemed to think Watergate was that big of deal, and the Soviet wheat deal, while covered extensively by the press as a scandal, was nonetheless viewed generally as a private transaction between the grain exporters and the Soviet Union."

Amber thought a lot about the questions she posed to Joshua about why the news media had not looked behind the Soviet Wheat deal for hidden meaning. As a news reporter, she still could not answer the question, but she agreed with Joshua that the media probably did not withhold the damaging news in terms of international relations out of any altruistic notion of protecting America's image in the international community. In her opinion, it was unlikely that members of the press, would ever withhold a story of that magnitude for altruistic reasons. Any reporter who discovered that linkage, would surely race to get it in news print first, and then expect some recognition and award for the article.

"Amber, let me ask you another question. Which newspaper led the way in reporting on Watergate?"

"I don't know of any reporters who worked more diligently than Carl Bernstein and Bob Woodward, the reporters at the *Post*," she commented. "I think we all relied upon them, maybe too much so."

"Have you ever thought that the *Washington Post* reporters might have been compromised by the White House?" Josh queried.

"What? No way!" she stated assertively as if she were offended and felt a need to defend her profession.

"Why not?"

"I don't know. I guess I want to think it would be impossible, or at least too hard for anyone to compromise an independent newspaper, much less a paper of the national stature of the *Washington Post*."

"Well, think about it," Josh suggested. Josh and Amber were walking down one of the dirt roads from Amber's parents' house that led to a clear stream, just as they used to do as kids and as teenagers. As they silently walked toward the creek, Josh shifted the subject. "Amber, it is hard to believe that the wheat deal with Russia was the thing that brought peace to Vietnam. That may have taken some drastic action, but many more American soldiers could have lost their lives in that war had President Nixon not been willing to finally take such drastic action."

"I agree," Amber responded. But she wanted to get back on the subject of the White House gaining control over the Watergate news content of the *Washington Post*. The very idea fascinated her, and also scared her.

"Josh, were you shifting the subject for some reason," Amber asked.

"Maybe!"

"Why?"

"I guess I thought the White House needed some justification for interfering with the free press. And ending the war in Vietnam with the wheat deal, even with the billion dollar illegal payoffs would be enough for this justification. Don't you agree?"

"I do, in the sense it brought peace," Amber said. "The only fault I have with the deal is that Nixon delayed the announcement of the end of the war, long after the wheat deal had been firmly in place. That delay was wrong," Amber stressed. "But the idea of exchanging wheat for peace was good and saved many lives."

"It was a brilliant plan," Josh agreed, "but it was sure costly, maybe a billion dollars in illegal payoffs."

"So was the war in Vietnam, costly," Amber added. "In the long run, the billion dollar illegal payoffs to the private grain exporters probably saved money, certainly saved lives, and ended that hated war."

"I wonder if anyone ever did a comparative cost/benefit analysis of the Soviet wheat deal's illegal payoffs, as compared it to a cost/benefit analysis of a continuation of the Vietnam war?" Josh added. "That is what justified Nixon's interference with the news reporting at the *Washington Post.*"

"You still believe that happened,?" Amber asked.

"It had to happen," Josh insisted. "Amber, all news about this international trade for peace had to be blacked out from the press, no exception, because it involved illegal conduct. President Nixon had given Dean the exclusive assignment of controlling every aspect of the Watergate investigation. That's the reason Dean, had to find a way to compromise the news content being reported by the *Washington Post*, through the young news reporters, Woodward and Bernstein."

"I'm beginning to understand the motivation," Amber added. She recalled that John Dean's assignment was keeping all investigations by the Senate Watergate Committee and others strictly limited to domestic politics. Dean's job was to make sure no foreign country would see the Soviet wheat deal as anything other than a private transaction that had nothing to do with the Nixon White House's international commitments. In accomplishing this, Dean realized it would not be enough to gain control over the Senate investigation, making sure that that official probe remained tightly confined to domestic politics.

Josh had to be in Washington again for a meeting on January 6 and 7. So Amber decided to head back also. She wanted to keep her dialogue with Josh continuing. Back in Washington, Josh suggested that they go to the pub he used to frequent when he worked at the White House. When they got to the pub, it was busy but not overly crowded and a few of the patrons were White House assistants, Josh knew. After they were seated and had ordered drinks, Josh went over to talk to a few of them. Since leaving the White House, he had kept in close contact with several of his former colleagues who had remained in their jobs after Gerald Ford became President. When he returned to the table, he told Amber, "They wanted to tell me that I was with a reporter who was attracting a lot of attention at the White House. Your articles are still raising eye brows."

"I consider that a compliment," Amber responded. "But, of course now, we have a new administration."

"You should," Josh agreed. "Those guys over there were saying it as a compliment and were impressed that we were together. So thanks for being here and lifting my status to new levels."

Amber smiled. "Josh, let's get back to your suggestion about Dean's efforts to gain control of the *Washington Post's* news content. Tell me what do you know about the White House's efforts to gain control over the contents of the *Post's* Watergate news coverage." As they sat in the pub, Amber began thinking about the *Post*, and its coverage of Watergate. She recalled the *Post* had seldom if ever gone beyond the version of Watergate offered by Dean. She suddenly realized that if Dean were to succeed in keeping the Watergate story tightly confined to domestic politics with no interaction with foreign policy, he would need to find a way to gain some level of influence over the *Washington Post's* news coverage. Thinking about this, Amber knew, as a journalist, that one of the best ways for John Dean to accomplish this would be to become a credible and indispensable news source for these reporters. "Tell me what you know about this, Josh."

"The idea had been mentioned before I left the White House. The talk I overheard was that John Dean had come up with a plan of becoming an insider news source to the *Post* reporters. A former colleague of mine told me that Dean had been boasting about how he planned to establish himself as the credible source to the *Washington Post's* reporters, Bob Woodward and Carl Bernstein. It helped him achieve this credibility as a news source when he transformed himself into his image of a Judas-type and betrayer of President Nixon." Josh paused and ordered another round of drinks.

"Josh, I am just imagining now," Amber explained, "I am finding it hard to imagine that Dean successfully and skillfully manipulated his way into an insider position within the heralded *Washington Post*, the newspaper that had become the official record and national chronicle for coverage of Watergate. What a coup!" Amber exclaimed. "Dean becoming a secret informer to the *Post*, passing sensitive information to Carl Bernstein, sounds so unreal. I remember your telling me about Dean's meetings with President Nixon on September 15, 1972, when Dean boasted about his ability to keep the Watergate investigations from spilling over into the President's foreign policy. If I recall correctly, he told the President that the press was playing it just as we expected."

Josh had always recognized the brilliant coup achieved through the skills of John Dean. "Imagine this Amber, Nixon gaining news-content control of the *Washington Post's* coverage of Watergate." Josh believed that Dean had succeeded in gaining entry into the *Post's* newsroom, and that Woodward and Bernstein had been deceived and ensnared into unknowingly becoming active participants in Nixon's Watergate cover-up.

"A true master stroke!" Amber observed.   "If it happened!"

"I agree."

"But, I am still finding it hard to believe it could ever happen," Amber observed.   "I'm a journalist, so maybe I don't want to think it could happen."

"It did though, and it came with a big twist of irony."

"What do you mean,?" Amber asked.

"The irony," Josh began to explain, "was that John Dean's infiltration into the *Post's* newsroom, made it possible for President Nixon to use the news's media he disliked so much.   He used the *Post* to his advantage."

"This would be the irony of all ironies," Amber added. "I know the *Washington Post's* coverage of Watergate remained tightly confined to domestic politics, just as Nixon wanted and needed.   This independent newspaper was trusted when it reported the narrow scope of the Watergate break-in, with no mention of Nixon's foreign policy being linked."

"It was indeed," Josh said with a chuckle.   "It was well known that Nixon had a love/hate relationship with the press and generally treated them with courteous, cool contempt. Sometimes, Nixon called for a game plan for an all-out, slam-bang attack on news people.   He particularly disliked the *New York Times* and the *Washington Post*.   So, now just imagine: his loyal legal counsel intruding into the private domain of the *Post's* Watergate reporting staff, and sitting at his inside spot, Dean kept the news coverage confined to domestic presidential politics."

"God," Amber began, "It really could have happened. Dean's containment strategy could be measured by the content of the *Post's* Watergate news coverage. Just like Dean's Senate testimony, the *Post's* always remained confined to domestic politics."

Josh had had to get back to Birmingham. He left on January 12, so Amber, accepted the challenge of finding the truth about John Dean's infiltration into the Washington Post's newsroom. Through her many sources, Amber, within a period of two weeks, had put the story together, and viewing it, she was surprised that Dean had in fact been so successful. She surmised that Dean had set out on his carefully designed course, knowing that the President and Henry Kissinger could not be effectively protected unless he were successful in convincing the *Washington Post* to keep Watergate confined to domestic politics. Toward this goal, he knew he needed to find a way to become a credible messenger, willing to share valuable insider information.

Transforming himself into a Judas type became part of his plan to gain credibility with the *Post*. Dean needed to get on the inside of the Post before he could ever expect to gain effective news-content control over the *Washington Post's* Watergate coverage. Amber unexpectedly received an anonymous call, telling her that an associate of John Dean had begun passing information to the *Post* through Carl Bernstein. This practice began sometime before Dean was scheduled to offer his testimony to the Senate Watergate Committee. With Dean's associate passing truthful but sanitized information to the *Post* reporter, Dean and the White House could check on the plan's effectiveness when the *Post* reported the information.

Once the White House became confident its plan was secured and firmly set, and after the *Post* became confident Dean's associate was credible, Dean's design took on a life of its own. Bernstein would call Dean's office and talk with his secretary who had been instructed to read a statement, issued earlier in Dean's name, that in substance made clear Dean had no intent on becoming a scapegoat in the Watergate case. The day after Dean's secretary had set the stage that he would not be a scapegoat, the *Washington Post* published an article under the byline of Woodward and Bernstein, reporting that "there were reliable reports that Dean is prepared to tell a federal grand jury all he knows about the Watergate bugging and that he will allege there was a cover-up by White House officials, including H.R. Haldeman." That reliable report was John Dean speaking through his associate.

Finding the accuracy he was looking for in the *Post's* reporting, as reflected in the Woodward and Bernstein article, Dean became convinced he was in, that the reporters were now accepting him as a credible source. With that, Dean was confident that, as an insider, he could effectively control the content of the *Washington Post's* Watergate reporting. Dean's circle had been completed. He had done what needed to be done to protect America's international image by insisting that the Watergate affair never reached into the international arena. Dean's ambitious containment plan to prevent Watergate from spilling out into this international arena worked its wonders.

Viewing the scene from the outside, Amber became convinced that Carl Bernstein, never suspected Dean of playing him and the newspaper, by passing on sanitized information intended to keep Watergate news coverage tightly confined to domestic politics. Unknowingly, the *Washington Post* had become part of a bigger White House containment strategy endorsed by President Nixon. Amber assumed that Bernstein and the *Post* thought they had discovered a defiant John Dean, willing to talk to the press and willing to sell out the President. Bernstein must have become convinced, Amber thought, that he had made this great discovery in identifying a prime insider and reliable source of information of the caliber of John Dean, the legal counsel to President Nixon. One day when Bernstein called, Dean's associate gave him the terms for the continuing flow of confidential information. Dean's associate told Bernstein that John welcomes the opportunity to tell his side of the story to the grand jury and the *Post*. The associate added that Dean was determined not to go down in flames for the activities of others. Amber was convinced that Bernstein took this statement to mean that Nixon's White House had lost all discipline and self-control, and that internally there was rapid disintegration."

     With the assumption that the White House had lost control over its staff, Carl Bernstein advanced a proposal to Dean's associate. If Dean would tell the Watergate story to the *Post*, the paper would defend him against attacks from other White House officials.   Now, for sure, Dean was more confident he had been accepted as an insider, and had gained entry into the reporting arm of the *Washington Post*. Carl Bernstein became Dean's designated handler, and, from that insider position, Dean stood in a firm position to insure for his President, that the *Post's* Watergate coverage would remain confined to domestic politics, with no implication into international affairs. As a continuing interest, it was all about protecting the international reputation of the United States. Dean was the person in charge. He made it all happen.

Dean's associate told Bernstein in substance that, Dean would prefer telling him the whole story, in person, except he needed to be able to tell the Senate Committee under oath, that, if asked, he had not talked to the press. But, then the associate added, that we are free to visit with each other. From that moment on Bernstein made a daily call to John Dean's associate for Watergate information. Amber became convinced that Dean in fact, had become Bernstein's "Deep Throat," equal to, if not greater than, Bob Woodward's secret source.

Amber became convinced that John Dean's loyalty toward President Nixon had continued unabated, and out of that loyalty, he was providing Woodward and Bernstein just enough facts to keep the focus of these young reporters away from Nixon's foreign policy surrounding the wheat for peace agreement, with that event standing as the central motivating factor behind the Watergate break-in. During one of many Bernstein-calls to Dean's associate, he was told, that Dean had collected and kept documentary evidence that would establish the involvement of his superiors in both the bugging and the cover-up. Then, the associate told Bernstein that John Dean had been loyal to Nixon and the White House, but now, they were willing to turn against him and send him up the river. Dean's associate then added that, "Dean's going to take some lieutenants and captains with him."

Through contacts made with Carl Bernstein and the *Post*, Nixon, through Dean was quite literally able to see their

tightly scripted containment strategy endorsed by and reported
in the *Washington Post*. That if the Post said it, then it must
be that Watergate was limited to domestic presidential politics.
Once Dean had been embraced by the Post's reporters as their
credible source, Dean's scheduled testimony before the Senate
Watergate Committee was by then made more credible. And
his carefully prepared story-line projected Watergate as an
incident resting solely with American domestic politics with
no involvement into Nixon's foreign policy.   With that
success, America's international image remained untarnished.
The plan worked.

On April 29, 1973, Woodward and Bernstein wrote a
story saying that H.R. Haldeman and John Ehrlichman had
supervised the cover-up in the Watergate bugging case. It was
another story Dean had supplied.   The *Washington Post*
reporters wrote, "A Dean associate commented yesterday:
'Haldeman and Ehrlichman have been trying to get John Dean
to take a dive and to convince the President that he should
save their skins and blame it all on Dean.'" The article went
on to disclose "that Dean has kept records and other
documents that he believes constitute circumstantial evidence
that Haldeman and Ehrlichman directed the cover-up."   It was
exactly as Dean's associate had said.

Clearly, John Dean had become an important insider
news source for the young reporters at the *Washington Post*.
Nixon's legal counsel must be credited for so skillfully
making certain that the newspaper's focus remained on the
domestic scene.   Through Bernstein's daily contacts with
Dean's associate, the White House had gained the
extraordinary power and influence over the *Washington Post*,

with the capability of planting stories that served their intended objective of keeping Watergate narrowly confined. On behalf of President Nixon, Dean was able to effectively gain the endorsement of the *Washington Post* of his self-created Watergate image: that the break-in was only an unplanned incident of a paranoid political campaign, growing out of a reaction to the publication of the Pentagon Papers. As portrayed, it was nothing more than American domestic politics run wild. And out of all this, no one at the *Post,* or anywhere else took the time to look beyond the stories John Dean was handing them. It was a fixed and continuing cover-up of the truth of Watergate, and the *Washington Post* unknowingly contributed to that cover-up.

Pouring over all the evidence she had collected, Amber Highlander became convinced Dean's carefully measured news stories leaked to the *Post* vitalized what she saw as the Nixon/Dean contrived containment strategy to keep secret any linkage between Watergate and Kissinger's Soviet wheat deal and Vietnam. Success in gaining his inside track into the *Washington Post* news room and managing the news content of the Watergate stories to fit President Nixon's needs, can in reality be measured by the continuing restrictive content of the *Post's* Watergate coverage.

When Dean came up with his idea of creating his Judas-type image to add to his credibility, he wanted Carl Bernstein to accept him as a credible source. This must surely have pleased the President. In one way, Amber thought, Nixon must have celebrated, even gloated, over Dean's success in keeping the *Washington Post* news coverage so tightly confined to the narrow scope of domestic politics. As she reviewed this setting, Amber theorized that the *Post's* reporters were equally pleased in discovering such a credible witness as Dean.   And with excitement, they may have forgotten to ask one important question: "If the Watergate break-in were a reaction to the publication of the Pentagon Papers, why did it take a year before the break-in occurred?"

As part of his celebration and perhaps a way to inflate his crowing, President Nixon issued a public apology to the *Post* and to the reporters Woodward and Bernstein for all the White House's criticism of their reporting.   It was May 1, 1973, less than two months before Dean's Senate testimony, when President Nixon publicly apologized to Bob Woodward and Carl Bernstein for calling their Watergate news stories "shabby journalism."   Quite clearly, Amber reasoned, Nixon's public apology served to further lift the credibility of the *Washington Post's* news coverage of Watergate.   This in return, increased the believability in Dean's contrived story of Watergate.   Amber could not help but marvel at the skills that went into the masterful plan and dream of a politician capturing a major newspaper's newsroom.

Richard Nixon's apology to the *Washington Post* was at the time surely surprising to Amber, as a freelance reporter. At first glance, she could not believe it was happening or even possible.   Yet, there it was.   Nixon's press secretary delivered the public apology, "When we're wrong, we're wrong, and I would have to say I was [wrong] in that case and other cases." Amber later saw it all as part of the White House strategy to reinforce its news content control over the *Washington Post's* coverage of Watergate.   As unrealistic as it might sound, the *Post* joined with the White House in creating as a lasting image, a picture of Watergate that rested solely within the confines of domestic politics, with the total exclusion of Nixon's foreign policy. This perfected image would exclude Kissinger's Soviet wheat deal, including the billion dollar illegal payoffs to the exporters.

President Nixon, Amber thought, had to be highly pleased with Dean's extraordinary success in breaking into the newsroom of the *Washington Post* and there controlling the substantive content of the news coverage of Watergate. His issuing the public apology only added to that pleasure. But the real highlight came when Katherine Graham, publisher of the *Washington Post*, acknowledged and accepted Nixon's apology on behalf of the *Post*. "We appreciated the apology and accepted it with pleasure," Ms. Graham stated. Hearing Graham's acceptance of his public apology, Richard Nixon must have gloated more than once with a smile as he watched John Dean's masterful form of deception, working its wonders.

CHAPTER FIFTEEN

*D*ean's skills of containment had served his President well. It kept the Watergate inquiry from spilling over into Nixon's foreign policy arena. He had negotiated agreements with the Watergate prosecutors and the Senate Watergate Committee that tightly contained the Watergate investigation to the narrow sphere of domestic presidential politics. And, so contained, the true cause of Watergate was excluded from consideration. Then to insure that the narrowly drawn sphere was never breached, he skillfully infiltrated into the news room of the *Washington Post*, gaining effective control over the *Post's* news coverage of Watergate. John Dean's effective containment strategy may have prolonged Nixon's tenure in office. But, Nixon's tenure in office, took a major hit when the House of Representative's Judiciary Committee adopted impeachment articles against the President.

The Judiciary Committee voted in favor of three articles of impeachment, thus opening the door to more investigations. An impeachment trial could have led to new and more extensive investigation with no bounds or limits. With no containment in effect, the impeachment trial could have uncovered the real truth about Watergate, the Soviet Wheat Deal, and the Vietnam peace agreement. President Nixon's savoring of the moments his loyal legal counsel had so skillfully and successfully gained effective influence over the *Washington Post's* news coverage of Watergate, the three articles of impeachment suddenly changed the scene. Within the halls of the House of Representatives, John Dean's skills of containment became meaningless and there they faced the uncertainty of that political body.

If Nixon expected to keep contained from public disclosure all his secrets during an impeachment hearing before the full House of Representatives, he would soon need to face his ultimate personal sacrifice. For their ultimate sacrifice, Nixon and Dean had built into the structured containment plan, Nixon's willingness to give up his most cherished position as President. This was a truly heavy price for him to pay, but one to which he had come to accept as a reality. For, as long as Nixon remained in office, the swirling investigations would continue with each, adding to the risks that some official probe might swing open the door to a discovery of the link connecting Watergate to Nixon's foreign policy. Nixon's resignation from office was the only thing that would more securely shut down the investigations, thus, bringing forth the only hope for a true sense of finality to the final chapter in the Nixon/Dean containment strategy.

Keeping Watergate out of the foreign policy arena became the bitter/sweet conclusion for John Dean and all the others who believed in Richard Nixon.

Amber Highlander had concluded after carefully studying the record that if the international image of America as an honest dealer were to be preserved, President Nixon's resignation became unavoidable and visually foreseeable. But, for Nixon and all those who believed in him, his resignation would not be seen as an act of personal disgrace, but rather as a form of personal sacrifice by this man of peace. Nixon had been preparing himself for the resignation spectacle. Viewing this from a wide-angle, Amber was now convinced that it was out of his deep love of America, that he accepted his resignation as a reality. Amber concluded that it had become a reality from the moment Nixon decided against defending himself against all the public charges by lifting his own sword or by retaining a skilled lawyer to fight the battle. As part of the overall containment plan, Nixon would know when the moment came, and he would be prepared to take that step forward into political exile.

Nixon understood that historians, writing history based on less than a full record, might preserve in their minds all the disparaging thoughts and words directed toward him by the politicians, the hungry news reporters and their media. But he was willing to carry on his shoulders alone this burden of dishonor and disgrace, knowing in his own mind that it had been the only way he could end the Vietnam war and still retain some legitimate claim of honor, the honor of not losing the Vietnam war to the Communists. Amber Nicole Highlander had come to understand this. She understood that

Nixon never wanted to resign from the office he loved, cherished and respected. But, she also understood and concluded that resignation stood only as his ultimate sacrifice to protect the international reputation of the United States. He would leave it to historians to see if and when they got it right.

Amber came to understand that neither Nixon nor Dean could ever tell the full truth at a time when the potential damage to America's international image was at its apex. The full truth could not be told until the passage of enough time that allowed the facts to fade into a panorama of history. Only then could the full truth be safely told. Amber was not sure, chronologically, when that would be, when the impact of facts do fade into history. She wasn't sure whether there was any measure of time that would offer a signal when the facts could be more safely told. During all the time she kept digging for more relevant facts, she could not get out of her head the words of John Dean, the words he gave in response to a question from Senator Joseph Montoya. She kept repeating Dean's words in her head: "I strongly believe," Dean had explained, "that the truth always emerges. I do not know if it will be during these hearings; I do not know if it will be as the result of the further activities of the special prosecutor. I do not know if it will be through the processes of the history. But the truth will be out someday." From the moment Amber heard Dean speak these words, she was captivated and spent long periods thinking about their ramification. Now, she thought, she understood them.

Amber understood why Nixon had reason to fear that some Watergate investigator might bring to the surface the

Watergate link to his international deal-making with Moscow and from there, discover the interlacing of the wheat deal, peace in Vietnam, and the Watergate break-in. It had been all about his concern over the nation's reputation in the world. Realistically though, Amber believed, Nixon had to know that it would be only a matter of time when the full truth emerged. He just didn't want that to come too quickly, for if it did, the truth could cause great harm to America's image among nations in the free world. He didn't want it to come during his lifetime! Amber had come to understand how the truth that Watergate was conceived and born out of Nixon's foreign policy over the Vietnam war could harm America's international reputation. In her mind, Nixon's fear was real.

Congress too had understood this, and did its part toward preventing this damage, keeping its investigation into Watergate tightly confined to domestic presidential politics with no link to Kissinger's directed foreign policy. This offered a front that helped extend the time before the full truth emerged. But then the House Judiciary Committee voted out three Articles of Impeachment against President Nixon, and that opened the door to more extensive investigation, as the full House began considering the Committee's report. This Committee action, Amber thought, potentially increased the risk facing the President that the full truth might emerge far too quickly, and surely so if he stood to fight the charges. In his mind, time had come to face the reality of his own personal, ultimate sacrifice – his resignation from office.

Going back to the moment when the critical decisions were being made on how to preserve the secrecy of the truth of Watergate, and who in the White House's inner circle might be indispensable, Amber found it fascinating that the one and only person identified as being indispensable was Henry Kissinger. Though he stood at the center of the complex interlacing events, he was still the only person inside the Nixon White House who received formal protection from the U. S. Senate. By way of formal Senate Resolution, Kissinger was cleared of any taint of guilt, without regard to his culpability. Kissinger was protected because he was the one in the forefront of America's international relations. Everything he did involved, affected and reflected on international politics. Consequently, Kissinger became the untouchable for the sake of protecting America's image, and he knew and used that unique status.

As the Senate was protecting Kissinger, they needed someone else to blame. Thus, Richard Nixon would be the one to take the fall. He was the only person who could be targeted and, at the same time, lower the cries of the public. As president, he was at the top, responsible for everything occurring in the White House, domestic and international. So, unlike with Kissinger in his role as Secretary of State, the U. S. Senate did not need to shield the President. Following what Amber saw as the script written by John Dean and the President, Nixon's expected role was resignation, thereby placing the interest of the nation ahead of his personal desire to protect himself and continue serving as President. Standing ready to make the ultimate sacrifice, President Nixon on August 9, 1974, resigned from office. This was the final step in his and Dean's Watergate containment strategy.

Less than two years after his impressive victory over George McGovern, Richard Nixon spoke to the nation from the East Room of the White House. "Good evening," President Nixon began as he had so many other times. "This is the 37th time I have spoken to you from this office, where so many decisions have been made that shaped the history of this Nation. . . . In all the decisions I have made in my public life, I have always tried to do what was best for the Nation. Throughout the long and difficult period of Watergate, I have felt it was my duty to persevere, to make every possible effort to complete the term of office to which you elected me.

"In the past few days, however, it has become evident to me that I no longer have a strong enough political base in the Congress to justify continuing that effort. As long as there was a base, I felt strongly that it was necessary to see the constitutional process through to its conclusion, that to do otherwise would be unfaithful to the spirit of that deliberately difficult process, and a dangerously destabilizing precedent for the future. But with the disappearance of that base, I now believe that the constitutional purpose has been served, and there is no longer a need for the process to be prolonged. . . . Therefore, I shall resign the Presidency effective at noon tomorrow. Vice President Ford will be sworn in as President at that hour in this office."

Richard Nixon signed his last official document as President on August 9, 1974. It was a terse, one sentence letter to Secretary of State Henry Kissinger: "I hereby resign the Office of President of the United States." With that, he left the White House, the first U.S. President ever to resign from office, and returned home to California for an indefinite period in political exile, allowing time to pass before the true damaging Watergate facts could be allowed to safely surface.

Ten days after Nixon made his final sacrifice by resignation, the full House of the Congress closed the official Watergate chapter with its vote of 412 to 3 to take official notice of the House Judiciary Committee's recommendation for impeachment.   With that, all official investigations into Watergate were halted, as the full House never officially voted on the Articles of Impeachment.   With the passage of enough time, Nixon hoped people might forget about Watergate and never consider even the notion that American grown wheat had ended a war that could not be won by bombs.   But, out of that complex international bartering the Watergate break-in became necessary and unavoidable.

      Amber Highlander had initially thought Nixon's resignation was his final act of disgrace that brought to an end his debased administration, and that this President would undoubtedly be forever remembered as our most corrupt politician.   But after spending so much time, investigating and talking with different insiders and collecting a massive volume of documents, she began to see Richard Nixon in a new, and brighter light.   Knowledge gained had changed how she viewed his image, modifying her Nixon image from a corrupt politician to a statesman and man of peace.   From all the evidence she now held, Amber began to see Nixon's resignation as his necessary personal sacrifice that was a critical part to a bigger plans to keep secret the linkage between the Watergate break-in and the financial fraudulent dimensions of the billion dollar illegal payoffs to the private grain exporters.   She remembered: this was the big financial thing that Nixon admitted to be the force that fueled the Watergate break-in.   She understood why his resignation had become such an indispensable part of the programmed cover-up. Amber theorized that, had Nixon remained in office and held on to his power as President, investigations would have persisted in increased numbers, and such continuation, would have increased the risks of serious disclosure of facts that could reveal the truth.

Amber Highlander understood and began to marvel at what she was discerning. She was particularly moved by President Nixon's clear love of country that prevented the trauma of the truth 'of Watergate from emerging too quickly. In an effort to avoid this premature disclosure, and to extend the time before the truth would ultimately emerge, he walked out of office into political exile, and endured all the vile, disparaging comments hurled at him personally and at his presidency, but none directed toward America. Richard Nixon had protected America's image, and the country could continue walking within and among the community of nations with respect and dignity.

When Richard Nixon walked out of the White House into political exile, he lifted his arms to give his well known victory sign. In his own mind, he knew the truth and could exit with his head held high. But with the public, he left office with a tarnished reputation as a corrupt politician who should be criminally charged for all he had done. Nixon had no choice but to accept all the charges and slurs, without putting up any defense. He knew it was too early for the full truth to be allowed to surface. Time needed to pass. And, until enough time had elapsed, the American people, with inadequate facts, would continue vilifying their former President.   From   the   time   of   Watergate,   the   Nixon investigators and historians have been writing on the basis of an incomplete record, portraying Nixon only as a crook and burglar, no better than those who performed the actual break-in at the DNC.

From the depth of her own studies, Amber knew that history would in time offer the final judgment on Richard Nixon and his final act of resignation.   Amber Nicole Highlander, with her expanded insight, was already seeing Nixon's resignation in a different light.   Based on her accumulated evidence, she saw Nixon's resignation as the highest statesman-like act of personal sacrifice to protect the international reputation of the United States.   She came to understand!

She came to understand the underlying dynamics of Nixon's resignation and his presidency.   She came to understand that this period of time, marked as a divided country with an ongoing Vietnam war, could be fairly judged only by those historians, looking back at those turbulent Nixon years with a more complete record.   Amber was confident she had assembled that record that had given her a deeper and truer insight of history.   She understood all the things, but knew that gaining access to that completed Nixon record had not been an easy task.   It turned out to be one of her biggest challenges.   Amber had thought it would have become easier to collect the relevant facts after Nixon's resignation, when he no longer possessed the power of the presidency to block access to information.   With his departure from office, there was a growing threat that information about the wheat deal's linkage to Watergate might be discovered, and the private grain exporters might be brought under prosecution.

Once Nixon resigned, and surrendered the power of the presidency, he could no longer protect the private exporters, against prosecution for their continuing PL 480 grain fraud and illegal governmental payoffs. He could no longer tell USDA special investigators, such as Special Agent Willard Griffin, or FBI agents to back off their investigation of the grain fraud. With Nixon no longer in office, there was an increased risk that an expanded industry-wide grain fraud investigation might be launched. There was no longer a guarantee that information about the billion dollar grain fraud could be suppressed. Even before Nixon resigned, the FBI had already launched its investigation. It was on January 24, 1974, when information about the grain fraud was leaked to the FBI. With this new investigation surfacing, Nixon's predicament could not end completely with his resignation, but would follow him in exile, with many calling for criminal prosecution.

CHAPTER SIXTEEN

*I*n February of '75, Amber could see an end to her long investigative journey that had first gotten a big boost back in Billings, Oklahoma. A group of Oklahoma wheat farmers had shown their trust in her, and spurred her journalistic search of President Nixon's secret use of American grown wheat to end the Vietnam war. Now, after this long and twisted journey, she had broken through Nixon's secrets of peace that had led him to accept the risk of the Watergate break-in. Amber hoped to soon have the final segments of the story to her newspapers, with the full story quite clearly linking the Soviet wheat deal to Vietnam and to

Watergate, or as some were phrasing it, the Nixon Trilogy.

Nixon and Kissinger had wanted to, they needed to, extend their secrecy into perpetuity if that were possible. Preserving the secrets of the Soviet wheat deal and its fraudulent component that had made the private grain exporters rich was a commitment the President had to make to protect the private companies, particularly Continental Grain and Cargill Incorporated. These two high officials in government had no realistic choice! And, to the extent Nixon was willing to go in securing his secrecy serves to reveal his personal deep loyalty to those private grain exporters that had helped him achieve peace in Vietnam. It also showed the depth of his concern. Toward his goal of perpetuating secrecy, Nixon, before releasing his hold to the power of the office of president, had set into motion plans to preserve all his secrets.

Amber discovered that before announcing his resignation, Nixon had entered into an agreement with the Administrator of the General Services Administration (GSA), the federal custodian of public records. Under that agreement, access to Nixon's presidential documents and tapes was tightly restricted up until their planned ultimate destruction, an act that would have taken the secrets into perpetuity. Nixon's agreement with the GSA called for all his tapes to be destroyed on September 1, 1984, or at the time of Nixon's death, whichever event first occurred. Amber kept reading this part of the agreement unable to accept it as a reality. Her mind just stopped, unable to get past the thought of an agency of the United States agreeing to destroy Nixon's secret White House tapes. Unbelievable: that is unbelievable, she kept saying to herself.

Irony then set in when Amber remembered Nixon boasting that his administration would be the best chronicled in history. This became his later explanation for first installing and maintaining his secret White House tapping system. But now, she thought, Nixon wanted the tapes destroyed; how does that preserve history? In time, she put the pieces together, realizing that Nixon's need to maintain strict secrecy trumped any desire to preserve history. It was all about the deep Nixon secrets and protection of the private grain exporters. Nixon was showing a willingness, as long as he had such power, to totally erase from history all the facts of Kissinger's exchange of wheat for peace. What a historic tragedy, Amber thought. With the White House tapes given a limited five-year life, they were virtually deprived of all their extraordinary historical value. As Amber viewed the scene, the very thought of the GSA agreement to physically destroy the irreplaceable Presidential material made no sense at all, unless viewed in the context of the deep-seated imperative to preserve absolute secrecy. It was with this sense of being that President Nixon was able to walk away from his cherished office, with some level of confidence that his private exporters would remain protected, and by that, America's image in the world would remain firm and untarnished.

As a journalist, Amber was bewildered over the official, government destruction- agreement; as a person, she was saddened because it would hide forever Nixon's brilliance. She understood how Nixon could be put down as being corrupt, evil, sinister and all that stuff by the public and even historians. She had been guilty of this same Nixonbashing and putdown in her role as a freelance reporter. It was only after she had accumulated and studied the whole historic record that she began to see a different Nixon. She freely admitted that her earlier viewed lowly image of Nixon had been shortsighted and made upon an incomplete record. Now, with more facts in front of her, Amber began to see President Nixon as a man of passion; a President in search of peace in Vietnam, no longer caring about the cost and personal risks of achieving that peace. Amber came to understand that it was only after the chance of peace in Vietnam seemed to be moving out of reach that Nixon finally stepped forward, with a willingness to take on more drastic and daring action, including illegal bribing of the Russians, all in the name of peace.

With Gerald Ford, as the new President, the door remained open for Nixon's destruction plan to continue. On September 6, 1974, President Ford approved Nixon's plan to destroy all the White House tapes, and two days later, on Sunday, September 8, 1974, he granted to Richard Nixon a formal, unconditional pardon. Reciting the troubles of Watergate and acknowledging the House's impeachment hearings, the new President granted Nixon "an absolute pardon against all offenses against the United States which Nixon may have committed." This shut down all the investigations into Watergate, and continued Nixon's secrecy. Amber wondered why President Ford had ever agreed with Nixon's desire to destroy the most critical of evidence of one of the most significant parts of American history. Speculating a bit, she thought Ford may have shared the concern about the potential injury to America's international reputation.

Whatever it was, she wanted to find the complete truth. She kept thinking and repeating to herself that there has to be answers, and in time, she would find the truth.

It was about three in the afternoon when she got back from her long walk along the C&O Canal. These long walks helped Amber sort though all her mental notes. Arriving back at her apartment, she poured herself a glass of wine and went out to the patio to relax and continue thinking. Looking up toward the sky and watching the clouds slowly move across a deep blue background, her eyes closed just for a moment, when the phone rang. She answered after the fifth ring. It was Bessie Grimes of Billings. She wanted to talk about her son Michael. "Hey Bessie," Amber greeted her. "I'm happy to hear from you." She was happy to hear from her. Amber was still interested in Bessie's son Michael and other veterans who had gone to Vietnam and come back with severe physical and mental injuries, including her fiancée RJ. "How's everything on the farm?"

"Everybody's doing good," Bessie spoke in her soft voice, revealing a calm excitement. "Yesterday, Michael walked the quarter mile stretch down to the mail box to check to see if the postal carrier had left us anything. He use to do that all the time when he was a kid. But this was the first time he has done it since getting back home."

"That's exciting," Amber said. "Has he started talking to you?"

"No, but I know he will one of these days. I still hold out faith. My hope and faith was renewed when he walked down to the mail box. For once, there was purpose in what he was doing. That's what made it so great," Bessie said. "He walks and runs a lot, but never for a purpose, like checking the mail. For us, this was truly exciting, so I had to call to tell you. I hope you don't mind."

"Bessie, I am delighted you called. You are free to call me at anytime. What you're saying about Michael, is a big step and should give you hope. I understand why you are so excited." From her ongoing studies and investigation, Amber was beginning to gain a better understanding of what parents of Vietnam veterans were going through with the problems brought on by their war experience in Vietnam. Toward this great tragedy of war, Bessie continued showing her unbending faith. In fact, Amber knew from her past visits that the wheat farmers of Noble County all held a lot of faith. This same faith and hope had helped the Grimes family cope with Michael. Faith seemed to be at the center of her universe and the universe of the farmers. Amber had learned that raising wheat in Oklahoma with its weather extremes, required a lot of faith, mental strength, and an enduring work ethic.

"Amber, when are you coming back to Oklahoma for a visit? Tyler and I would like you to come for a visit and stay with us, as our guest."

"Thanks for the invitation. I have been wanting to come again to visit you and the farmers. Maybe I can come during your next wheat harvest."

This did not sound much like a firm commitment to Bessie, but it still made her happy, for she found Amber so easy to talk with. "I know all the wheat farmers would like for you to come down," Bessie assured her. "And, maybe, this time Michael might be brought into a conversation. Amber, you know you are always welcome on our farm."

"Thanks." With that, their conversation ended, and Amber, who did think she was making a commitment, immediately marked her calendar, May 15, 1975: "Trip to Oklahoma." With her calendar marked with a committed date, Amber returned to her patio, just as the sky began turning darker, with sounds of thunder rumbling in the background. As her eyes turned toward the sky, a bolt of lightning streaked across the horizon, then a second and then a third. She was enraptured. When the rain came, she took shelter in her apartment where she could still hear the thunder. As she listened ever so intently, her mind drifted back to her remaining unanswered questions. What could Ford do? What should he do?

Gerald Ford now had the power of the presidency behind him, carrying with it the power to make public the whole truth of Nixon's wheat for peace exchange, and its resulting illegal payoffs to the private exporters. Amber thought a long time about this. She began considering that the FBI's presence on the scene of the grain industry might be causing problems for the Ford administration. What if the FBI's investigation result in prosecution, with lengthy criminal and civil trials appearing on the horizon? This could lead to a full ventilation of Nixon's Watergate secrets. But now, it was for President Ford. He held the power to make it happen or not happen. As President, he could disclose the facts to the public or extend the secrets of Richard Nixon until a later day.

Ford had the power to delay prosecution arising from the multiple FBI investigations. Through his prosecutors in the Justice Department, he could tell the court that the White

House had been a victim of the fraudulent acts committed by the private grain dealers. Or, he could avoid that open confession by settling all the civil claims. By that stroke, the President could avoid any ventilating criminal or civil trials, keeping Nixon's secrecy intact. Amber remembered the potential threat to keeping intact all the secrecy Nixon left behind from the possible litigation growing out of the FBI's investigation. She remembered Ford's statement about this litigation when he pardoned Nixon. During his expanded explanation, President Ford suggested that "the litigation might challenge the credibility of our free institutions of government at home and abroad. He knew the full risk." Secrecy could end or be extended; it was all within the power of President Ford.

Amber had become convinced that President Ford knew all the details of the Soviet wheat deal's linkage to the Vietnam war settlement, and, with this knowledge came a duty to preserve Nixon's secrecy all in the name of America's international image. That is what was at stake! The new President experienced equal concern over the potential damage to America's international relationship within the Community of Nations, had the truth behind the Soviet wheat deal ever became public. Such concern would explain the need to go along with Nixon's extraordinary destruction plans to secure his continuing secrecy. Still, Amber found it hard to believe that Gerald Ford went along with the plan. It made no sense to her.

Amber learned that the debate over Nixon's historic materials had quickly shifted over to Capitol Hill, when Senators Gaylord Nelson of Wisconsin and Sam Ervin of

North Carolina, and Representative Jacob Javits of New York introduced legislation to nullify the Nixon/Sampson destruction agreement. Their emergency bill to preserve Nixon's presidential materials against destruction, which Senator Nelson arguing for quick passage, stressed the historic need to preserve Nixon's secrets for all to discover, in time. And in time, the full truth about the Watergate scandals would be revealed to the public. This is what Amber had been working toward during the last three years and now she was close to the end.

In Congress, preservation was considered essential if the American people might, sometime in the future, learn the full story behind the Watergate scandal and the Nixon presidency. Passage of the Presidential Materials Preservation Act, however, did not result in all the Nixon tapes and documents suddenly becoming open and available to the public. Amber learned this lesson the hard way, when her efforts to gain access to the documents relating to the Soviet wheat deal were met by a wall of resistance from the former President. Then she saw an opening, when in early 1975, some 100 employees of the private grain exporters were criminally indicted for grain fraud in the industry-wide PL 480 stealing scheme. These indictments were followed by indictments of the same private grain exporters which had carried forward Henry Kissinger's Soviet wheat exchange for peace.

Criminal prosecution, Amber thought, could provide a true ventilating series of trials that would bring to the public all the evidence of the grain exporters' fraud on the government albeit in the name of peace. As she waited for the

beginning of these ventilating criminal trials with all the
highly guarded secrets Nixon's wheat deal and Watergate, all
the private grain exporters stepped forward and entered pleas
of guilty. With that, Nixon's secrets remained intact. But,
then another chance opened. President Ford's Justice
Department gave off signals of an intent to force the private
exporters to make full restitution of the billion-dollar illegal
payoffs.

Amber saw the move toward these civil trials for
restitution to recover the full billion dollars from the private
grain exporters as offering one more chance toward revealing
the full truth behind the Soviet wheat deal and the illegal
payoffs. Toward gaining this full restitution through the
courts, the Justice Department through the Department of
Agriculture established a special joint investigative task force
to factually determine the full extent of the government's
financial losses. She learned that this investigative task force,
staffed with 150 full and part-time people, was charged with
investigating all the fifty export grain elevators in this country.
Amber was impressed by the apparent seriousness in the plan,
shown by the creation of the task force. With this 150
member task force, it was appearing to her that the Ford
administration was demonstrating a level of seriousness about
recapturing all the public money stolen by the private grain
exporters.

But, suddenly, the seriousness was gone; the 150
member investigative task force was disbanded; and the
ambitious plan to gain full restitution fell apart. After much
thought and reflection, Amber Highlander concluded in her
mind that President Ford may not have had the freedom to go

full force against the private grain exporters regardless of their culpability. He was stopped out of concern about causing a damaging blemish on the image of America as a honest international trader. Translated, this meant that his administration did not have the freedom to pursue civil claims against the private exporters. Whether he liked it or not, President Ford shared with his predecessor a deep concern over America's international image. For protection of this image, Ford was made to realize that he needed to find a way to dispose of the grain fraud cases as quickly as possible, and with the least amount of publicity. When Amber inquired of the Ford White House, she was told that the Administration had decided to play no role whatsoever in the Department of Justice's inquiry into the wheat deal. She was told that she needed to direct her inquiries to the Attorney General, but there, she found only a clamp of secrecy.

What the hell is going on, Amber thought. Refusing to stop looking, she turned to her USDA insider, Ken Downing, for help. She called, and Ken agreed to meet her at the C & O Bar and Grill that next Friday. Ken arrived first, took their table at the C & O, and waited. As she approached, Ken spoke, "Hey Amber, it's been a long time."

"Too long," Amber replied.

After an extended period of silence and casual conversation, Amber asked Ken, "Why did the USDA back away from its investigative task force, and let the private exporters keep all the money they had been stealing over a five-year period? It seems to me," Amber continued, "that without the task force, the Justice Department would not be able to gain the necessary evidence needed to claim full restitution. If Justice really expected to gain reimbursement of the billion dollars, it needed hard evidence! Without that evidence, the private exporters would get away with stealing the billion dollars in PL 480 grain, something to which they admitted when they entered their pleas of guilty to the criminal indictments."

"Your right, Amber. But think about this! To gain full restitution, there would have been an extensive trial, and what defenses do you think the private exporters would have advanced?"

"I hadn't thought about that," Amber said. "Most likely the exporters would have disclosed Nixon and Kissinger's role as their defense, had they faced a trial. Everything would then have been opened up, with the secrecy gone."

"Right," Ken commented. "And with that, America's international reputation could have been seriously damaged. I think it all came down to the administration's recognition of the vital need to protect the international integrity and reputation of the United States," Ken opined. "Had the Justice Department taken the exporters to trial in an effort to recover the true measure of damages, the private exporters' lawyers would surely have claimed as a defense that it was all part of Nixon and Kissinger's foreign policy. Nixon knew he could not afford for this to happen, and President Ford, now with the responsibilities of the presidency on his shoulders, had no realistic choice but to go along with the plan to preserve Nixon's secrets."

"So what did he do?" Amber asked.

"The Justice Department took the easy way and

entered into friendly settlements with the private grain exporters, thereby avoiding the publicity of civil trials. With this, Nixon's secrets remained firm! Here is one example of the token settlements," Ken offered. "Continental Grain, the largest of the six private exporter, which probably reaped hundreds of millions of dollars, settled with the government for the paltry sum of $392,500."

"Oh my god!" Amber exclaimed, "$392,500, that is unreal. A fraud claim of over a hundred million dollars. What did Continental Grain get in return for its payment of this paltry sum?"

"It's embarrassing to say," Ken replied. "Continental Grain was released and discharged from all causes of action, claims for damages, administrative claims, claims for sanctions, claims for refund, and claims whatsoever, including claims for costs, interest, attorneys' fees and penalties, which the United States may have against Continental Grain arising out of, or in any way relating to Continental's grain operations. All this for $392,500."

"Were there other settlements like Continental's?" Amber asked.

"All but Cook Industries' settlement of $4 million." Ken rattled off the other settlements. Bunge Corporation settled the government's claim for $550,000, Garnac Grain paid $110,000, and Louis Dreyfus Corporation paid $61,000."

"What about Cargill?" Amber asked.

"Cargill paid nothing and avoided all charges of wrongdoing by the Justice Department," Ken explained.

"Why did Cook Industries pay the higher settlement?" Amber asked. "I remember that company operated only one of the fifty total export grain elevators compared to Continental's multiple export elevators through which the stealing took place. So, why such a huge disparity? Had each of the fifty export grain elevators in the country paid been treat the same as Cook, the government would have collected as some recovery the sum of $200 million. So, again, why the disparity?"

"Quite simply, the Justice Department's negotiations with Cook Industries were conducted in virtual-public since Cook was a public corporation, the only one among the private grain exporters. That with Cook being subject to the reporting requirements of public corporations under rules of the Securities Exchange Commission, the Justice Department needed to disclose a level of seriousness when dealing with Cook Industries." Ken then explained, "that because Cook's settlement had to be filed with the SEC as public information, that settlement had to appear more realistic."

"Wow!" Amber responded. "That was brilliant on the part of the Justice Department if the plan was to preserve Nixon's secrecy for the sake of America's image. Little Cook Industries paid $4 million to settle the false claims lawsuit for the PL 480 grain it stole through its single export grain elevator, and the two giant grain exporters pay little or nothing. That surely calls for a Wow!" she exclaims.

"It does indeed," Ken concurred. "Continental Grain, the largest exporter, paid only $392,500; and Cargill Incorporated, the second largest, paid nothing. But, because these were private corporations, not subject to the Securities Exchange Commission, their favored treatment could remain secret. And, all the other settlements, with the exception of

Cook, the settlement negotiations and amount of settlement were confidential."

"The power of secrecy," Amber murmured silently. "Ken, let's have another drink and then go to your place."

"I'm ready!" he said. "With all the information I have been throwing at you, you probably have had enough. It is truly a fascinating story that reveals how the gigantic financial thing occurring during the Nixon administration brought on so much torture to the presidency, and yet remained secret for so many years."

"Yeah," Amber murmured, "but hopefully not too much longer."

"You're the one who has broken the deep secrets of the Nixon administration," Ken boasted. "It has been like a Nixon trilogy."

CHAPTER SEVENTEEN

*I*t had been a long, lonely journey. A journey for peace! And when her war against the war ended, with Kissinger's wheat for peace agreement, Suszette Andrew set out on her long journey in search for her way back home. It was an early Spring day in March of 1975, just as the daffodils were showing their full glory, when Suszette finally arrived back home in Billings, Oklahoma. She showed up unannounced and unnoticed at her home at about four o'clock in the afternoon. Nobody was there. Her parents, Douglas and Sandra Andrew, had driven to Stillwater to have dinner with friends. She remembered that the extra key to the house was kept in a small crevice at the top of the third from the left porch column, and there it was after all this time. Slipping the key out of the crack as she had done many times before, Suszette opened the door and slowly entered as if she were not sure she was supposed to be there, feeling a little bit like a trespasser.

She was tired from her long journey and began to listlessly walk through the house, checking out every corner, going into the kitchen, to the den, to her father's home office, and then to her old bedroom. She wanted to make sure this was her home. When she opened the door, she saw nothing in her bedroom had been changed. She even saw a vase of fresh flowers on her dresser as if her parents knew she was coming home. As she stood frozen, in the doorway, tears rolled down her cheeks. Then taking one step into her bedroom, she stood there, just looking for the longest time it seemed and she began to cry. Her bed had its same bright quilt, the same pictures were hanging on the wall, and her night slippers were at the side of her bed. As she kept crying, Suszette fell in her bed and went to sleep. She was finally home!

Douglas and Sandra arrived back home at about ten that night, and as they turned into the long drive to the house, they were taken aback when they saw lights on in the house and some strange, old beat-up car in the drive way. Expecting a possible burglary in progress, Doug picked up a big stick as he and his wife slowly walked to the front door that was unlocked. Yet, when they opened the door, there was silence as they delayed stepping into the house. Then, stepping through the front door, they stopped and continued listening. They heard only the silence of an empty house. Maybe we left the lights on and the front door open, they thought, but we didn't drive an old clunker up the drive way.

Finally, they began slowly, deliberately and cautiously walking through the house until they came to their daughter's bedroom. When they looked into the room, they were shocked. Their daughter was home, sleeping in her own bed. They froze, their mouths opened but no sounds came out. Tears rolled down the cheeks of Douglas, a big burly man, and his wife Sandra. They took a step toward their daughter's bed, and Doug wanted to wake her, but Sandra touched her husband's arm and shook her head no, signaling that they let her sleep. So, they left the room and went to the kitchen, knowing that neither of them would be getting any sleep that night. Both were deliriously happy.

Sandra made a pot of coffee as the two of them sat at the kitchen table, not saying a word, not needing to say a word. Their silence told it all. Expressions on their faces alone revealed their happiness, relief and contentment. For them, everything was good with the world. Neither Sandra or Douglas moved from that kitchen table for over two hours. Then, at about two in the morning, they looked up and there she stood, looking tired, dazed, bewildered, groggy and hurt. Her head was lowered as if she was still not sure her parents wanted her in their home after being away for over two years. But when they saw her standing in the doorway, Suszette's father and mother began openly weeping with joy, as they got up from the table and took their daughter into their arms. The three of them just stood there in the kitchen, crying and holding on to each other, not saying a word. Finally, Douglas broke the silence, "Welcome home honey," and they started crying again. Suszette is home, and they hoped she was here to stay.

As the morning sun began to rise, Sandra began making a big breakfast of ham and eggs and grits, with her homemade biscuits. Everybody helped fix breakfast and then helped clean the kitchen. And then they went into the den where for the first time, they began talking.

"Suszette," her dad said, "we are so happy you are

home and proud of what you have been doing to end the Vietnam war. We even want to shout the news to all in Billings that our daughter is home, but we don't want to rush you at all."

"That's right," her mom agreed. "We are so happy to have you home, and we want you to take your time settling back down and deciding what you want to do. You have our support."

"Thanks, mom and dad. I needed to hear that! I have been leading a hectic life in fighting that damn Vietnam war. Right now I am so tired, both physically and mentally. I am confused and I don't know what I want to do, except to rest. But, I have missed you, and I am so happy to be home where everything has always been so peaceful. For a while though, I just need to rest with nobody else knowing I am here. Is that OK with you?"

"Take your time," her dad said. "And anything you need, let me or your mom know. This is your home, and we are so glad you are here. Do you want us to call anybody in town to let them know your back?"

"No, but thanks. I need a few days, maybe a week, to just stay home with you'll and unwind, then I think I will be OK."

"That's fine," her mom replied. "How ever much time you need, you take and know that we will be here for you."

"Right now, I think I am going to shower and go back to bed. I am so tired."

"OK," her mom said. "Your pajamas are in the same drawer you always kept them, We knew that one day you would be coming home, so we changed nothing in your room."

"Thanks mom." That made Suszette feel good, knowing that she was really back home, and was wanted.

Suszette went to her room and bathroom and got in the shower, with the water as hot as she could stand. As the hot water flowed over her sore body, that had not fully healed from the police clubbing, she began thinking about the peacefulness of home and the gentleness of her parents. After a long restful shower, she got out and got ready for bed, though it was not yet noon. She pulled out her favorite flannel nightgown, and crawled back in bed and went to sleep. Her mom and dad were still in the kitchen, sipping on coffee, and planning for Suszette's favorite foods for dinner. Both of them were feeling good, and it mattered not what was to be. Whatever might happen, will happen.

Douglas went out and pushed Suszette's old clunker car into the garage so her friends would not think she was home. He wanted to give her the time she needed to heal and rest. When she is ready, she can call her friends. He simply did not want anything to interfere with her continuing journey to reach home, realizing that her physical body might be back home, but her mind and spirit may not have yet arrived. Her dad though was confident she would soon be home, with a bright future ahead of her. Deep down, he was hoping his daughter would go back to Oklahoma State University in the Fall.

Over the next several weeks, Suszette slept much of the time with only a little conversation with her parents. She slept and ate and watched television with her mom and dad. Then, suddenly on April 20, a Sunday, Suszette got up before her parents and fixed breakfast for them, and after breakfast, she cleaned the kitchen and made another fresh pot of coffee. They then went to the backyard patio with their coffee and began talking about her antiwar activities, about the peace announcement and about the future. She told her parents she wanted to go back to OSU and complete her degree in history and then go on to law school. "I will find the way to accomplish this," Suszette told her parents. "I am a determined person."

"You have proven your determination. And Suszette, I am so very happy to hear that you want to head back to OSU," her dad said. "We still have the money we set aside for your college, so as far as your undergraduate work, we will be able to help. We will have to wait to see how much we can help for law school. But we are sure happy with your plans."

"Mom, Dad, do you think, sometime, we could drive around the countryside? It's been a long time since I have seen a field of wheat."

"Sure," her mom answered.

"Maybe," her dad added, "we can also drive to Stillwater and have a nice dinner."

"That would be great," Suszette said. "That will give me a chance to see my old school."

"I need to run to the hardware store," Doug said. "So I'll leave you women to yourselves for a while." He then left to drive to Blackwell, and returned home at about one o'clock in the afternoon with a huge flower arrangement for Suszette.

After Suszette received the flowers, a smile came to her face. "Thank you dad." More and more she was feeling at home and she liked that feeling. Her war was over and she had finally won.   During the next couple of weeks, Suzette and her mom spent a lot of time talking. Then, on Saturday, May 17, Suzette told her parents that she was ready to get out of the house.

Toward mid-afternoon, the three of them left the house for a drive through wheat country's back roads.   Suszette remembered the beauty and peacefulness of the flowing wheat fields reaching to the horizon and looking like fields of gold. She could still tell that the wheat was close to ready for harvest. Just as they passed the Grimes farm, she remembered the times she had worked the wheat harvest with Michael. Those were her fond memories, but she did not want to stop and visit, not just yet.

One more diversion Amber wanted her dad to take as they were heading to Stillwater was a stop in Perry. She remembered as a teenager driving to Perry, not far from Billings, and just driving around the square. That had been part of their socializing scene, as teenagers. After about three trips around the town square, they headed on into Stillwater for dinner and a visit to the OSU Campus.

On the way back home, Suszette finally asked about Michael and whether he got back from Vietnam safely. That's when she learned for the first time that Michael had been seriously wounded, that he had recovered physically, but mentally, he was still suffering from that battle- field disorder, called post traumatic stress disorder. Neither Douglas or Sandra had seen the Grimes family for a long time and did not know if Michael was getting any better. "Do you think it would be OK for me to go visit Michael?" Suszette asked.

"I am sure it would," her dad said. "Your visit might

help him pull out of his stress. That would be the greatest gift ever for Tyler and Bessie. When do you think you might go?"

"I don't know yet. But I don't think I can plan for it. Someday, I will just decide and then go."

"Good!"

• • • •

A week before Suzette ventured out of the house with her parents, Amber, back in Washington was getting ready for her trip to Oklahoma. It had been a cold winter and Amber had stayed in much of the time, though she still took her frequent long walks along the path overlooking the Potomac River, as well as the C & O Canal path. These walks always refreshed her spirit, increased her energy level and released her creative juices. During that winter past, she had been able to get a lot of work done, and was getting close to reaching some level of finality. She had been looking forward to her visit to Oklahoma and the wheat farmers.

Amber's final road to travel would take her from wheat country to the aftermath of the Vietnam war, the veterans of that war and their families. She wanted to learn and write about how veterans and their families were able or not able to handle the stress of war brought home to them. She wanted to study Michael Grimes, the Vietnam vet from Billings, a high school football star who had dreamed of becoming a wheat farmer, but whose dreams had been shattered by that war. Michael, she thought, was not unlike the many other veterans who survived war in terms of life, but who came home physically and mentally scarred. He and so many other veterans came home from Vietnam, suffering from post traumatic stress disorder (PTSD). She couldn't tell where that part of the story might take her. She did expect, however, to find a close linkage to the bigger picture dominated by the Soviet wheat deal, Vietnam and Watergate, Nixon's trilogy that delivered peace. It was not a cause and effect linkage but nonetheless a linkage tied together with a common thread that ran through and interlinked all the component parts. It all needed to be sorted out, and she was ready to accept the challenge.

Amber's calendar reminded her that she would soon be back in Oklahoma. She arrived there on May 15, this time for a casual visit and another opportunity to work on the wheat harvest. But though casual, Amber wanted an opportunity to talk to the farmers at their grange hall and then spend an evening with them at Jake's Place. Her plane landed in Oklahoma City at 1:15 in the afternoon, she rented a car, and began driving straight through to the farm on the Interstate, rather than taking the back roads. On this trip, she had been anxious to see her friends at the Grimes farm, and when there, once again to touch the magic of wheat.

As she drove up the dirt road to the house, Bessie came out to meet her. She had been watching for her out the window and when she saw a strange car coming up the drive she assumed it was Amber. Bessie was so happy to see her. In an impulse, she gave Amber a big hug. "Do you want a glass of iced tea?" Bessie asked.

"That would be great. Is it sun tea?"

"That's the only way I ever make tea during the spring

and summer."

"I knew that," Amber said.

Bessie followed Amber into the house and led her to the guest room and left her to get settled in. Soon though, Amber returned to the kitchen where she found that Bessie had already poured them a glass of iced tea. As they sat and talked at the kitchen table, Michael walked in.

"Do you remember Amber?" Bessie asked her son.

"Yea," came Michael's one word response.

"Hi Michael," Amber greeted him with a big smile and with her extended hand, hoping he would shake her hand.

"Hey," he responded as he hurried back to his room without any hand shake.

"Well, I got a word out of him this time," Amber said, "and that pleased me."

"Little by little, Michael is showing some slight improvement," Bessie said, as she lowered her head to hide her display of sadness. "I think your visit might help," she told Amber.

"I hope so. Where's your husband?"

"Tyler will be home soon. He knows you're coming in. He headed out to the fields early this morning, getting ready for the harvest."

"I would like to trace the steps that Michael use to take

when he ran down the dirt road to your mail box," Amber said. "You want to walk with me?"

"Sure, I actually need to check the mail."

As they walked down the dirt road, Amber moved closer to the edge of the wheat field that ran along the road. She reached out and ran her hand along the top of the ripened wheat. Amber was always so impressed with how the sun turned a standing wheat field into a bed of gold that constantly flowed with the rhythm of the wind. Now she was touching it once again. As they walked slowly down the road, Bessie talked about how Michael use to run his hands along the top of the wheat. "He loved the wheat fields and dreamed of becoming a farmer and working with his dad and grandpa. When he walked this path toward the mail box, he would often dart in and out of the wheat fields." Hearing this, Amber darted into the wheat field and then back to the road, and she and Bessie began laughing, just as they reached the mail box. Bessie had a nice laugh. Amber thought.

Bessie checked the mail and then they headed back to the house. As they approached the house, Amber noticed that Michael was peeking out his window. What he might have been thinking at that moment, Amber could only guess. When they entered the kitchen, Tyler was sitting at the kitchen table drinking tea, but stood up when they entered the room and greeted Amber to the farm, and invited her and Bessie to sit down and have a glass of iced tea.

"We are all glad you came down for a visit Amber. When you called, you indicated that you would like a chance to talk to the farmers at the grange hall. I passed this on and everybody was happy that you were willing to speak to us.

So, for this purpose, the president called a special meeting for tomorrow evening, if that's OK with you."

"That's perfect," Amber confirmed.

"Amber, after your talk at the grange hall, do you plan to hang around and work the wheat harvest with us?"

"Absolutely, I timed my visit just for that."

The next day, Amber asked Tyler to drive her around the countryside to the highest point where she would be surrounded by wheat fields. He knew the exact spot in Noble County and headed for the big hill in his farm truck. When they reached the hill, Amber got out of the truck with her camera and for the longest time stood amazed at the beauty and peacefulness of the view, spread majestically before her eyes. As she stood on that hill, she was filled with awe at the inspirational power of the silence. She closed her eyes and listened to the silence broken only by the light rustling sound of wheat. She then started taking pictures, knowing that the photographs would never equal the extraordinary physical beauty she was seeing on top of that hill in the center of a wheat field ready for harvest. As she stood there, Amber saw no end to the fields of gold that seemed to flow into the deep blue sky marked only by a few scattered clouds that filled in the panorama. She would never forget the sight, the sounds of silence, or the experience. It was magic.

Back at the house, Bessie had already fixed a light lunch of sandwiches, fresh fruit and of course her iced sun tea. Tyler just grabbed a couple of sandwiches and a jug of iced tea and headed back to the fields, leaving the women to their more leisurely lunch. They did not mind. After Tyler left,

Amber and Bessie took their sandwiches and fresh fruit out to the green chairs where they slowly ate and just sat in silence looking up at the same blue sky and feathery clouds Amber had been watching when she went to the top of the big hill surrounded by wheat fields. Amber was sitting in Michael's green chair and as she sat down, she began feeling like a trespasser. When she glanced up at the house, she saw Michael peeking out the window. Maybe he is thinking Amber is invading his personal space.

"Has Michael ever come back to the green chairs since coming back from Vietnam?" Amber asked Bessie.

"No!"

"Well, I see him peeking out the window at me sitting in his green chair. Do you think he might be considering coming out?"

"I don't know," Bessie answered. "It would be so great if he did."

After about an hour in the green chairs that seemed only about fifteen minutes, Amber and Bessie returned to the house and together, they quickly cleaned the kitchen. Amber then excused herself and went to her room to get ready for her presentation to the farmers. As she reviewed her planned remarks, she looked out her window at the long extended wheat fields. She then showered and took a short nap, only to be awakened by the smell of the pork roast Bessie had put in the oven. They would have an early dinner today because of Amber's scheduled talk before the farmers.

Dinner was to be pork roast, sweet potatoes, a green

vegetable and a small salad. When Amber came out of her room and to the kitchen, Bessie and her daughter Kathy Ann, now 17, were in the kitchen getting everything ready. Sarah Jean and Cindy Kay were still at college. Amber talked with Kathy Ann about her plans for college, and inquired about her sisters. When dinner was ready, Kathy called out in a loud voice for her brother Michael to come to dinner. When all the girls were at home, they called for Michael in a unison choir of voices of young girls. But, the girls never yelled for their dad to come to the table. For their dad, the three of them would walk to where he was and politely tell him that dinner was ready. Now, with only Kathy Ann at home, she continued that custom. But Michael was just their brother. When he heard his sister call, he immediately came in and took his regular seat at the table. Michael was very polite, but Amber, as much as she tried could not draw him into conversation. He would talk more freely with his younger sisters, but nothing serious. Sometimes, Michael would go to college with his sisters and spend the night at Sarah Jean's apartment.

After dinner, Bessie told Amber to go on to her meeting with the farmers and that she and Kathy Ann would take care of the kitchen. So Amber and Tyler headed to the grange hall and when they arrived, Amber was once again warmly greeted by the farmers. Tonight, Amber would bring to the farmers her final chapter of the Soviet wheat deal that had made it necessary for the President to sacrifice the farmers' 1972 wheat harvest. She reminded them of the extraordinary worldwide power of wheat that had finally brought to an end the war in Vietnam. She reminded them that the wheat deal had been built upon the framework of a financial scheme involving illegal payoffs to the private grain exporters. Then she told the farmers that it was this wheat deal that had led the White House into a need to break into the Democratic National Headquarters to learn whether anyone had leaked confidential information to the Democrats.

At the end of her talk that went for some thirty minutes, the farmers gave her another standing ovation. Then after the meeting adjourned, Amber stayed in the hall talking with individual farmers and brushing off several marriage proposals she took as personal compliments, but nothing else. After visiting with the farmers, she climbed in Tyler's truck and they headed for Jake's Place where a number of the farmers had planned to go. When they arrived, the owner of Jake's recognized her and announced her arrival. Amber was hard to forget once you met her. Her stunning beauty made her stand out in any crowd and this was truly so when the crowd was a bunch of wheat farmers.

After a few beers, the farmers began drifting out, knowing that harvest time was about to begin. Tyler and Amber arrived back at the farm about 10:00 p.m. and found Bessie waiting up. After Amber changed into something more comfortable, Bessie fixed them a nightcap and the three of them went out and sat in the green chairs. It was a moonless night with not a cloud in the sky. It was a sky, filled with so many more stars visible to the naked eyes. Looking up at a sky fully occupied with the splendor and luster of stars, Amber felt a grandness that gave her a sense of inner peace and tranquility. It was after midnight before the three let go of the stars and came back into the house to get ready for bed.

When Amber put her head on the pillow, she almost

immediately drifted off into a deep and peaceful sleep that she had seldom experienced. The next morning after breakfast, Amber and Bessie took off in the rental car to visit other wheat farms in Noble County. Amber wanted to visit with some of the farm women. After visiting several farms, they were invited to stay for lunch at the farm they were visiting at about the farmer's lunch time. That evening, Tyler, Bessie and Amber sat around the kitchen table talking about the wheat harvest that would begin the next day. The talk in the house was all about the upcoming harvest, and Tyler told Bessie and Amber he was looking forward to the 1975 crop, hoping it would be as good as his two past years of 1973 and 1974.

Bessie then added another bit of good news on the Grimes wheat farm, that Michael was showing signs of improving. He was staying in the kitchen much longer and talking with his mom a little and a lot more with his sisters. During early spring, Bessie explained, Michael had started venturing out of the house and occasionally walking down to the mail box to check to see if the rural postal carrier had left anything. She had earlier told Amber about this. She just needed to repeat herself. He would walk that quarter of a mile down the dirt road from the farm house, but not nearly as fast as he made the loop as a teenager. But walking his old familiar path seemed to be bringing Michael full circle with a ray of hope for the future. Still, Bessie murmured, "he has a long way to go."

CHAPTER EIGHTEEN

*A*s Tyler, Bessie and Amber sat around the kitchen table talking, Michael had once again ventured out of the house that evening, unnoticed by his mom or dad. Outside, he began walking slowly toward the green chairs, as if he needed to reclaim his chair from that intruder from Washington. This was the very first time he had even come close to the three green chairs, but earlier in the day, he had seen Amber sitting in his green chair when he peeked out the window. The chairs were still in the same spot they were when he had left to go to Vietnam. When he approached the chairs, he paused as if he could not sit down unless grandpa was in his chair. He just stood there as if he had forgotten what the green chairs represented. He continued standing as storm clouds began building in the western sky and moving fast toward the east. As Michael looked at those fast moving clouds, he began remembering the years he had spent with his grandpa and the times the two of them just sat in the chairs watching the Oklahoma sky. Now, Michael thought, it is OK for him to sit down in his own green chair, next to his grandpa's chair.

As he slowly sat down, he gave out a long sigh, as he kept his eyes focused on the storm clouds. But as he sat down, Michael grew uneasy and yet at peace with himself for the first time. Suddenly, sharp flashes of lighting streaked across the sky, followed by repeated claps of thunder. This went on for a good thirty minutes. But Michael could not move from his chair. He could not take his eyes off the clouds and the lightning flashes. Then, surely only in his mind, Michael saw in one of the storm clouds the image of his grandpa. Grandpa Mose was looking down at the three green chairs and Michael with the same kind expression he remembered. He then heard the stern voice of his grandpa, "Michael, it is time for you to come home. The war is over!" Sitting there alone, Michael was so afraid! But he kept looking, wanting to reach out and touch his grandpa and to talk to him just as he use to before going to Vietnam. But nothing would come out of his mouth, he was speechless. Then another bolt of lightning stretched across the sky, followed by a louder eruption of thunder. And the image of his grandpa once again returned, and once again, Michael could hear the same kind but stern voice coming out of the growing storm clouds, "Michael," the gentle voice said again, " The war is over, you can come home!"

Michael remained frozen in his seat, feeling lost with his grandpa gone. Feeling lost and frightened, Michael did not move as the thunder and lightning continued with increasing force, but without rain. Unable to move from his chair, Michael's eyes remained fixed on the clouds as if he were waiting for another message from his grandpa. For once since coming home from the war, peace had come to Michael's mind as he sat in his green chair watching the display of nature's power. For awhile, everything turned peaceful, as Michael gave a big sigh of relief. But then another bolt of lightning struck that seemed so much closer, followed by the sound of more thunder. Right then, a hand touched his shoulder, sending chills down his body with a feeling of such fright that his entire body froze. Then, when another bolt of lightning flashed, Michael was finally able to move and look up.

Standing behind him and touching his shoulder, Michael saw Suszette or an image of Suszette. Everything seemed to stop again, as her hand remained on his shoulder and they continued looking into each other's eyes. Finally, Suszette spoke, and Michael knew it was not another image. Suszette had just recently returned home herself, and continued to stand behind her old friend with her hand on his shoulder. Then she spoke, "Michael, the war is over!" And so it was. The war was finally over for Michael and Suszette, as they both kept searching, trying to find their way back home.

After the longest moment as the clouds in the sky kept churning as if they were about to erupt again, Suszette came around and sat down in grandpa's chair. They sat there, the two of them, saying nothing, just looking out over the wheat fields ready for harvest that still looked golden when the lighting flashes cast off enough light. And with the darkness that came in between the flasks of lightning when the wheat field faded into the night, Michael and Suszette kept their focus on the storm clouds. They sat there, still saying nothing, not caring what they had both experienced during the last few years as a result of the Vietnam war. As they sat in silence, the brightest flash of lightening brightened the sky and lingered for the longest time.   Both of these veterans of the Vietnam war were, at that moment, feeling at peace within themselves and with each other and maybe with the world.

Finally, Michael was about ready to tell Suszette he was glad she had come, but before he spoke a word to her, another bolt of lightning came out the clouds, this one hitting the ground, setting fire to the wheat fields.   As the fire began to race across the wheat fields, Michael suddenly sprang to his feet and screamed out as loud as he could, "Dad, the wheat fields are on fire!"   And as he called out, the fire kept spreading and he and Suszette raced toward the farm's water truck as they had done before, years ago.   Once again Michael yelled out, "Dad, the wheat fields are on fire!"   He started the truck's motor and raced to the back door of the house, yelling out once again,   "Dad, the wheat fields are on fire!"

Tyler, inside the kitchen, talking with Bessie and Amber, had heard Michael's call the first time.   Everybody at the kitchen table had heard Michael's call.   But nobody could move, not even the tough free lance reporter from Washington.   They all seemed frozen and unable to move. Bessie was crying uncontrollably.   Tyler, the tough wheat farmer, stood with his body trembling, tears running down his cheeks.   And, Amber Highlander stood frozen, unable to believe that all this was happening right in front of her.   At that moment, Tyler and Bessie knew their son had come home.   Right at that moment, Tyler didn't care if his entire wheat crop burned.   It was enough that he heard the voice of his son. Then the cry came out again, "Dad, the wheat fields are on fire!"

Right then, after what appeared to be the longest moment, Tyler raced out of the house and jumped in the back of the truck as he had done many times before. It was as if time had gone backward, giving him an opportunity to relieve the past. Without any words being spoken, Tyler, Michael and Suszette raced toward the fire as the three had done before. Bessie and Amber came out of the house and saw them drive off toward the fire and the two of them raced on foot after the truck. Neither could take their eyes off of what was going on. It was like a miracle, happening before their very eyes.

When they reached the fire, Tyler directed the fire hose from the back of the truck, as Michael slowly drove the parameters of the burning field, as he had been taught before going to Vietnam. He knew exactly what had to be done. The team of three worked rapidly and brought the fire under control with only a loss of about ten acres. Just as the spread of the fire was stopped with the danger over, the storm clouds opened up and brought torrential rains, but as the rains fell the three of them stood out there without moving to the shelter of the truck. Bessie and Amber finally reached the spot of the fire, with the rain streaming down Bessie's face washing away her tears. Bessie stood there with her fixated eyes looking at her son who had finally come home. Michael walked toward her, and for the first time in so long, her son wrapped his arms around his mother. And Bessie could not stop crying, as her tears competed with the rain. As all of this magic was taking place in the wheat fields, Amber stood on the sideline, totally mesmerized at what she had just witnessed as a person, as a friend and as a freelance news reporter.

The rains kept coming but no one was leaving the

burnt wheat fields, now the place of the miracle. Then Tyler, Bessie, Michael and Suszette came together in a group embrace and cried. Soon, the circle opened and Amber was invited to join them, as she too began to cry. So the five of them continued in their family embrace as the rains kept coming until it stopped as abruptly as it began. The clouds parted to bring a return to the brilliance of the star filled sky that, on that night, seemed more brilliant than ever, as if telling the world that on that day, a miracle had occurred on the Grimes wheat farm, in Billings, Oklahoma. Finally, Michael and his dad took the truck back to the house and refilled the water tank, so that it was always ready for the next fire.

Bessie, Amber and Suszette walked back to the house while the men serviced the farm's fire truck. After everyone dried off, and changed into dry clothes, they all came to the kitchen for a late breakfast Bessie was fixing. After breakfast, Michael and Suszette went out to the green chairs and just sat there saying nothing, but yet saying a lot by their silence. They kept looking up at the sky that was now filled with stars that seemed even brighter as the rain had moved farther east. As they sat in the green chairs, Michael and Suszette had both been on long journeys, but their journeys were coming to an end. The circles of hope were almost complete for both Michael and Suszette, and in time, maybe very soon, their circles would be complete, as they reached the end of their journey, ready to come home to begin a new future.

Back in the kitchen, Tyler and Bessie were also sitting in silence until broken by the faint sound of Tyler's soft, low voice under his breath, "Thank God, our son is home and a new hope has been brought to the Grimes farm." Bessie looked at Amber and just said, "thank you." All of this had coincided with Amber's visit to the Grimes wheat farm, so Bessie was giving Amber's mere presence a lot of praise. So was Tyler. But Amber remained in silence, and for the first time could not talk. As a newspaper reporter, she still could not believe what she had witnessed with her own eyes.

Later, Tyler told Amber that the rain had caused a delay in the harvest which meant she probably would not get to work the wheat harvest this year. She didn't care after what she had seen. She was ready to get back to Washington and start writing about the miracle in an Oklahoma wheat field. Imagine, Amber thought, it was wheat that had served the noble deed of bringing to an end the Vietnam war, and now it was the wheat field that had finally brought Michael back home from Vietnam. As Amber prepared to head home, she told Tyler that next year will be better, and she would be back if they let her. Before leaving, she had already reserved her room at the Grime's farm for next year's harvest.

The three green chairs on the Grimes' farm had not been used for so long, and now they were. They were being used once again by Michael and this time by his close friend, Suszette. With the Vietnam war over for the two of them, Michael and Suszette sat in the green chairs not saying a thing and just listening to the nighttime silence. Earlier in their lives, grandpa had taught them how to listen and be able to hear the night time silence. Those who can hear the silence are the lucky ones he would always say. It was as if they were listening to the music that was only the silence of the night, just as if grandpa were sitting there with them. For them, their circles of hope were complete and yet it was still only the beginning.